Lecture Notes in Artificial Intelligence 9442

Subseries of Lecture Notes in Computer Science

More information about this series at http://www.springer.com/series/1244

Yohei Murakami · Donghui Lin (Eds.)

Worldwide Language Service Infrastructure

Second International Workshop, WLSI 2015
Kyoto, Japan, January 22–23, 2015
Revised Selected Papers

 Springer

Editors
Yohei Murakami
Unit of Design
Kyoto University
Kyoto
Japan

Donghui Lin
Kyoto University
Kyoto
Japan

ISSN 0302-9743   ISSN 1611-3349   (electronic)
Lecture Notes in Artificial Intelligence
ISBN 978-3-319-31467-9   ISBN 978-3-319-31468-6   (eBook)
DOI 10.1007/978-3-319-31468-6

Library of Congress Control Number: 2016934198

LNCS Sublibrary: SL7 – Artificial Intelligence

This Springer imprint is published by Springer Nature
The registered company is Springer International Publishing AG Switzerland

Preface

Language technologies and tools (hereafter called language resources) increasingly require sophisticated infrastructures to share, deploy as services, and combine for supporting research, development, innovation, and collaboration. To meet this need, several infrastructures have been already established over the past few years, such as Language Grid, Language Application Grid, META-SHARE, MLi, and PANACEA. The main theme of the International Workshop on Worldwide Language Service Infrastructure (WLSI) is technological and institutional challenges that are significant for constructing a worldwide interoperable language service infrastructure. The first workshop focused on language service infrastructures in Asian areas, and a related workshop, Language Technology Service Platforms: Synergies, Standards, Sharing (LTSP 2014), was held at the ninth edition of the Language Resources and Evaluation Conference (LREC 2014). The aim of LTSP 2014 was to provide a forum to enhance international cooperation and sustainable collaboration among worldwide initiatives. The second workshop was held during January 22–23, 2015, in Kyoto, Japan.

The workshop featured five prominent invited speakers: Toru Ishida from the Department of Social Informatics, Kyoto University, who introduced intercultural collaboration activities of the Language Grid; Nancy Ide from the Department of Computer Science, Vassar College, who presented the Language Application Grid framework to create custom natural language processing applications; Khalid Choukri from the Evaluations and Language Resources Distribution Agency, who explained the MLi Hub Project that aims at compiling the specification of the next generation of language grids; Núria Bel from the Department of Translation and Language Sciences, University of Pompeu Fabra, who reported characteristics of users in humanities and social sciences in the Spanish CLARIN Center; and Nicoletta Calzolari from the European Language Resource Association, who summarized policy issues related to language service infrastructures. The first four invited speakers are leaders of each ongoing project in Asia, the USA and Europe, and the last one is a representative of the association to promote language resources. The workshop included 11 oral presentations, and four posters. Participation in the workshop was by invitation only, and there were 29 professionals from 10 countries: China, France, Greece, Indonesia, Italy, Japan, Spain, Thailand, the USA, and Vietnam.

This volume includes 14 selected papers presented at the workshop. The papers are categorized into four parts. The first part introduces metadata and annotations to describe what kind of functionalities and annotations language services provide, and how to invoke the language services and convert the output of a language service to the input of another service. In META-SHARE, Piperidis et al. have focused on processing language datasets with appropriate linguistic annotation services such as tokenization, POS tagging, lemmatization, dependency parsing, and so on. On the other hand, in the Language Application Grid, Ide and Verhagen have addressed the language service interoperability to combine various services by defining Web Service Exchange

Vocabulary (WS-EV), which specifies a terminology for a core of linguistic objects exchanged among linguistic annotation services, and LAPPS Interchange Format (LIF), which represents linguistically annotated data including WS-EV for Web service invocations.

The second part provides technologies for service platforms that compose atomic language services across different interfaces, policies, and licenses. Ide et al. have proposed the Language Application Grid platform that enables language service composition using Galaxy workflow engine in workflow layer, LIF in messaging layer, and WS-EV in vocabulary layer. To solve licensing issues, Cieri and DiPersio have proposed the Language Application Grid license schema by establishing two classes of enforcement, requirement and notification. Mai et al. have tackled policy-aware language service composition by modeling the parallel execution policy of atomic language services. Moreover, Otani et al. have introduced Language Mashup to combine different licensed services, commercial language services, and open-sourced language services.

The third part focuses on the development of language resources and services, especially low-resource languages. Aili and Wushouer describe how to build Uyghur language resources such as dependency Treebank and grammatical information dictionary. Martadinata et al. explain how to implement a language identification tool with Wikipedia corpus and Twitter data. This tool is useful for classifying social media posts like Twitter into several regional languages in Indonesia, which can contribute to monolingual corpora creation in those languages.

The fourth part collects reports on language service application. Luong et al. have developed a Vietnamese multimedia agricultural information retrieval service using a Vietnamese agricultural thesaurus. Liu and Gao have proposed an approach to mine the opinion polarity of songs based on song lyrics in a multilingual environment. Gratta et al. have presented the Cooperative Philology WordNet Platform (CoPhiWordNet) that connects different WordNets in both modern and classical languages such as the Ancient Greek WordNet, the Latin WordNet, the Italian WordNet, the Croatian WordNet, and the Arabic WordNet. Sornlertlamvanich and Kruengkrai have applied a semantic relation extraction approach based on simple relation templates to the Thai cultural database for generating knowledge maps and infoboxes.

We hope this book will strongly support and encourage researchers who are willing to utilize various language services worldwide to create customized language applications and multilingual environments. We are grateful to all the participants and those who have supported this workshop.

January 2016   Yohei Murakami
                                                                            Donghui Lin

Organization

WLSI 2015 was organized by the Language Grid Project, Ishida and Matsubara Laboratory, Department of Social Informatics, Kyoto University.

Organizing Committee

Workshop Co-chairs

Yohei Murakami	Kyoto University, Japan
Donghui Lin	Kyoto University, Japan

Program Committee

Mirna Adriani	University of Indonesia, Indonesia
Mairehaba Aili	Xinjiang University, China
Núria Bel	Universitat Pompeu Fabra, Spain
Nicoletta Calzolari	CNR-ILC, Italy
Khalid Choukri	ELDA, France
Luca Dini	Ho2S, France
Riccardo Del Gratta	CNR-ILC, Italy
Zhiqiang Gao	Southeast University, China
Nancy Ide	Vassar College, USA
Hitoshi Isahara	Toyohashi University of Technology, Japan
Toru Ishida	Kyoto University, Japan
Yoshinobu Kano	NII, Japan
Monica Monachini	CNR-ILC, Italy
Weinila Mushajiang	Xinjiang University, China
Masayuki Otani	Kyoto University, Japan
Stelios Piperidis	ILSP, Greece
James Pustejovsky	Brandeis University, USA
Vu Hai Quan	University of Natural Sciences, Vietnam National University, Vietnam
Virach Sornlertlamvanich	SIIT, Thailand

Workshop Secretariat

Terumi Kosugi	Kyoto University, Japan
Hiroko Yamaguchi	Kyoto University, Japan

Sponsor

Grant-in-Aid for Scientific Research (S) (No. 24220002), JSPS

Contents

Language Service Applications

Metadata and Annotation
for Language Services

Combining and Extending Data Infrastructures with Linguistic Annotation Services

Stelios Piperidis[✉], Dimitrios Galanis, Juli Bakagianni, and Sokratis Sofianopoulos

Athena RC/ILSP, Athens, Greece
{spip,galanisd,julibak,s_sofian}@ilsp.athena-innovation.gr

Abstract. This paper reports on a first prototype implementation for combining and extending a data infrastructure with linguistic processing services, bringing language datasets and basic language processing services together in a unified platform thus boosting the organic growth of data and facilitating language technology research and development. The META-SHARE data infrastructure is enhanced by providing a language processing mechanism for annotating content with appropriate NLP services that are documented with the appropriate metadata. Atomic services are combined into workflows modeled as an acyclic directed graph where each node corresponds to an NLP processing service (e.g. sentence splitting, part-of-speech tagging). Services run either locally or remotely. Currently, the language processing layer implements services and workflows for processing monolingual and bilingual content/resources in raw text, xces, tmx formats. From the legal framework point of view, a simple operational model is adopted by which only openly licensed datasets can be processed by openly licensed services and workflows.

Keywords: Data infrastructures · Distributed repositories · Metadata standards · Language resources licensing · Linguistic processing services · Workflows · Web services

1 Introduction

Contemporary methods for language technology research and development rely on the deployment of appropriate resources more than ever before. Despite this strong dependence on language resources (language datasets, tools and services) the respective landscape has been scattered, unorganised and highly fragmented. To tackle these issues, a number of initiatives (FLaReNet [1], CLARIN [2], Language Grid [3], Panacea [4], LAPPS Grid [5]) have been launched aiming at improving accessibility and visibility of resources and tools, as well as lawful re-use, re-purposing, interlinking and direct deployment in modern computational environments. Inspired and in most cases collaborating, at different degrees and stages, with these initiatives, META-SHARE[1] was launched in 2012 [6], aiming at creating a data infrastructure, in the form of a pan-european network of repositories of language resources, broadly conceived as encompassing datasets and language tools.

---

[1] www.meta-share.eu/org/net.

© Springer International Publishing Switzerland 2016
Y. Murakami and D. Lin (Eds.): WLSI 2015, LNAI 9442, pp. 3–17, 2016.
DOI: 10.1007/978-3-319-31468-6_1

Following the successful deployment and use of the platform's software and metadata model as well as its licensing and operational model [7], we have recently moved on to enhance the data infrastructure with linguistic processing services, thus bringing language datasets and basic language processing services together in a unified platform and boosting the organic growth of both data and language technology research and development. This paper reports on the first prototype implementation of such combination and extension. Sect. 2 briefly introduces the basics of META-SHARE as an infrastructure and the supporting software implementation. Sects. 3 and 4 describe the metadata model and management aspects, while Sect. 5 briefly introduces the user management aspects. Sect. 6 elaborates on the operations of the new language processing layer and presents its limitations and the work on our agenda for the future. Finally, Sect. 7 summarizes the main points of the paper.

2 META-SHARE Platform and Repository Software

META-SHARE is designed as a network of distributed repositories of language data, tools and web services, documented with high-quality metadata, aggregated in central inventories allowing for uniform search and access to resources and services. Its repositories can have a local or hosting role. Local repositories are being set up by organisations participating in the META-SHARE network and are used to store and provide access to their own resources. On the other hand, hosting repositories except from providing access to own resources they are also used as storage and documentation facilities for donated or orphan resources and for resources that are developed in organisations not wishing to set up their own repository. Language resources are described according to the META-SHARE metadata schema. Actual resources and their metadata reside in the local or hosting repositories. Each repository undertakes the responsibility to maintain a local inventory with all the metadata records of its resources, export them and allow their harvesting. Every resource in META-SHARE has to be primarily assigned to one of the network's repositories, implementing the notion of a master copy of a resource, with the member maintaining that repository undertaking its curation. Metadata records are harvested and stored in the META-SHARE central servers (also called Managing Nodes). Central servers share metadata, create, host and maintain a central inventory including metadata of all resources available in the distributed network.

Consumers of language resources are able to: register and create a user profile, log-in to the repository network, browse and search the central inventory using multifaceted search facilities (simple and advanced search), access the actual resources by visiting the local (or hosting) repositories, get information about the usage of specific resources, their relation (e.g. compatibility, suitability, etc.) to other resources, download resources accompanied by easy-to-use licensing templates, exploit additional language processing functionality in the form of web services.

Providers of resources are able to: create, store and edit resource descriptions by using a metadata editor implementing the META-SHARE metadata model, get support through mapping services from an existing metadata schema into the META-SHARE model, upload actual resources to the repository storage, get reports and statistics on number of views, downloads, types of consumers, etc. of LRs, get support for making available additional functionality (e.g. web services).

2.1 META-SHARE Repository Software

META-SHARE has opted for platform independent, open source solutions for its implementation [8]. Likewise, all software generated by META-SHARE is open source, released under a BSD licence and available on GitHub repository[2]. The META-SHARE platform has been developed using the Django framework[3], a Python-based[4] web framework, and it has been tested with lighttpd 1.4.29, while other web servers can be used. For database software, PostgreSQL[5,6] is used. All Python-related dependencies together with a Linux/Unix/Mac install script are provided with META-SHARE v3.0. The repository software package comes with a pre-configured Apache Solr server, which is used to index the META-SHARE database for browsing and searching. Extensive documentation on software dependencies and their versions, local and global configuration settings, as well as a set of frequently asked questions and answers is included in the Installation Manual of the package.

Organisations wishing to set up their own repository are invited to use the META-SHARE repository implementation. Other software solutions are also possible, as long as basic responsibilities of creating an inventory, exporting and allowing harvesting of metadata are borne. Recently, repositories of the Language Grid infrastructure[7] [3] have been successfully harvested into META-SHARE, while conversely two META-SHARE repositories have been successfully harvested and integrated in the CLARIN VLO[8].

3 Language Resources Formal Description

The META-SHARE metadata model [9] builds upon previous initiatives [10] so as to be easily, fully and immediately adopted by the target community. In the design of the model, central is the principle of a minimal core subset of metadata; the elements that form this minimal set are considered indispensable in the process of language resource description and are, thus, obligatory. The minimal level of description is the one at which interoperability with other schemas and typologies takes place. The META-SHARE metadata schema includes elements (most are linked to ISOcat Data Categories [11]),

---

[2] https://github.com/metashare/META-SHARE.

[3] www.djangoproject.com.

[4] http://www.python.org/about/.

[5] SQLite can also be used. SQLite comes built-in with Python 2.7. Since SQLite has a number of limitations, including missing transaction management and access permission management, the preferred database is PostgreSQL.

[6] *PostgreSQL 9.0.5.*

[7] http://langrid.org/en/index.html.

[8] http://www.clarin.eu/content/virtual-language-observatory.

as well as relations used to link together resources that are both included in the META-SHARE repository (e.g. original and derived, raw and annotated resources, a language resource and the tool that has been used to create it etc). The schema comprises all elements and relations required for the description of language resources, including related tools and services; it refers to any kind of information, including identification parameters, administration information (creation, distribution, licensing), technical information required for their manipulation, information as to the production and usage (intended and actual), etc.

The elements of the schema belong to two basic levels of description: (a) an initial level providing the basic elements for the description of a resource (minimal schema), and (b) a second level with a higher degree of granularity (maximal schema), providing more detailed information on each resource. These two levels contain four classes of elements: (1) the first level contains Mandatory and Condition-dependent Mandatory elements (i.e. they have to be filled in when specific conditions are met), while, (2) the

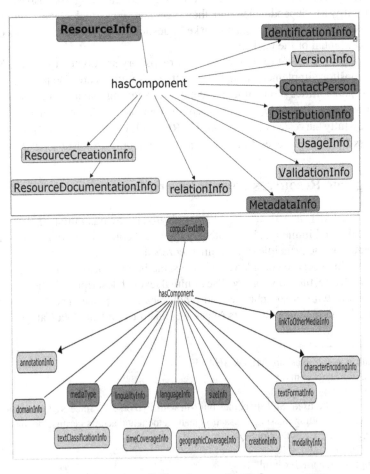

Fig. 1. The *resourceInfo* and *corpusTextInfo* components

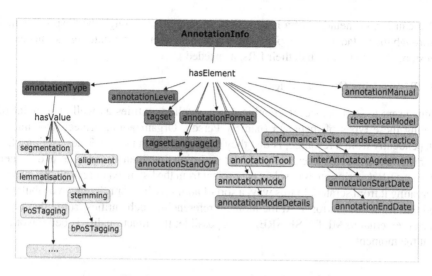

Fig. 2. The *AnnotationInfo* component

second level includes Recommended (i.e. LRs producers are advised to include information on these elements) and Optional elements. Following the ISOcat DCR model, elements are grouped together into semantically coherent "components" which, in turn, can include other components.

The core of the model is the resourceInfo component (Fig. 1 on the top), which contains all the information relevant for the description of a LR. It subsumes components and elements that combine together to provide this description.

Obviously, certain components (e.g. the identification, contact and the rights component) are common to all types of language resources, as the elements they contain can be used to describe a resource regardless of type. The content component, e.g. the corpusTextInfo component (Fig. 1, bottom), the annotation component (Fig. 2) etc., being modality dependent, differ across types. The modality of each type determines the description component, which is used not only for resources but also for resource parts, and is critical for extending the data infrastructure with processing services.

4 Managing Metadata in META-SHARE

There are three ways to enter metadata in META-SHARE. Registered providers with appropriate rights (cf. Sect. 5) can use the metadata editor and by following the steps indicated document their resources using the META-SHARE metadata schema. A second way of importing metadata is provided by the "Upload" functionality of the editor, using which users can provide schema compliant individual XML files or zip files (containing XML files). Last, META-SHARE comes with a command line tool[9] to import XML metadata files into the platform. Likewise, providers with appropriate

---

[9] import_xml.py.

rights can export metadata of a LR to XML format either through the "export" action or through the metadata editing page. Last, providers with appropriate rights can delete, ingest, publish and unpublish their LRs, as needed.

4.1   Referencing Other Entities

Editor users have a choice of creating other, satellite, entities as well. The point of creating these types of metadata (namely Person, Organization, Project, Document) independently from a resource, is that they can be reused in many LR descriptions. So, if for example a provider creates a project description first, then all (s)he has to do, when creating a LR description, is to select the project from the list of existing projects, instead of creating it from scratch. In this way, a sort of authority lists or reference vocabularies are built inside the platform. At the moment referencing such entities from other repositories, external to META-SHARE, is not possible; this functionality is being worked on at the moment.

4.2   Documenting Rights of Use

Central to META-SHARE is the precise documentation of the rights of use of a dataset, tool or service, using one of the options offered by its licensing scheme. The licensing scheme is organised on the axes of Creative Commons licenses and variations of them (META-SHARE Commons and No Redistribution licences) for datasets, and existing standard open source software (FOSS) licences for tools and services. Details about the concepts, implementation and use of these licences is presented in [6] and at the respective META-SHARE page[10].

5   User Management in META-SHARE

Distinct user profiles have been defined, including related authorisations which enable certain actions and ensure the security of transactions. Users may be registered or unregistered, where the former may be divided into end users, providers or administrators of a META-SHARE node. With the exception of unregistered users, every user is given a specific profile containing the information about their rights and obligations. META-SHARE knows the following user roles:

- *anonymous user:* used for non-logged in users; no user account; may browse published LR descriptions and can download free LRs; can see node statistics.
- *registered user:* personalized user account tied to an e-mail address; in addition to the rights of an anonymous user, a registered user may also contact LR maintainers for obtaining LRs which are not freely downloadable; can apply for editor group membership and for organization membership; can use the language processing services offered for annotating his own datasets or datasets residing in the repository up to 5 MB (cf. Sect. 6)

---

[10] http://www.meta-net.eu/meta-share/licenses.

- *editor group member:* a registered user who is a member of one or more editor groups; may create his/her own LR descriptions and may upload smaller data files for them; may alter LR entries belonging to his/her editor group; may add owned resources to the editor groups (s)he is member of; can use the language processing services offered for annotating his own datasets or datasets residing in the repository up to 35 MB (cf. Sect. 6)
- *editor group manager:* a registered user who manages a certain editor group; may accept or turn down applications for the managed editor group; may ingest, publish, unpublish and delete LRs belonging to the managed editor group.
- *organization member:* a registered user who is member of an internally known organization; gets the rights of the organization.
- *organization manager:* a registered user who manages an internally known organization; may add and remove registered users to/from the managed organization group.
- *superuser:* a registered user who has all possible permissions of the META-SHARE web application; a superuser account is usually created during the installation of a node; superusers are especially needed for creating editor groups, for making registered users editor managers, for creating organizations and for making registered users organization managers.
- *node administrator:* the person who administers the META-SHARE node installation; not a META-SHARE web application role but the administrator should have a superuser account; apart from the node installation, a node administrator may be needed for uploading larger LR data sets.

6   Extending META-SHARE Through a Language Processing Layer

For the purposes of research projects where META-SHARE was to be used as the language resource sharing platform, notably the QTLaunchPad project[11] and the Greek CLARIN infrastructure initiative[12], its functionalities have been extended, at a prototype level, by providing an additional language processing mechanism for processing language datasets with appropriate natural language tools. In what follows, we take as example and focus on the language processing (LP) layer implementation for the QTLaunchPad project, for which a dedicated QT21 META-SHARE compliant repository has been created. Language processing tools are documented with the appropriate metadata in the QT21 repository[13] and are provided as web services through the LP layer (Fig. 4). As the software/hardware infrastructure necessary for extended use of the LP was not yet in place, use has been restricted to users with specific rights; therefore, users should be registered and/or assigned editor group member status (cf. Sect. 5). When such a user selects to process a dataset, a list of all available annotation services for each relevant

---

[11] http://www.qt21.eu/launchpad/.

[12] http://www.clarin.gr.

[13] http://qt21.metashare.ilsp.gr/.

annotation level (e.g. tokenization and sentence splitting, POS tagging, lemmatization, dependency parsing, text alignment) are provided for the given language, and resource type (Fig. 3). As soon as the user selects a service, the server invokes the LP layer that dispatches the corpus to the specific web service(s) for processing. The system (based on the messaging service of the platform) informs the user via the META-SHARE web interface about the progress of the requested job. When the processing has been completed, the new (annotated) dataset is automatically stored and indexed in the repository, and the user is appropriately informed (on the interface and by an e-mail). Newly created resources as a result of processing are publicly available to all users of the repository. If the user, for any reason, requests to process a dataset with a specific tool, and this dataset has already been processed by the specific tool, then the system will just forward the user to the processed dataset that has been created and stored in the repository.

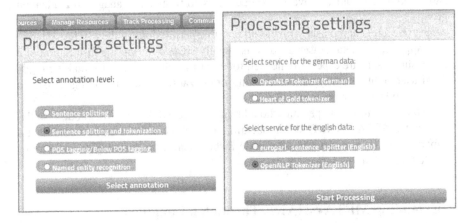

Fig. 3. Dynamically generating relevant annotation levels and annotation services per level.

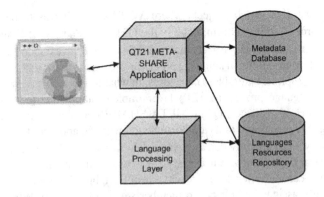

Fig. 4. QT21 repository architecture

In view of integrating the language processing layer, the existing data infrastructure and the supporting software were adapted and extended so that (1) the metadata model caters for documenting language processing services as well as processing related properties of datasets, and (2) mechanisms for automatically creating the metadata records of the newly generated datasets, as a result of processing using an annotation service or workflow, are in place. Automatic creation of metadata records for newly-created datasets consist in automatically naming the annotated resource following a [<ResourceName> annotated by <ServiceName(s)>] pattern, filling in annotation information in the *AnnotationInfo* component of the record, creating relations between the original dataset and the annotated one (in the *RelationInfo* component) and updating contact information by aggregating information from the *ContactInfo* components of the original dataset and the annotation service.

Certain extensions concern the providers of Language Resources who wish to deposit their LRs to the QT21 repository and make them processable. A user can also discover a processing service for a particular language and annotation level by querying the repository using either a simple query or the faceted search, and input a user-owned dataset to the processing mechanism, if it complies with the following specifications: (i) the user should upload (Fig. 5) the actual dataset to the QT21 repository storage, (ii) the dataset should be compressed and must not exceed 5 MB or 35 MB in size, depending on the user's status, i.e. *registered* or *editor group member* respectively, (iii) the user specifies the data format of the dataset, by choosing one of the supported data formats (information regarding every data format is available by clicking the help buttons of the metadata editor, which accompany each data format choice).

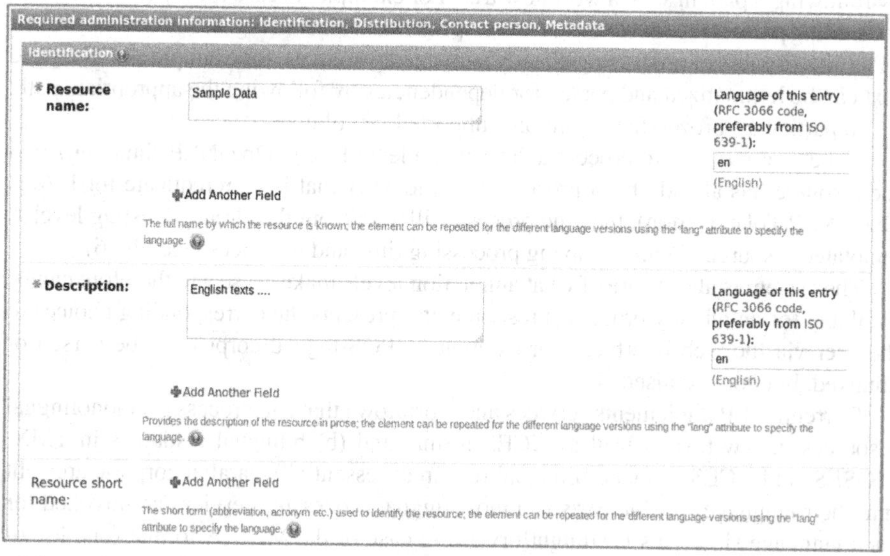

Fig. 5. Describing and uploading user owned data

User-owned processed datasets are temporarily stored in the repository storage and are available for download for 48 h. After this period, the processed dataset and the original data are permanently deleted. If, however, the user wishes to permanently store his/her processed dataset, (s)he can choose to do so on condition that (1) (s)he becomes an editor group member and (2) (s)he verifies that (s)he has cleared the rights of use of the specific dataset.

6.1 Language Processing Layer Implementation

The Language Processing (LP) layer has been implemented in Java, based on the Apache Camel framework[14]. Camel is an open-source project that provides libraries which enable the easy integration of different components and technologies and the creation of (data) processing workflows. The implemented LP is bundled as a web application and can be deployed in a standard java-based web container[15].

LP's workflows are implemented based on a variety of natural language processing services. These services run either locally within the application environment (loc), or they are accessed via remote services (rmt). Currently, OpenNLP services (loc) are deployed for English, German and Portuguese, Panacea-DCU services (rmt) for English, LX-Center/University of Lisbon services (rmt) for Portuguese, Heart of Gold/DFKI services (rmt) for German, ILSP NLP services (loc) for Greek, and Hunalign text alignment services for aligning parallel corpora at sentence level (loc).

Each set of workflows, for example the UIMA-based ones for the Greek language (see Fig. 6, top), can be modelled as an acyclic directed graph (tree) where each node corresponds to a processing service (tool). The processing of a data chunk is performed by following a path in such a workflow tree. For example, in case the input is a raw text the starting point is the root of the tree (e.g. splitter/tokenizer in Fig. 6, bottom). However, LP is also capable of processing already annotated resources, for example a POS tagged text can be lemmatized and parsed for dependencies by following the appropriate path.

In particular, processing chains are supported, as follows:

If the user requests to process a dataset at a level L (e.g. OpenNLP chunking), and the resource has already been processed at a level A that is a prerequisite for L (e.g. Open NLP Tokenization), then the process will start from the already existing level A annotated resource, therefore saving processing time and resources (see Fig. 6).

The system is also aware of what annotation levels make sense and therefore can be available for an already processed resource and presents the corresponding choices to the user via the web interface. For example, a POS-tagged corpus can be parsed or chunked, but not tokenised.

Currently, LP implements services and workflows that can process (a) monolingual resources in raw text as well as XCES format and (b) bilingual resources in TMX, MOSES, and XCES formats. Bilingual resources, essentially parallel corpora, are split into their language specific parts and monolingual processing services are invoked for each language side. This is straightforward in case of the MOSES format (one file of raw text for each language), by parsing the folder structure of the parallel corpora, while in the case of TMX input it necessitates parsing, extracting text from the relevant

---

[14] http://camel.apache.org/.

[15] In our tests, we used Jetty, which is small, fast and embeddable server that powers many software projects (e.g. Solr).

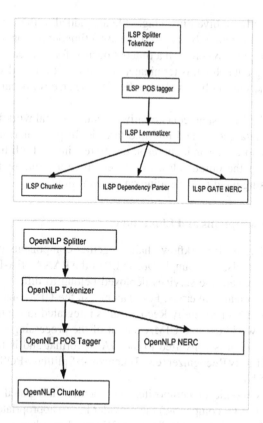

Fig. 6. Workflow trees for the Greek Language (on the top), for OpenNLP pipelines (on the bottom).

translation unit variant elements[16] and creating language specific files. The resources are stored in the QT21 repository in a compressed format (e.g. .zip, tar.gz, .gz). Initially, a service decompresses the specified resource file and then uses an appropriate reader that splits the content of the extracted files in smaller text (data) chunks, so that any file size constraints that a service might have can be met. These chunks are then forwarded to the appropriate NLP service/workflow. A symmetric service that collects the data chunks after the processing and merges them in a single compressed resource is initiated as soon as the service/workflow has completed the data processing.

The output format for the produced annotations of the LP is pertinent to the specific workflow that is executed. For example, the annotations of a UIMA-based pipeline are serialized in the XML Metadata Interchange format (XMI) whereas in OpenNLP and DCU workflows the output is stored in a custom XML representation and in a text-based format, respectively.

In all cases, the files with the annotations which are produced from the processing of a language resource are checked for potential software errors (e.g. number of files

---

[16] <tuv> tags.

processed as expected), archived in a single file and added to the QT21 repository. In the cases where a tool is remotely accessed, we use a timeout mechanism to prevent the application from hanging. When such a timeout occurs, for any reason, the processing of the corresponding data chunk is terminated, i.e., it is not forwarded to the next step of the workflow. The same policy is also applied in case an error occurs in a service that runs locally.

To ensure that the LP system concurrently executes several workflows or parts of a workflow, we use data queues and multiple threads. In particular, there are separate threads for (a) decompressing an input resource, (b) reading and splitting the input files, and (c) for archiving the output files. Moreover, there are one or more threads for executing a processing pipeline depending on the workflow.

6.2 Workflow Assumptions and Limitations

Currently, each QT21 NLP workflow chains together components or services of the same suite/family of tools, for example OpenNLP or the PANACEA-DCU services. To accommodate cases where the services deployed belong to different suites, we have developed the appropriate converters. For example, in the UIMA-based tree of Fig. 6, where a GATE-based Named Entity Recognizer is integrated in the respective Named Entity Recognition workflow, the UIMA output of the processing services preceding named entity recognition is converted to the GATE format and is fed to the GATE-compatible Named Entity Recognizer (e.g. Tokenizer->Splitter->POSTagger->UIMA-GATE Converter->NERC).

For adding new atomic or composite, interoperable integrated services (SOAP, OpenNLP, UIMA, GATE compatible) the provider has to appropriately document his/ her services/workflows using the META-SHARE metadata schema, i.e. at least service name and location, platform and service version, languages, acceptable input/output formats, while the LP has to be appropriately enhanced with a mechanism that dynamically creates the appropriate workflows based on the given description.

Enabling the user to define and deploy custom workflows, cross-suite or not, is on our agenda for the immediate future. The implementation of cross-suite workflows requires the development of several data format converters for each pair of different technologies (e.g. UIMA-GATE, DCU-OpenNLP). Understandably, there are several performance, compatibility and above all interoperability issues that arise in such cases and have to be investigated and addressed, especially in the light of Language Grid [3] and LAPPS Grid [5] developments. For example, the machine learning models on which the tools are based, have been trained and optimized using the output of a specific tool. This fact, may lead to significant drop in the performance of a tool. Moreover, in a mixed workflow it is possible, not to say highly expected, that a tool may use a different tagset than the one required as input in the next step. This may lead to either a software error or to an output of low quality.

In addition, worthwhile noting is the dependence of the LP application on the design properties of individual, remotely called workflows. Such properties may constrain the amount of data a workflow can process per unit time (workload), as some workflows are:

- deployed in a single machine which might also have limited processing and memory capabilities.
- inherently designed and implemented to serve only non-concurrent requests.

To assess the stability, performance and scalability of the LP application we have tested it with resources of various lengths depending on the workflow. Locally running services (tools that run within our application) were tested with resources of 1 MB, 10 MB and 50 MB. Remote services were tested with smaller resources of 500 KB, 5 MB and 10 MB. First, each tool/service was tested separately (not concurrently) so as to assess its processing efficiency. Then, we initiated concurrent workflows. All performed tests, concurrent or not, were completed successfully generating the expected output. The tests have also shown that LP application can handle in parallel at least 4 workflows and 200 MB of data.

Last, but not least, considering the experimental QT21 repository operations from the legal framework point of view, we have adopted a rather simple operational model by which only openly licensed, with no no-derivatives (ND) restriction, datasets can be processed by openly licensed services and workflows. In future versions, in collaboration with other infrastructure providers, we intend to elaborate on a business logic that will allow processing of otherwise licensed datasets and services supporting the appropriate business models.

7   Conclusions and Future Work

This paper presented a data sharing infrastructure which is able to process (annotate) datasets with appropriate NLP tools (e.g. tokenization, parsing). An initial set of tests has shown that the LP layer of the infrastructure can be easily used (via the interface) by the users and it can handle and process a significant amount of input data. However, performance also depends on the available processing resources (e.g. memory, CPU, number of machines), the requested workflow (e.g. dependency parsing is usually more time consuming that tokenization) and the service implementation. Currently, the processing layer is appropriately enhanced so as to run on multiple machines in a Hadoop cluster. This will enable the processing of large volumes of data. In addition, in the immediate future we plan to focus on interoperability and deployment issues and enable the execution of custom and mixed (cross-suite) workflows.

Acknowledgements. This paper presents work done in the framework of the projects T4ME (GA no. 249119), QTLaunchPad project (GA no. 296347), funded by DG INFSO of the European Commission through the FP7 and ICT-PSP Programmes. The infrastructure described in the paper is maintained and further extended in the framework of the Greek CLARIN Attiki project (MIS 441451), Support for ESFRI/2006 Research Infrastructures, of the Greek Government.

References

1. Soria, C., Bel, N., Choukri, K., Mariani, J., Monachini, M., Odijk, J., Piperidis, S., Quochi, V., Calzolari, N.: The FLaReNet strategic language resource agenda. In: Calzolari, N., Choukri, K., Declerck, T., Doğan, M.U., Maegaard, B., Mariani, J., Odijk, J., Piperidis, S. (eds.) Proceedings of the Eighth International Conference on Language Resources and Evaluation (LREC 2012), European Language Resources Association (ELRA), Istanbul, 23–25 May 2012
2. Wittenburg, P., Bel, N., Borin, L., Budin, G., Calzolari, N., Hajicova, E., Koskenniemi, K., Lemnitzer, L., Maegaard, B., Piasecki, M., Pierrel, J.M., Piperidis, S., Skadina, I., Tufis, D., Veenendaal, R.V., Váradi, T., Wynne, M.: Resource and service centres as the backbone for a sustainable service infrastructure. In: Calzolari, N., Choukri, K., Maegaard, B., Mariani, J., Odijk, J., Piperidis, S., Rosner, M., Tapias, D. (eds.) Proceedings of the Seventh International Conference on Language Resources and Evaluation (LREC 2010), European Language Resources Association (ELRA), Valletta (2010)
3. Ishida, T. (ed.): The Language Grid: Service-Oriented Collective Intelligence for Language Resource Interoperability. Springer, Heidelberg (2011)
4. Poch, M., Bel, N.: Interoperability and technology for a language resources factory. Article Presented in the Workshop on Language Resources, Technology and Services in the Sharing Paradigm at IJCNLP 2011, Chiang Mai, 12 November 2011
5. Ide, N., Pustejovsky, J., Cieri, C., Nyberg, E., Wang, D., Suderman, K., Verhagen, M., Wright, J.: The language application grid. In: Calzolari, N., Choukri, K., Declerck, T., Loftsson, H., Maegaard, B., Mariani, J., Moreno, A., Odijk, J., Piperidis, S. (eds.) Proceedings of the Ninth International Conference on Language Resources and Evaluation (LREC 2014), European Language Resources Association (ELRA), Reykjavik (2014)
6. Piperidis, S.: The META-SHARE language resources sharing infrastructure: principles, challenges, solutions. In: Calzolari, N., Choukri, K., Declerck, T., Doğan, M.U., Maegaard, B., Mariani, J., Odijk, J., Piperidis, S. (eds.) Proceedings of the Eighth International Conference on Language Resources and Evaluation (LREC 2012), European Language Resources Association (ELRA), Istanbul, 23–25 May 2012
7. Piperidis, S., Papageorgiou, H., Spurk, C., Rehm, G., Choukri, K., Hamon, O., Calzolari, N., del Gratta, R., Magnini, B., Girardi, C.: METASHARE: one year after. In: Calzolari, N., Choukri, K., Declerck, T., Loftsson, H., Maegaard, B., Mariani, J., Moreno, A., Odijk, J., Piperidis, S. (eds.) Proceedings Of The Ninth International Conference On Language Resources and Evaluation (LREC 2014), European Language Resources Association (ELRA), Reykjavik (2012)
8. Federmann, C., Georgantopoulos, B., Girardi, C., Hamon, O., Mavroeidis, D., Minutoli, S., Schröder, M.: META-SHARE v2: an open network of repositories for language resources including data and tools. In: Calzolari, N., Choukri, K., Declerck, T., Doğan, M.U., Maegaard, B., Mariani, J., Odijk, J., Piperidis, S. (eds.) Proceedings of the Eighth International Conference on Language Resources and Evaluation (LREC 2012), European Language Resources Association (ELRA), Istanbul, 23–25 May 2012
9. Gavrilidou, M., Labropoulou, P., Desypri, E., Piperidis, S., Papageorgiou, H., Monachini, M., Frontini, F., Declerck, T., Francopoulo, G., Arranz, V., Mapelli, V: The META-SHARE metadata schema for the description of language resources. In: Calzolari, N., Choukri, K., Declerck, T., Uğur Doğan, M., Maegaard, B., Mariani, J., Odijk, J., Piperidis, S. (eds.) Proceedings of the Eighth International Conference on Language Resources and Evaluation (LREC 2012), European Language Resources Association (ELRA), Istanbul, 23–25 May 2012

10. Broeder, D., Kemps-Snijders, M., Van Uytvanck, D., Windhouwer, M., Withers, P., Wittenburg, P. Zinn, C.: A Data category registry- and component-based metadata framework. In: Calzolari, N., Choukri, K., Maegaard, B., Mariani, J., Odijk, J., Piperidis, S., Rosner, M., Tapias, D. (eds.) Proceedings of the Seventh Conference on International Language Resources and Evaluation (LREC 2010), European Language Resources Association (ELRA), Valletta (2010)

11. ISO 12620. Terminology and other language and content resources – Specification of data categories and management of a Data Category Registry for language resources. (2009). http://www.isocat.org

The Language Application Grid Web Service Exchange Vocabulary

Nancy Ide[1(✉)], Keith Suderman[1], Marc Verhagen[2], and James Pustejovsky[2]

[1] Vassar College, Poughkeepsie, NY, USA
ide@cs.vassar.edu, suderman@cs.vassar.edu
[2] Brandeis University, Waltham, MA, USA
marc@cs.brandeis.edu, jamesp@cs.brandeis.edu

Abstract. In the context of the Linguistic Applications (LAPPS) Grid project, we have undertaken the definition of a Web Service Exchange Vocabulary (WS-EV) specifying a terminology for a core of linguistic objects and properties exchanged among NLP tools that consume and produce linguistically annotated data. The goal is not to define a new set of terms, but rather to provide a single web location where terms relevant for exchange among NLP tools are defined and provide a "sameAs" link to all known web-based definitions that correspond to them. The WS-EV is intended to be used by a federation of six grids currently being formed but is usable by any web service platform.

Keywords: Linguistic standards · Interoperability · Web services · Service grids

1 Introduction

There is clearly a demand within the community for some sort of standard for exchanging annotated language data among tools.[1] This has become particularly urgent with the emergence of web services, which has enabled the availability of language processing tools that can and should interact with one another, in particular, by forming pipelines that can branch off in multiple directions to accomplish application-specific processing. While some progress has been made toward enabling *syntactic interoperability* via the development of standard representation formats (e.g., ISO LAF/GrAF [11,13], NLP Interchange Format (NIF) [7], UIMA[2] Common Analysis System (CAS)) which, if not identical, can be trivially mapped to one another, *semantic interoperability* among NLP tools remains problematic [8]. A few efforts to create repositories, type systems, and ontologies of linguistic terms (e.g., ISOCat[3], OLiA[4], various repositories for UIMA

---

[1] See, for example, proceedings of the recent LREC workshop on "Language Technology Service Platforms: Synergies, Standards, Sharing" (http://www.ilc.cnr.it/ltsp2014/).

[2] https://uima.apache.org/.

[3] http://www.isocat.org.

[4] http://nachhalt.sfb632.uni-potsdam.de/owl/.

© Springer International Publishing Switzerland 2016
Y. Murakami and D. Lin (Eds.): WLSI 2015, LNAI 9442, pp. 18–32, 2016.
DOI: 10.1007/978-3-319-31468-6_2

type systems[5], GOLD[6], NIF Core Ontology[7]) have been undertaken to enable (or provide) a mapping among linguistic terms, but none has yet proven to include all requisite terms and relations or be easy to use and reference. General repositories such as Dublin Core[8], schema.org, and the Friend of a Friend project[9] include some relevant terms, but they are obviously not designed to cover all the kinds of information found in linguistically annotated data. There have been recent efforts to address semantic interoperability among NLP web services [15,16], but the solutions deal only with meta-data and high-level elements (e.g., text); more precise specification of information types are deliberately left underspecified and left to the service provider to determine.

In the context of the Linguistic Applications (LAPPS) Grid project [10], we have undertaken the definition of a Web Service Exchange Vocabulary (WS-EV) specifying a terminology for a core of linguistic objects and properties exchanged among NLP web services that consume and produce linguistically annotated data. The work is being done in collaboration with ISO TC37 SC4 WG1 in order to ensure full community engagement and input. The goal is not to define a new set of terms, but rather to provide a single web location where terms relevant for exchange among NLP tools are defined and provide a "sameAs" link to all known web-based definitions that correspond to them. A second goal is to define relations among the terms that can be used when linguistic data are exchanged. The WS-EV is intended to be used by a newly-formed federation of grids, including the Kyoto Language Grid[10], the Language Grid Jakarta Operation Center[11], the Xinjiang Language Grid, the Language Grid Bangkok Operation Center[12], LinguaGrid[13], MetaNet/MetaShare[14], and LAPPS, but is usable by any web service platform.

This paper describes the LAPPS WS-EV, which is currently under construction. We first describe the LAPPS project and then overview the motivations and principles for developing the WS-EV. We then describe its use in the JSON-LD LAPPS Interchange Format (LIF) to enable semantic interoperability among web services in the LAPPS Grid.

2   The Language Application Grid Project

The Language Application (LAPPS) Grid project establishing a framework that enables language service discovery, composition, and reuse, in order to promote

---

[5] E.g., http://www.julielab.de/Resources/Software/UIMA+type+system-p-91.html.
[6] http://linguistics-ontology.org.
[7] http://persistence.uni-leipzig.org/nlp2rdf/ontologies/nif-core/nif-core.
[8] http://dublincore.org.
[9] http://www.foaf-project.org.
[10] http://langrid.org.
[11] http://langrid.portal.cs.ui.ac.id/langrid/.
[12] http://langrid.servicegrid-bangkok.org.
[13] http://www.linguagrid.org/.
[14] http://www.meta-share.eu.

sustainability, manageability, usability, and interoperability of natural language Processing (NLP) components. It is based on the service-oriented architecture (SOA), a more recent, web-oriented version of the pipeline architecture that has long been used in NLP for sequencing loosely-coupled linguistic analyses. The LAPPS Grid provides a critical missing layer of functionality for NLP: although existing frameworks such as UIMA and GATE provide the capability to wrap, integrate, and deploy language services, they do not provide general support for service discovery, composition, and reuse.

The LAPPS Grid is a collaborative effort among US partners Brandeis University, Vassar College, Carnegie-Mellon University, and the Linguistic Data Consortium at the University of Pennsylvania, and is funded by the US National Science Foundation (NSF). The project builds on the foundation laid in the NSF-funded project SILT [9], which established a set of needs for interoperability and developed standards and best practice guidelines to implement them. LAPPS is similar in its scope and goals to ongoing projects such as The Language Grid [12], PANACEA[15], LinguaGrid[16], and CLARIN[17], which also provide web service access to basic NLP processing tools and resources and enable pipelining these tools to create custom NLP applications and composite services such as question answering and machine translation, as well as access to language resources such as mono- and multi-lingual corpora and lexicons that support NLP. The transformative aspect of the LAPPS Grid is therefore not the provision of a suite of web services, but rather that it orchestrates access to and deployment of language resources and processing functions available from servers around the globe, and enables users to easily add their own language resources, services, and even service grids to satisfy their particular needs. The specific goals of the LAPPS project are to: (1) design, develop, and promote a Language Application Grid (LAPPS Grid) based on Service Grid Software to support the development and deployment of integrated natural language applications and enable federation of grids and services throughout the world; (2) provide an open advancement (OA) framework (Ferrucci et al., 2009a) for component- and application-based evaluation; (3) provide access to language resources for members of the NLP community as well as researchers in a wide range of social science and humanities disciplines; (4) enable easy navigation through licensing issues; and (5) actively promote adoption, use, and community involvement with the LAPPS Grid.

One of the most unique innovations in the LAPPS Grid is the provision of an open advancement (OA) framework (Ferrucci et al., 2009a) for component- and application-based evaluation of NLP tools and pipelines. The availability of this type of evaluation service will provide an unprecedented tool for NLP development that could, in itself, take the field to a new level of productivity. OA involves evaluating *multiple possible solutions* to a problem, consisting of different configurations of component tools, resources, and evaluation data, to find the

---

[15] http://panacea-lr.eu/.
[16] http://www.linguagrid.org/.
[17] http://www.clarin.eu/.

optimal solution among them, and enabling rapid identification of frequent error categories, together with an indication of which module(s) and error type(s) have the greatest impact on overall performance. On this basis, enhancements and/or modifications can be introduced with an eye toward achieving the largest possible reduction in error rate [2, 20]. OA was used in the development of IBM's Watson to achieve steady performance gains over the four years of its development [3]; more recently, the open-source OAQA project has released software frameworks which provide general support for open advancement [5, 20], which has been used to rapidly develop information retrieval and question answering systems for bioinformatics [14, 20].

The fundamental system architecture of the LAPPS Grid is based on the Open Service Grid Initiative's Service Grid Server Software[18] developed by the National Institute of Information and Communications Technology (NICT) in Japan and used to implement Kyoto University's Language Grid, a service grid that supports multilingual communication and collaboration. Like the Language Grid, the LAPPS Grid provides three main functions: language service registration and deployment, language service search, and language service composition and execution. The LAPPS Grid project has adopted Galaxy [6] as a workflow engine, which provides a graphical interface where data inputs and computational steps are selected from dynamic menus, and results are displayed in plots and summaries that encourage interactive workflows and the exploration of hypotheses. The LAPPS Grid produces relevant component-level measures for standard metrics, given gold-standard test data, for each component in a pipeline, which facilitates error analysis. In addition, the Grid automatically generates metrics measurements plus variance and statistical significance calculations for each possible pipeline, using a service-oriented version of the Configuration Space Exploration (CSE) algorithm [20]. The LAPPS Grid also implements a dynamic licensing system for handling license agreements on the fly[19], provides the option to run services locally with high-security technology to protect sensitive information where required, and enables access to grids other than those based on the Service Grid technology.

We have adopted the JSON-based serialization for Linked Data (JSON-LD) to represent linguistically annotated data for the purposes of web service exchange. The JavaScript Object Notation (JSON) is a lightweight, text-based, language-independent data interchange format that defines a small set of formatting rules for the portable representation of structured data. Because it is based on the W3C Resource Definition Framework (RDF), JSON-LD is trivially mappable to and from other graph-based formats such as ISO LAF/GrAF and UIMA CAS, as well as a growing number of formats implementing the same data model. Most importantly, JSON-LD enables services to reference categories and definitions in web-based repositories and ontologies or any suitably defined concept at a given URI. JSON-LD provides *syntactic interoperability* among services

---

[18] http://servicegrid.net.

[19] See [1] for a description of how licensing issues are handled in the LAPPS Grid.

in the LAPPS Grid, while *semantic interoperability* is provided by the LAPPS Web Service Exchange Vocabulary, described in the next section.

3   LAPPS Web Service Exchange Vocabulary

3.1   Motivation

The WS-EV addresses a relatively small but critical piece of the overall LAPPS architecture: it allows web services to communicate about the content they deliver, such that the *meaning*–i.e., exactly what to do with and/or how to process the data–is understood by the receiver. As such it performs the same function as a UIMA type system performs for tools in a UIMA pipeline that utilize that type system, or the common annotation labels (e.g.,"Token","Sentence", etc.) required for communication among pipelined tools in GATE. These mechanisms provide semantic interoperability among tools as long as one remains in either the UIMA or GATE world. To pipeline a tool whose output follows GATE conventions with a tool that expects input that complies with a given UIMA type system, some mapping of terms and structures is likely to be required.[20] This is what the WS-EV is intended to enable; effectively, it is a *meta-type-system* for mapping labels assigned to linguistically annotated data so that they are understood and treated consistently by tools that exchange them in the course of executing a pipeline or workflow. Since web services included in LAPPS and federated grids may use any i/o semantic conventions, the WS-EV allows for communication among any of them–including, for example, between GATE and UIMA services[21].

The ability to pipeline components from diverse sources is critical to the implementation of the OA development approach described in the previous section, it must be possible for the developer to "plug and play" individual tools, modules, and resources in order to rapidly re-configure and evaluate new pipelines. These components may exist on any server across the globe, consist of modules developed within frameworks such as UIMA and GATE, and/or be user-defined services existing on a local machine.

3.2   WS-EV Design

The WS-EV was built around the following design principles, which were compiled based on input from the community:

1. The WS-EV will not reinvent the wheel. Objects and properties defined in the WS-EV will be linked to definitions in existing repositories and ontologies wherever possible.

---

[20] Within UIMA, the output of tools conforming to different type systems may themselves require conversion in order to be used together.

[21] Figure 6 shows a pipeline in which both GATE and UIMA services are called; GATE-to-GATE and UIMA-to-UIMA communication does not use the WS-EV, but it is used for communication between GATE and UIMA services, as well as other services.

2. The WS-EV will be designed so as to allow for easy, one-to-one mapping from terms designating linguistic objects and properties commonly produced and consumed by NLP tools that are wrapped as web services. It is not necessary for the mapping to be object-to-object or property-to-property[22]

3. The WS-EV will provide a *core* set of objects and properties, on the principle that "simpler is better", and provide for (principled) definition of additional objects and properties beyond the core to represent more specialized tool input and output.

4. The WS-EV is not LAPPS-specific; it will not be governed by the processing requirements or preferences of particular tools, systems, or frameworks.

5. The WS-EV is intended to be used *only* for interchange among web services performing NLP tasks. As such it can serve as a "pivot" format to which user and tool-specific formats can be mapped.

6. The web service provider is responsible for providing wrappers that perform the mapping from internally-used formats to and/or from the WS-EV.

7. The WS-EV format should be compact to facilitate the transfer of large datasets.

8. The WS-EV format will be chosen to take advantage, to the extent possible, of existing technological infrastructures and standards.

As noted in the first principle, where possible the objects and properties in the WS-EV are drawn from existing repositories such as ISOCat and the NIF Core Ontology and linked to them using the taxonomy of relation types defined in RELcat [19], which accommodates multiple vocabularies for relation predicates, including those from the Web Ontology Language (OWL) [17] and the Simple Knowledge Organization System (SKOS) [18], as shown in Fig. 1.

However, many repositories do not include some categories and objects relevant for web service exchange (e.g., "token" and other segment descriptors), do include multiple (often very similar) definitions for the same concept, and/or do not specify relations among terms. We therefore attempted to identify a set of (more or less) "universal" concepts by surveying existing type systems and schemas–for example, the Julie Lab and DARPA GALE UIMA type systems and the GATE schemas for linguistic phenomena–together with the I/O requirements of commonly used NLP software (e.g., the Stanford NLP tools, OpenNLP, etc.). Results of the survey for token and sentence identification and part-of-speech labeling[23] showed that even for these basic categories, there exists no "standard" set of categories and relations.

---

[22] We follow the terminology used in RDF/OWL and JSON-LD: the term "objects" (in RDF, nodes in the Semantic Web graph) refers to common linguistic labels or types, and "properties" denote what are often referred to as "features" or "attributes" of an object (in RDF, these are labels of edges between object nodes). We emphasize that our assignment of linguistic labels as objects and properties, while principled to the extent possible, is otherwise arbitrary and may therefore differ from existing type systems and schemas. This does not, however, impede mapping to object and properties in the WS-EV.

[23] Available at http://www.anc.org/LAPPS/EP/Meeting-2013-09-26-Pisa/ep-draft.pdf.

```
1. Related (rel:related)
1.1. Sameas(rel:sameAs)
1.2. Almost same as (rel:almostSameAs)
1.3. Broader than(rel:broaderThan)
1.3.1. Superclass of (rel:superClassOf)
1.3.2. Has part (rel:hasPart)
1.3.2.1. Has direct part (rel:hasDirectPart)
1.4 Narrower than (del:narrowerThan)
1.4.1. Sub class of (rel:subClassOf)
1.4.2. Part of (rel:partOf)
1.4.2.1. Direct part of (rel:directPartOf)
```

Fig. 1. Relation types in RELCat

Perhaps more problematically, sources that do specify relations among concepts, such as the various UIMA type systems and GATE's schemas, vary widely in their choices of what is an object and what is a property; for example, some treat "token" as an object (label) and "lemma" and "pos" as associated properties (features), while others regard "lemma" and/or "pos" as objects in their own right. Decisions concerning what is an object and what is a property are for the most part arbitrary; no one scheme is right or wrong, but a consistent organization is required for effective web service interchange. The WS-EV therefore defines an organization of objects and properties solely for the purposes of communication among web services in the LAPPS Grid. It is irrelevant if a given scheme treats, say, "pos" as an object or type in its own right, as long as it is mapped to the correspondingly defined WS-EV object or property for the purposes of web service exchange.

In addition, the WS-EV is intended to provide a *core* set of terms, augmented as needed when services are added to the LAPPS Grid, but it is by no means intended to be comprehensive. The WS-EV includes *sameAs* and *similarTo* mappings that link to like concepts in other repositories where possible, thus serving primarily to group the terms and impose a structure of relations required for web service exchange in one web-based location.

In addition to the principles above, the WS-EV is built on the principle of orthogonal design, such that there is one and only one definition for each concept. It is also designed to be very lightweight and easy to find and reference on the web. To that end we have established a straightforward web site (the Web Service Exchange Vocabulary Repository[24]), similar to *schema.org*, in order to provide web-addressable terms and definitions for reference from annotations exchanged among web services. Our approach is bottom-up: we have adopted a minimalist strategy of adding objects and properties to the repository only as they are needed as services are added to the LAPPS Grid. Terms are organized in a shallow hierarchy, with inheritance of properties, as shown in Fig. 2.

---

[24] http://vocab.lappsgrid.org.

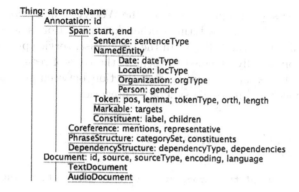

Thing: alternateName
  Annotation: id
    Span: start, end
      Sentence: sentenceType
      NamedEntity
        Date: dateType
        Location: locType
        Organization: orgType
        Person: gender
      Token: pos, lemma, tokenType, orth, length
      Markable: targets
      Constituent: label, children
    Coreference: mentions, representative
    PhraseStructure: categorySet, constituents
    DependencyStructure: dependencyType, dependencies
  Document: id, source, sourceType, encoding, language
    TextDocument
    AudioDocument

Fig. 2. Fragment of the WS-EV type hierarchy (associated properties in gray)

Note that the WS-EV does not provide a repository of specific categories for part-of-speech or syntactic and semantic roles; rather, a specific label may be referenced in the JSON-LD representation using a URI for one of the several locations where such information resides on the web. Alternatively, a string providing the information may be used (see, for example, the JSON-LD sample in Sect. 4.1). Metadata specifying the tags and/or software that produced a given labeling can be checked to ensure that the labels required by a consumer service conform to those generated by the provider.

4   WS-EV and JSON-LD

We have defined the *LAPPS Interchange Format (LIF)*[25] using JSON-LD for interchange among LAPPS Grid web services. References in LIF point to URIs providing definitions for specific linguistic categories in the WS-EV. They may also reference documentation for processing software and rules for processes such as tokenization, entity recognition, etc. used to produce a set of annotations, which are often left unspecified in annotated resources thus inhibiting reproducibility of results (see for example [4]). While not required for web service exchange in the LAPPS Grid, the inclusion of such references can contribute to the better replication and evaluation of results in the field. Figure 4 shows the information for *Token*, which defines the concept, identifies application types that produce objects of this type, cross-references a similar concept in ISOCat, and provides the URI for use in the LIF representation. It also specifies the common properties that can be specified for a set of Token objects, and the individual properties that can be associated with a Token object. There is no requirement to use any or all of the properties in the LIF representation, and we foresee that many web services will require definition of objects and properties not included in the WS-EV or elsewhere. We therefore provide mechanisms for (principled)

---

[25] For a full description of LIF, see Verhagen, *et al.*, "The LAPPS Interchange Format", elsewhere in this volume.

definition of objects and properties beyond the WS-EV. Two options exist: users can provide a URI where a new term or other documentation is defined, or users may add a definition to the WS-EV. In the latter case, service providers use the name space automatically assigned to them at the time of registration, thereby avoiding name clashes and providing a distinction between general categories used across services and more idiosyncratic categories.

```
"@context" : "http://vocab.lappsgrid.org/",
"metadata" : { },
"text" : {
    "@value" : "Some of the strongest critics of our welfare system..."
}
"views" : [ {
    "metadata" : {
        "contains" : {
            "Token" : {
                "producer" : "org.anc.lapps.stanford.SATokenizer:1.4.0",
                "type" : "tokenization:stanford"
            }
        }
    }
} ],
"annotations" : [ {
    "@type" : "Token",
    "id" : "tok0",
    "start" : 18,
    "end" : 22
} ],
    . . .
```

Fig. 3. JSON-LD fragment referencing the LAPPS Grid WS-EV

Figure 3 shows a fragment of the LIF representation that references terms in the WS-EV. The *context* statement at the top identifies the URI that is to be prefixed to any unknown name in order to identify the location of its definition. For the purposes of the example, the text to be processed is given inline. Our current implementation includes results from each step in a pipeline, where applicable, together with metadata describing the service applied in each step (here, org.anc.lapps.stanford.SATokenizer:1.4.0) and identified by an internally-defined type (tokenization:stanford). The annotations include references to the objects defined in the WS-EV, in this example, *Token* (defined at http://vocab.lappsgrid.org/Token), with (inherited) properties *id, start,* and *end* defined at http://vocab.lappsgrid.org/Token#id, http://vocab.lappsgrid.org/Token#start and http://vocab.lappsgrid.org/Token#end. The web page defining these terms is shown in Fig. 4.

Thing > Annotation > Span > Token

Definition	A string of one or more characters that serves as an indivisible unit for the purposes of morpho-syntactic labeling (part of speech tagging).
Similar to	http://www.isocat.org/datcat/DC-1403
URI	http//vocab.lappsgrid.org/Token

Metadata

Metadata from Annotation

Properties	Type	Description
producer	List of URI	The software that produced the annotations.
rules	List of URI	The documentation (if any) for the rules that were used to identify the annotations.

Properties

Properties	Type	Description
pos	String or URI	Part-of-speech tag associated with the token.
lemma	String or URI	The root (base) form associated with the token. URI may point to a lexicon entry.
tokenType	String or URI	Sub-type such as word, punctuation, abbreviation, number, symbol, etc. Ideally a URI referencing a pre-defined descriptor.
orth	String or URI	Orthographic properties of the token such as LowerCase, UpperCase, Upperinitial, etc. Ideally a URI referencing a pre-defined descriptor.
length	Integer	The length of the token

Properties from Span

Properties	Type	Description
start	Integer	The starting offset (0-based) in the primary data.
end	Integer	The ending offset (0-based) in the primary data.

Properties from Annotation

Properties	Type	Description
id	String	A unique identifier associated with the annotation.

Properties from Thing

Properties	Type	Description
alternateName	String	An alias for the item.

Fig. 4. Token definition

4.1   Mapping to JSON-LD

As noted above in Sect. 1, existing schemes and systems for organizing linguistic information exchanged by NLP tools vary considerably. Figure 5 shows some variants for a few commonly used NLP tools, which differ in terminology, structure, and physical format. To be used in the LAPPS Grid, tools such as those in the list are wrapped so that their output is in JSON-LD format, which provides syntactic interoperability, terms are mapped to corresponding objects in the WS-EV, and the object-feature relations reflect those defined in the WS-EV. Correspondingly, wrappers transduce the LIF representation to the format used internally by the tool on input. This way, the tools use their internal format as usual and map to LIF for exchange only.

For example, the Stanford POS tagger XML output format produces output like this:

```
<word id="0" pos="VB">Let</word>
```

Name	Input	Form	Output	Form	Example
Stanford tagger	pt	n/a	word_pos	opl	box_NN1
	XML	n/a	XML	inline	<word id="0" pos="VB">Let</word>
NaCTeM tagger	pt	n/a	word/pos	inline	box/NN1
CLAWS (1)	pt	n/a	word_pos	inline	box_NN1
CLAWS (2)	pt	n/a	XML	inline	<w id="2" pos="NN1">Type</w>
CST Copenhagen	pt	n/a	word/pos	inline	box/NN1
TreeTagger	pt?	n/a	word pos lem	opl	The DT the
TnT	token	opl	word pos	opl	der ART
			word (pos pr)+	opl	Falkenstein NE 8.00 NN 1.99
Twitter NLP	pt	opl	word pos conf	opl	smh G 0.9406
NLTK	pt	s, bls	[('word', 'pos')]	inline	[('At', 'IN'), ('eight', 'CD'),]
OpenNLP splitter	pt	n/a	sentences	ospl	I can't tell you if he's here.
OpenNLP tokenizer	sent	ospl	tokens	wss, ospl	I can 't tell you if he 's here .
OpenNLP tagger	token	wss, ospl	word_pos	ospl	At_IN eight_CD o'clock_JJ on_IN

pt = plain text
opl = one per line
wss = white space separated
ospl = one sentence per line
bps = blank line separated

Fig. 5. I/O variants for common splitters, tokenizers, and POS taggers

This maps to the following LIF representation:

```
{
    "@type" : "Token",
    "id" : "0",
    "start" : 18,
    "end" : 21,
    "features" : {
        "pos"    : "VB"
    }
}
```

The Stanford representation uses the term "word" as an XML element name, gives an id and pos as attribute-value pairs, and includes the string being annotated as element content. For conversion to JSON-LD/WS-EV, "word" is mapped to "Token", and the attributes *id* and *pos* map to properties of Token with the same names. Because the LIF representation uses standoff annotation, the properties *start* and *end* are included in order to provide the offset location of the string in the primary data.

Services that share a format other than JSON-LD need not map into and out of LIF when pipelined in the LAPPS Grid. For example, two GATE services would exchange GATE XML documents, and two UIMA services would exchange UIMA CAS, as usual. This avoids unnecessary conversion and at the same time allows including services consisting of individual tools or entire composite workflows from other frameworks. Figure 6 gives an example of the logical flow in the LAPPS Grid, showing conversions into and out of LIF where needed.

Each service in the LAPPS Grid is required to provide metadata that specifies what kind of input is required and what kind of output is produced. For example, any service as depicted in the flow diagram in Fig. 6 can require input with specific content (tokens, sentences, etc.), reduced according to certain specifications (stanford-style tokenization, penn pos tags, etc.), and in a particular format (gate-document, uima-cas, LIF).

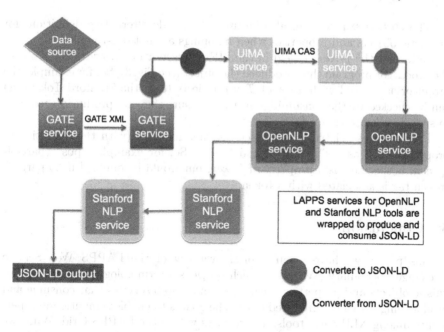

Fig. 6. Logical flow through the LAPPS Grid (client-server communication not represented) (Color figure online)

We have created the WS-EV to provide a basic, common terminology that can handle the basic types that are exchanged among LAPPS Grid services, regardless of the internal representations they use, with the intention that where possible, commonly used linguistic types (whatever their names, and whether they are objects or properties in the original scheme) are mapped to terms in the WS-EV. However, services may provide their own definitions for any object or property, or use names other than those in the WS-EV. This is achieved by using the optional JSON-LD @CONTEXT key to reference a set of user-defined context elements or redefine the names that refer to WS-EV terms. For example, in the fragment below, a service provides an alternative definition for *Token* by associating it with a different URI (where, presumably, an alternative definition is provided). It also renames the properties "start" and "end" to "startOffset" and "endOffset", by associating these names with the URIs for the former names in the WS-EV:

```
{
  "@context": {
          "Token":"http:/www/example.com/MyToken",
          "startOffset":"http://vocab.lappsgrid.org/Token#start",
          "endOffset":"http://vocab.lappsgrid.org/Token#end",
          },
  "annotations": [
     {"@type":"Token","id":"t0","startOffset": 0,"endOffset": 5}
  ]
}
```

The @CONTEXT key can also be used to provide alternative definitions for linguistic objects and properties when mappings are not one-to-one.

Note that the *producer* field in the LIF representation provides the name of the process or program that produced the object (see Fig. 3). So, for example, the producer associated with a set of *Token* objects (e.g., the Stanford Tokenizer) can be checked by the consuming service to ensure they are produced according to specific tokenization rules.

Properties associated with objects are not required (with the exception of properties such as "id", "start", and "end"). So, for example, "pos" (part-of-speech) is specified as a property of *Token*, but would be omitted if no part-of-speech tag is associated with a token.

5   Conclusion

In this paper, we have given a brief overview of the LAPPS Web Service Exchange Vocabulary (WS-EV), which provides a terminology for a core of linguistic objects and properties exchanged among web services that consume and produce linguistically annotated data. The goal is to enable semantic interoperability among NLP data, tools, and services within the LAPPS Grid. While we recognize the inherent problems of defining a type system for linguistic objects, the LAPPS Grid cannot operate without semantic interoperability among services, and the WS-EV is our means to fulfill that requirement. Our approach is therefore notably bottom-up (adding objects and properties as needed) and treads a fine line between over- and under-specification. Ideally, the WS-EV will be useful to others, either web service providers or users of systems like UIMA, as a point of departure for defining type systems etc., and potentially provide a base upon which others can usefully build.

Acknowledgements. This work was supported by National Science Foundation grants NSF-ACI 1147944 and NSF-ACI 1147912.

References

1. Cieri, C., DiPersio, D., Wright, J.: Intellectual property rights management with web services. In: Proceedings of the Workshop on Open Infrastructures and Analysis Frameworks for HLT, Dublin, Ireland, August 2014
2. Ferrucci, D., Nyberg, E., Allan, J., Barker, K., Brown, E., Chu-Carroll, J., Ciccolo, A., Duboue, P., Fan, J., Gondek, D., Hovy, E., Katz, B., Lally, A., McCord, M., Morarescu, P., Murdock, B., Porter, B., Prager, J., Strzalkowski, T., Welty, C., Zadrozny, W.: Towards the open advancement of question answering systems. Technical report, IBM Research, Armonk, New York (2009)
3. Ferrucci, D.A., Brown, E.W., Chu-Carroll, J., Fan, J., Gondek, D., Kalyanpur, A., Lally, A., Murdock, J.W., Nyberg, E., Prager, J.M., Schlaefer, N., Welty, C.A.: Building Watson: an overview of the DeepQA project. AI Mag. **31**(3), 59–79 (2010)

4. Fokkens, A., van Erp, M., Postma, M., Pedersen, T., Vossen, P., Freire, N.: Offspring from reproduction problems: what replication failure teaches us. In: Proceedings of the 51st Annual Meeting of the Association for Computational Linguistics, vol. 1, pp. 1691–1701. Association for Computational Linguistics, Sofia, Bulgaria, August 2013. http://www.aclweb.org/anthology/P13-1166
5. Garduno, E., Yang, Z., Maiberg, A., McCormack, C., Fang, Y., Nyberg, E.: CSE framework: a UIMA-based distributed system for configuration space exploration unstructured information management architecture. In: Klgl, P., de Castilho, R.E., Tomanek, K. (ed.) UIMA@GSCL, CEUR Workshop Proceedings, pp. 14–17. CEUR-WS.org (2013)
6. Giardine, B., Riemer, C., Hardison, R.C., Burhans, R., Elnitski, L., Shah, P., Zhang, Y., Blankenberg, D., Albert, I., Taylor, J., Miller, W., Kent, W.J., Nekrutenko, A.: Galaxy: a platform for interactive large-scale genome analysis. Genome Res. 15(10), 1451–1455 (2005)
7. Hellmann, S., Lehmann, J., Auer, S., Brümmer, M.: Integrating NLP using linked data. In: Alani, H., Kagal, L., Fokoue, A., Groth, P., Biemann, C., Parreira, J.X., Aroyo, L., Noy, N., Welty, C., Janowicz, K. (eds.) ISWC 2013, Part II. LNCS, vol. 8219, pp. 98–113. Springer, Heidelberg (2013). http://svn.aksw.org/papers/2013/ISWC_NIF/public.pdf
8. Ide, N., Pustejovsky, J.: What does interoperability mean, anyway? toward an operational definition of interoperability. In: Proceedings of the Second International Conference on Global Interoperability for Language Resources, ICGL (2010). http://www.cs.vassar.edu/~ide/papers/ICGL10.pdf
9. Ide, N., Pustejovsky, J., Calzolari, N., Soria, C.: The SILT and FlaReNet international collaboration for interoperability. In: Proceedings of the Third Linguistic Annotation Workshop, ACL-IJCNLP, August 2009
10. Ide, N., Pustejovsky, J., Cieri, C., Nyberg, E., Wang, D., Suderman, K., Verhagen, M., Wright, J.: The language application grid. In: Proceedings of the Ninth International Conference on Language Resources and Evaluation LREC 2014. European Language Resources Association (ELRA), Reykjavik, Iceland, May 2014
11. Ide, N., Suderman, K.: The linguistic annotation framework: a standard for annotation interchange and merging. Lang. Resour. Eval. 48(3), 395–418 (2014)
12. Ishida, T. (ed.): The Language Grid: Service-Oriented Collective Intelligence for Language Resource Interoperability. Springer, Heidelberg (2011)
13. ISO-24612: Language Resource Management - Linguistic Annotation Framework. ISO 24612 (2012)
14. Patel, A., Yang, Z., Nyberg, E., Mitamura, T.: Building an optimal QA system automatically using configuration space exploration for QA4MRE 2013 tasks. In: Proceedings of CLEF 2013 (2013)
15. Poch, M., Bel, N.: Interoperability and technology for a language resources factory. In: Proceedings of the Workshop on Language Resources. Technology and Services in the Sharing Paradigm, Asian Federation of Natural Language Processing, Chiang Mai, Thailand, pp. 32–40, November 2011
16. Villegas, M., Bel, N., Bel, S., Rodrguez, V.: A case study on interoperability for language resources and applications. In: Proceedings of the Seventh International Conference on Language Resources and Evaluation, LREC 2010, Valletta, Malta, May 2010
17. W3C OWL Working Group: OWL 2 Web Ontology Language: Document Overview. W3C Recommendation (2012)
18. W3C SKOS Working Group: SKOS Simple Knowledge Organization System Reference. W3C Recommendation (2009)

19. Windhouwer, M.: RELcat: a Relation Registry for ISOcat data categories. In: Calzolari, N., Choukri, K., Declerck, T., Dogan, M.U., Maegaard, B., Mariani, J., Odijk, J., Piperidis, S. (eds.) LREC. European Language Resources Association (ELRA), pp. 3661–3664 (2012)
20. Yang, Z., Garduno, E., Fang, Y., Maiberg, A., McCormack, C., Nyberg, E.: Building optimal information systems automatically: configuration space exploration for biomedical information systems. In: Proceedings of the CIKM 2013 (2013)

The LAPPS Interchange Format

Marc Verhagen[1]([✉]), Keith Suderman[2], Di Wang[3], Nancy Ide[2], Chunqi Shi[1],
Jonathan Wright[4], and James Pustejovsky[1]

[1] Brandeis University, Waltham, MA, USA
{marc,shicq,jamesp}@cs.brandeis.edu
[2] Vassar College, Poughkeepsie, NY, USA
{suderman,ide}@cs.vassar.edu
[3] Carnegie Mellon University, Pittsburgh, PA, USA
diwang@cs.cmu.edu
[4] Linguistic Data Consortium, Philadelphia, PA, USA
jdwright@ldc.upenn.edu

Abstract. We describe and motivate the LAPPS Interchange Format,
a JSON-LD format that is used for data transfer between language services in the Language Application Grid. The LAPPS Interchange Format
enables syntactic and semantic interoperability of language services by
providing a uniform syntax for common linguistic data and by using the
Linked Data aspect of JSON-LD to refer to external definitions of linguistic categories. It is tightly integrated with the Web Services Exchange
Vocabulary, which specifies a terminology for a core of linguistic objects
and features exchanged by services.

Keywords: Language services · Interoperability · Linguistic resources ·
Web services · JSON-LD · Natural Language Processing

1 Introduction

The Language Application (LAPPS) Grid project is establishing a framework
that enables language service discovery, composition and reuse. It promotes sustainability, manageability, usability, and interoperability of Natural Language
Processing (NLP) components, provides access to basic NLP processing tools
and resources, and enables pipelining these tools to create custom NLP applications and composite services. The LAPPS Grid is based on the Service Grid
Server Software [6] and has currently deployed a suite of services for applications
that typically appear in NLP pipelines, including multiple tokenizers, sentence
splitters, POS taggers, named entity recognizers, coreference resolution modules,
phrase structure parsers and dependency parsers. The LAPPS philosophy and
its implementation is described in more detail in [4].

An essential aspect of composing services is to provide a vehicle for data
exchange. We have designed the LAPPS Interchange Format (LIF) to represent
linguistically annotated data for the purposes of web service exchange. Services
that implement or wrap a linguistic application may be required to consume LIF

© Springer International Publishing Switzerland 2016
Y. Murakami and D. Lin (Eds.): WLSI 2015, LNAI 9442, pp. 33–47, 2016.
DOI: 10.1007/978-3-319-31468-6_3

objects and are responsible for creating LIF objects.[1] LIF is an instantiation of JSON-LD (JavaScript Object Notation for Linked Data), a method for transporting Linked Data using JSON. JSON is a lightweight, text-based, language-independent data interchange format that defines a small set of formatting rules for the portable representation of structured data. JSON-LD extends JSON by enabling services to reference categories and definitions in web-based repositories and ontologies or any suitably defined concept at a given URI.[2]

Although the pipeline architecture has been implemented in several NLP frameworks over the past decades, including self-contained (non-service) frameworks such as GATE and UIMA, no accepted standard for module description or input/output interchange exists to support service discovery, composition and reuse in the language application domain. To address this, we have defined a Web Service Exchange Vocabulary (WS-EV), which specifies a terminology for a core of linguistic objects and features exchanged among NLP tools that consume and produce linguistically annotated data. As such, it addresses a need to not only identify a standard terminology, but also indicate the relations among them. Where possible, the core is drawn from existing repositories such as ISOCat; however, because many categories and objects relevant for web service exchange are not included in such repositories, we have attempted to identify a set of more or less universal concepts by surveying concepts, type systems and schemas used in, for example, the Julie Lab and DARPA GALE UIMA type systems and the GATE schemas for linguistic phenomena, together with the I/O requirements of commonly used NLP software (for example, the Stanford NLP tools and OpenNLP). WS-EV is described in more detail in [5] and all current definitions are available online at http://vocab.lappsgrid.org, also see *The Language Application Grid Web Service Exchange Vocabulary* elsewhere in this volume.

The LAPPS Interchange Format is in essence a vehicle for transporting information between NLP web services. The core of this information consists of linguistics annotation objects and features, as well as metadata associated with these annotation objects and features. Many of these objects, features and meta data properties are described in the WS-EV (also known as the LAPPS Vocabulary, and we will use these two terms interchangeably), but LIF allows services to use its own definitions and annotation objects. In spirit, LIF is similar to the Linguistic Annotation Framework [3], the CAS format used in UIMA [2] and the format used by the GATE architecture [1].

In the following sections, we describe the structure of LIF objects and the relation between LIF and the LAPPS Vocabulary. We also provide some examples with extensive comments. Throughout, we motivate our choices and explain some of the trade-offs.

---

[1] The USE of LIF objects is actually not a strict requirement imposed for LAPPS Services. For example, services based on an existing pipeline of GATE components may choose to use the GATE format until the output of the very last component. We have created a suite of translation services that translate common linguistic objects between LIF and common existing formats.

[2] See http://www.json.org/ and http://json-ld.org/.

2   The Structure of LIF Objects

The top-level structure of a LIF object contains keys to represent contextual information, meta data, the text being processed and a list of views. A minimal LIF object looks as follows:

```
{
  "@context": "http://vocab.lappsgrid.org/context-1.0.0.jsonld",
  "metadata": { },
  "text": { },
  "views": [ ]
}
```

2.1   The @CONTEXT Key

The @context key holds a special meaning in JSON-LD. It is used to define the short-hand names called terms that are used throughout a JSON-LD document. In the case of LIF, the value of the @context key is a fixed URL that points to an external context file with abbreviations into various parts of the LAPPS vocabulary. We allow services to provide their own context in a LIF object, but we require that services do this by adding contexts to individual views or to add elements to existing contexts in individual views.

While not recommended, services can use local contexts in views to redefine terms that are also defined in the external context file. The drawback here is that some annotation objects or properties would have different meanings depending on what view they are in. For example, if we have two definitions for Token, one in the top-level context and one in a view, then the Token annotation type in two different views would be expanded to two different full URIs with different associated definitions. While this can be considered to impede interoperability in the sense that these two types are now not the same thing anymore, allowing different expansions does reflect the reality that different definitions exist, allows services to use either definition, and makes this transparent to the user.

2.2   The METADATA Key

In the current LAPPS Grid, there is no use case for what should be in this metadata object. LIF objects are created and consumed by services and metadata added by services are typically relevant to individual views only and are therefore included as metadata inside the views, as described in Sect. 2.4. Nevertheless, we allow a metadata key here for future use.

2.3   The TEXT Key

This is a JSON-LD value object containing @value and @language keys. The value associated with @value is a string and the value associated with @language follows the rules in [7], which for our current purposes boils down to using the

ISO 639 code. Note also that `language` is defined as a meta data property in the vocabulary.[3]

2.4 The VIEWS Key

This is where all the annotations live with their associated meta data. The value is a JSON-LD array of views where each view specifies what information it contains and what service created that information. Views are similar to annotation layers and annotation tasks as used by several mainstream annotation tools, formalisms and frameworks. They contain structured information about a text but are separate from that text. Views also provide flexibility in structuring annotations. One example of this flexibility is that the results of two separate part of speech taggers can be stored in two different views. These taggers could use different tag sets or different rules or even different training data. The important point here is that from the perspective of the services in a pipeline, this flexibility allows the services to add exactly what they want to add without them being restricted by views already in the LIF object.

A note on the nature of the `views` array. JSON-LD arrays are by default unordered lists, but we have added context definitions to the external file to ensure this is an ordered list. The order is interpreted to reflect when views were added. So we require that any view added by a service has to be appended to the end.

There are a few general principles that apply to views:

1. For each view, the metadata section specifies what kind of information objects are in the view. Information objects are Annotation objects as defined in the vocabulary or subtypes thereof.[4]
2. Annotation objects in views can refer to annotation objects in other views.
3. There is no limit to the number of views and services may create as many new views as they want.
4. Services may add information to existing views by adding annotation objects or by adding features to annotation objects. If annotation objects added are of a type that does not yet occur in the view, then the view's metadata section may need to be updated.
5. Services may even overwrite or delete information in existing views, but this is generally not recommended and such services should make it obvious that they are overwriting data.

This last principle deserves some elaboration. One side effect of allowing non-monotonic operations is that the meta data on a view (described a few paragraphs below) cannot fully describe what data are available in a view, which is suboptimal. We allow this because the current versions of some of our evaluation services need to overwrite data. Note however that the vast majority of services

---

[3] See http://vocab.lappsgrid.org/Document.html#language.
[4] See http://vocab.lappsgrid.org/Annotation.

will not overwrite data and many pipelines can be constructed without fear of impacted annotation integrity.

Each view object has four keys: @context, id, metadata and annotations. Below is a minimal example of a view with just one annotation element.

```
"views": [
    {
        "@context": {},
        "id": "v0",
        "metadata": {
            "contains": {
                "Token": {
                    "producer": "lappsgrid.brandeis.opennlp.Tokenizer:0.0.4",
                    "rules": "tokenization:opennlp_basic" }}},
        "annotations": [
            { "@type": "Token",
              "id": "t0",
              "start": 0,
              "end": 5,
              "features": {} } ]
    }
]
```

The @context key in a view is an optional key that can be used for user-defined context elements. The LAPPS Vocabulary is considered a recommendation for commonly used linguistic types, but services may provide their own definitions and link to them in the local context. For example, a service that has a non-standard definition for Token could either use another name for this annotation type or use the same term yet redefine its meaning:

```
{
    "@context": { "Token": "http://www.example.com/MyToken" },
    "annotations": [
        { "@type": "Token", "id": "t0", "start": 0, "end": 5 } ]
}
```

Note that annotations of type Token in other views are still governed by the definition of Token in the LAPPS Vocabulary. Clearly, full semantic operability between the two types of tokens carrying the same is not automatically enforced, but at least there is transparency in what terms are used in each view.

Amongst the general principles listed above was that services may add contexts and information to existing views. Nothing prevents services from taking an existing view with Token annotations, copy those to a new view and redefine the meaning of Token for that view. We have chosen to allow this flexibility, while recognizing that there may be value in not allowing services to redefine terms that are already used in a view.

Services are not required to spell out user-defined properties in the context of the view, but, if they do not, full URIs must be used for the values of the @type key.

The **id** key is required and its value should be unique relative to all view objects. If annotation elements refer to an annotation element in another view then they have to use the view identifier as part of the reference. An example of this will be given in Sect. 3.2.

The **metadata** key contains information to describe the annotations in a view. At this point, its only key is `contains`. Other keys may be added, including `timestamp` or a key like `dependsOn`, which would spell out what other views a view is dependent on. The `contains` dictionary has keys that refer to annotation objects in the LAPPS vocabulary or properties of those annotation objects (they can also refer to user-defined objects or properties). And the value of each of those keys is a JSON object with `producer`, `type` and `rules` keys. The relevant part of the example above is repeated here:

```
{
  "contains": {
    "Token": {
      "producer": "lappsgrid.brandeis.opennlp.Tokenizer:0.0.4",
      "type": "tokenization:opennlp",
      "rules": "tokenization:opennlp_basic" }}
}
```

The `producer` key contains a string that gives an indication what service created this particular annotation category in this view and its value is generated by the service itself. It is considered good practice to add a versioning number of the wrapped component. A guiding principle on the current LAPPS Grid is that older versions of components remain in operation, even while newer versions are added.[5] This key is not a unique identifier for the service. In the current implementation of the LAPPS Grid, this string cannot be the unique name that the LAPPS grid has for this service, nor can it be the URL where the service resides. The reason for this is that the service itself has no access to this information and it is the service that adds information to the LIF objects.

The `type` key is used to specify what kind of token we are dealing with. It allows several tokenizers to specify the same type, for example if two tokenizers are both implementations of the OpenNLP tokenization. In the example here the type key has the compact IRI value `tokenization:opennlp` and `tokenization` is defined in the external context file, helping to expand the value of `type` to a full URL that contains a definition of this tokenization scheme. This particular definition resides in the WS-EV.

The `rules` key inside of `Token` can be used to specify a rule set, and, similarly to the `types` key, its value expands to a URL with a rule set definition. In the LAPPS vocabulary, `producer`, `type` and `rules` are all defined as metadata properties on Token (albeit inherited from Annotation)

---

[5] A related issue is that versioning not only applies to the version of the wrapped NLP component, but also the version of the wrapper itself as well as to versions of definitions in the vocabulary. This issue is currently under discussion.

Finally, the value of **annotations**, the fourth key in a view object, is a list of annotation objects. The relevant part of the view printed above is repeated here:

```
"annotations": [
  { "@type": "Token",
    "id": "t0",
    "start": 0,
    "end": 5,
    "features": {}
  }
```

As with other LIF objects, the keys allowed are specified in the JSON LIF Schema at http://vocab.lappsgrid.org/schema/lif-schema.json, in this case in the definitions for **annotations** and **annotation**.

The **@type** key is another special JSON-LD key and it is used to set the data type of a node or typed value. The value of **@type** is an element of the LAPPS vocabulary or an annotation category added by the user. But, as mentioned above, note that if a user-definition is added it would be defined outside of the LAPPS vocabulary. In that case the user should either use the full URI or add a context to the view in which this new annotation category lives. Each annotation object has a **id** key, which is an identifier unique to the view as well as **start** and **end** keys, which indicate the character offsets in the text. Annotations that do not refer to a text segment can have **-1** as the start and end.

The **features** dictionary holds all features of the annotation object. Technically all that is required of the keys in the features dictionary is that they expand to a URI. In most cases, the keys reflect properties in the LAPPS vocabulary and we prefer to use the same name. So if we have a property **pos**, we will use **pos** in the features dictionary. This implies that **pos** needs to be defined in the context so that it can be expanded to the correct URI in the vocabulary. This in turn implies that in the vocabulary each property should be only defined once.

It may be instructive here to expand a bit on how elements of a LIF object relate to elements in the WS-EV. One of the differences between WS-EV and LIF is in where properties of annotation objects are expressed. LIF is governed syntactically by its schema. A fragment of the schema, the specification for the **annotation** object, is printed below.

```
"annotation": {
  "type": "object",
  "properties": {
    "id": { "type": "string" },
    "@type": { "type": "string" },
    "start": { "type": "integer", "minimum": -1 },
    "end": { "type": "integer", "minimum": -1 },
    "features": { "$ref": "#/definitions/map" },
    "metadata": { "$ref": "#/definitions/map" }
}
```

The WS-EV pages for `Annotation` and its subtypes define many properties that cannot be expressed on the top-level of the LIF `annotation` object, like `pos` and `lemma`. In LIF, these are all expressed in the `features` dictionary, which is not restricted in any way and which can also be used by user-services to put in any property it wants.

3   Examples

To illustrate the principles and descriptions above, we now give some examples of LIF objects that would be generated by services that add common annotation types. In particular, we look at sentences, tokens, parts of speech, coreference and phrase structure.

3.1   Tokens and Parts-of-Speech

This section contains examples on how to represent tokenized and split text. It also elaborates on how to represent token-level information, in particular part of speech tags. Sentence splitters create annotation objects of type `Sentence` and tokenizers create objects of type `Token`, these are both defined in the LAPPS vocabulary.[6] POS taggers fill in the `pos` property in the `features` dictionary on the token (but note that some taggers create token objects as part of that process).[7] There are many potential pipelines for creating sentences, tokens and part of speech tags. For our example, we take a pipeline where the OpenNLP splitter service on the Brandeis University LAPPS Grid Node is followed by the Stanford tokenizer and the Stanford POS tagger, both implemented as services on the Vassar LAPPS Grid Node. Note that in this case the Stanford tokenizer and tagger are wrapped as separate services. The LIF object handed into the pipeline is as follows:

```
{
  "@context": "http://vocab.lappsgrid.org/context-1.0.0.jsonld",
  "text": { "@value": "Fido barks." },
  "views": []
}
```

With this object as input, the sentence splitter will append a sentence view to the views array and the tokenizer a token view, as exemplified on the next page. Recall from Sect. 2.4 that wrapped components are expected to add views to the end of the views array and that each view has a unique identifier.

---

[6] See   http://vocab.lappsgrid.org/Sentence.html   and   http://vocab.lappsgrid.org/Token.html.

[7] An alternative to this approach is to make PosTag a kind of annotation rather than a feature of an annotation, which can help in reducing potential redundancies that will become obvious later in this section. However, it was important to us to keep the number of annotation categories in the vocabulary as low as possible. We also felt that conceptually a part-of-speech tag is a natural feature of a token and not a standalone category.

```
{
  "@context": "http://vocab.lappsgrid.org/context-1.0.0.jsonld",
  "text": { "@value": "Fido barks." },
  "views": [
    {
      "id": "v1",
      "metadata": {
        "contains": {
          "Sentence": {
            "producer": "lapps.brandeis.opennlp.Splitter:0.0.4",
            "type": "splitter:opennlp" }}},
      "annotations": [
        { "@type": "Sentence", "id": "s0", "start": 0, "end": 11 } ]
    },
    {
      "id": "v2",
      "metadata": {
        "contains": {
          "Token": {
            "producer": "lapps.anc.stanford.SATokenizer:1.4.0",
            "type": "tokenization:stanford" }}},
      "annotations": [
        { "@type": "Token", "id": "tok0", "start": 0, "end": 4 },
        { "@type": "Token", "id": "tok1", "start": 5, "end": 10 },
        { "@type": "Token", "id": "tok2", "start": 10, "end": 11 } ]
    }
  ]
}
```

The Stanford tagger, the third step in the pipeline, could add part-of-speech information to an existing view, in which case the view with the identifier "v2" will be amended by the tagging service (not all meta data are printed):

```
{
  "id": "v2",
  "metadata": {
    "contains": {
      "Token": { ... },
      "Token#pos": {
        "producer": "lapps.anc.stanford.SATagger:1.4.0",
        "posTagSet": "penn",
        "type": "postagging:stanford" }}},
  "annotations": [
    { "@type": "Token", "id": "tok0", "start": 0, "end": 4,
      "features": { "pos": "NNP" } },
    { "@type": "Token", "id": "tok1", "start": 5, "end": 10,
      "features": { "pos": "VBZ" } },
    { "@type": "Token", "id": "tok2", "start": 10, "end": 11,
      "features": { "pos": "." } } ]
}
```

In the vocabulary, `posTagSet` is defined as a meta data property on Token and `penn` is a term defined in the external context file that points to a URL with information on this tag set. Note the use of `Token#pos` and `pos`. These are two alternative ways of pointing to the same URL in the vocabulary and again depend on term definitions in the external context file.

The second way for the tagger to add to the LIF object is to add a view and not change the existing token view. While the views with identifier "v1" and "v2" would remain the same, the next view would be appended to the views list:

```
{
  "id": "v3",
  "metadata": {
    "contains": {
      "Token": {
        "producer": "lapps.anc.stanford.SATokenizer:1.4.0",
        "type": "tokenization:stanford" },
      "Token#pos": {
        "producer": "lapps.anc.stanford.SATagger:1.4.0",
        "posTagset": "penn",
        "type": "postagging:stanford" }}},
  "annotations": [
    { "@type": "Token", "id": "tok0", "start": 0, "end": 4,
      "features": { "pos": "NNP" } },
    { "@type": "Token", "id": "tok1", "start": 5, "end": 10,
      "features": { "pos": "VBZ" } },
    { "@type": "Token", "id": "tok2", "start": 10, "end": 11,
      "features": { "pos": "." } } ]
}
```

This view's annotation list is identical to the previous one shown because annotation elements from the view with identifier "v2" are copied and the tagger does not overwrite existing information, rather, it fills in slots in the feature dictionary. There are other cases though where existing information could be overwritten. One example would be a cascade of taggers all writing to the same view and where later taggers are allowed to overwrite results of earlier taggers. In those cases, the provenance of a particular part-of-speech tag is not clear anymore. Adding a view with merged information would have the benefit of introducing that clarity again at the cost of extra views and some redundancy.

3.2   Coreference

Coreference provides an example where (1) elements in a view refer to elements in other views and (2) the feature dictionary contains non-atomic values. The examples below are all for the simple phrase *Sue sees herself.* The JSON-LD used in this section is fairly informal, just showing the bits and pieces that are relevant to the discussion.

First assume an existing LIF object that contains tokens, that is, the coreference module applies in a pipeline after a tokenizer, and consumes a LIF object generated by the tokenizer. Below we print just the relevant view with its annotations.

```
{
  "id": "v1",
  "metadata": {
    "contains": {
      "Token": {
        "producer": "lapps.brandeis.opennlp.Tokenizer:1.4.0",
        "type": "tokenizer:opennlp" }}},
  "annotations": [
    { "@type": "Token", "id": "tok0", "start": 0, "end": 3 },
    { "@type": "Token", "id": "tok1", "start": 4, "end": 8 },
    { "@type": "Token", "id": "tok2", "start": 9, "end": 16 } ]
}
```

A view added by a coreference component introduces two new annotation objects: Coreference and Markable, both defined in the LAPPS Vocabulary. Both objects refer to other annotation elements, which for the Markable object are outside of the view.

```
{
  "id": "v2",
  "metadata": {
    "contains": {
      "Markable": {
        "producer": "lapps.brandeis.opennlp.coref:1.0",
        "type": "coreference:opennlp" },
      "Coreference": {
        "producer": "lapps.brandeis.opennlp.coref:1.0",
        "type": "coreference:opennlp" }}},
  "annotations": [
    { "@type": "Markable", "id": "m0",
      "features": { "targets": [ "v1:tok0" ] } },
    { "@type": "Markable", "id": "m1",
      "features": { "targets": [ "v1:tok2" ] } },
    { "@type": "Coreference", "id": "coref0",
      "features": {
        "mentions": [ "m0", "m1" ],
        "representative": "m0" }}]
}
```

The Coreference and Markable definitions in the LAPPS vocabulary include definitions for the mentions, representative and targets properties. These properties allow for a common representation that abstracts away over the representations produced by common coreference components in GATE, OpenNLP or the Stanford tools.

The markables are required and the mentions list cannot refer directly to other views. There is a slight redundancy penalty to pay because other views may already have the objects that are co-referring. But it appeared conceptually cleaner to do it this way. In the example above, the `targets` property in the `Markable` annotation object contains a list of pointers to annotation objects in another view. The reference "v1:tok0" contains both a view identifier and an annotation object identifier, the latter is unique to the view it occurs in.

Here is an example where the coreference service applies to virgin data, that is, it is the first and only component in a pipeline. In that case, there is no other view to refer to. Again, the input text is *Sue sees herself* and we print just the view added by the coreference service. For brevity, we also decline to fill in all the structure inside the `contains` key.

```
{
  "id": "v1",
  "metadata": {
    "contains": {
      "Markable": { },
      "Coreference": { } }},
  "annotations": [
    { "@type": "Markable", "id": "m0", "start": 0, "end": 3 },
    { "@type": "Markable", "id": "m1", "start": 9, "end": 16 },
    { "@type": "Coreference",
      "id": "coref0",
      "features": {
        "mentions": [ "m0", "m1" ],
        "representative": "m0" }}]
}
```

The annotation elements here are very similar to the ones used in the previous example. The only difference is that the `Markable` objects have a `start` and `end` key instead of the `targets` key.

If a coreference component generates actual annotations that can be used, but that are not available in other views, then we put them in the coreference view. These could be named entities like persons (which is what the ANNIE Coreference module in GATE produces), noun chunks or tokens. These can all be added to the coreference view. Below we have an example where token annotations are added to the coreference view.

```
{
  "id": "v1",
  "metadata": {
    "contains": {
      "Token": { },
      "Markable": { },
      "Coreference": { } }},
  "annotations": [
    { "@type": "Token", "id": "tok0", "start": 0, "end": 3 },
    { "@type": "Token", "id": "tok2", "start": 9, "end": 16 },

    { "@type": "Markable",
```

```
    "id": "m0",
    "features": {
      "targets": [ "tok0" ] }},
  { "@type": "Markable",
    "id": "m1",
    "features": {
      "targets": [ "tok2" ] }},
  { "@type": "Coreference",
    "id": "coref0",
    "features": {
      "mentions": [ "m0", "m1" ],
      "representative": "m0" }}]
}
```

Sometimes, coreference modules will have all kinds of other information on the annotations that are linked. For example, the ANNIE Coreference component has an attribute ENTITY_MENTION_TYPE with value PRONOUN on one of the annotations. We can put these in the features directory of the Markable.

```
{
  "metadata": {
    "contains": {
      "Token": { },
      "Markable": { },
      "Coreference": { } }},
  "annotations": [
    { "@type": "Token", "id": "tok0", "start": 0, "end": 3 },
    { "@type": "Token", "id": "tok2", "start": 9, "end": 16 },
    { "@type": "Markable", "id": "m0",
      "features": {
        "targets": [ "tok0" ] }},
    { "@type": "Markable", "id": "m1",
      "features": {
        "targets": [ "tok2" ],
        "ENTITY_MENTION_TYPE": "PRONOUN" } },
    { "@type": "Coreference", "id": "coref0",
      "features": {
        "mentions": [ "m0", "m1" ],
        "representative": "m0" }}]
}
```

The features dictionary can be used for any feature generated by a service. Note however that each key in the dictionary needs to resolve to a full URI and that the service is now responsible for adding a statement to the context that does this.

3.3   Syntactic Structure

As a final example we show how a tree structure is represented in LIF. Let's assume the syntactic parser service consumes as input the output of a tokenizer (here printed without the metadata for the view):

```
{
  "text": "Sue sees herself",
  "views": [
    { "id": "v1",
      "annotations": [
        { "@type": "Token", "id": "tok0", "start": 0, "end": 3 },
        { "@type": "Token", "id": "tok1", "start": 4, "end": 8 },
        { "@type": "Token", "id": "tok2", "start": 9, "end": 16 } ]}],
}
```

We introduce an annotation object of type PhraseStructure. This object contains a list of constituents for some text span, typically for a sentence. It introduces the constituents feature which contains a list of identifiers pointing at annotations of type Constituent in the same view. A Constituent has a label reflecting the category and in the feature dictionary a list of children. Again, these annotation types are defined in the vocabulary. The view added by the parser looks as follows.

```
{
  "id": "v2",
  "metadata": {
    "contains": {
      "PhraseStructure": {
        "producer": "edu.brandeis.cs.lappsgrid.SimpleParser:1.0.0",
        "categorySet": "categories:PTBcategories",
        "type": "PhraseStructure:SimpleParser" }}},
  "annotations": [
    { "@type": "PhraseStructure",
      "id": "phrase0",
      "start": 0,
      "end": 16,
      "features": {
        "constituents": [ "c0", "c1", "c2" ] } },
    { "@type": "Constituent", "label": "S", "id": "c0",
      "features": { "children": [ "c1", "c2"] } },
    { "@type": "Constituent", "label": "NP", "id": "c1",
      "features": { "children": [ "v1:tok0" ] }},
    { "@type": "Constituent", "label": "VP", "id": "c2",
      "features": { "children": [ "v1:tok1", "v1:tok2" ] }}]
}
```

This example highlights an important feature of the constituents list in the view, which is that all annotation objects on the view are top-level elements in the constituents list. Annotation objects can refer to other annotation objects but cannot contain them. We decided to not represent the tree structure directly using deeper embedding. This is part of a more general issue which is whether we LIF structures are structurally as close as possible to encoded data structures like trees, linked lists and graphs. We flatten out all these structures.

4 Conclusion and Future Work

We have described the LAPPS Interchange Format and have given examples of what kind of LIF objects need to be generated by language services in order to promote interoperability amongst services. While the specifications for many types of language data are mature, the LAPPS Interchange Format is a work in progress and updated versions of the specifications will be available on the LAPPS Grid website at http://www.lappsgrid.org/interoperability/. We are working on a set of Java classes that provide an API for quickly reading and generating LIF objects, thereby facilitating the work of developers who wrap services for the LAPPS Grid. In addition, we continue to explore other processing modules including temporal and spatial processors.

Acknowledgements. This work was supported by two National Science Foundation grants: NSF-ACI 1147944 and NSF-ACI 1147912.

References

1. Cunningham, H., Maynard, D., Bontcheva, K., Tablan, V.: GATE: a framework and graphical development environment for robust NLP tools and applications. In: Proceedings of the 40th Anniversary Meeting of the Association for Computational Linguistics (2002)
2. Ferrucci, D., Lally, A.: UIMA: an architectural approach to unstructured information processing in the corporate research environment. Nat. Lang. Eng. **10**(3–4), 327–348 (2004). Cambridge University Press
3. Ide, N., Suderman, K.: The linguistic annotation framework: a standard for annotation interchange and merging. Lang. Resour. Eval. **48**(3), 395–418 (2014)
4. Ide, N., Pustejovsky, J., Cieri, C., Nyberg, E., Wang, D., Suderman, K., Verhagen, M., Wright, J.: The language application grid. In: The Ninth Language Resources and Evaluation Conference (LREC 2014), Reykjavik, Iceland
5. Ide, N., Pustejovsky, J., Suderman, K., Verhagen, M.: The language application grid web service exchange vocabulary. In: Workshop on Open Infrastructures and Analysis Frameworks for HLT (OIAF4HLT), Held in Conjunction with COLING, Dublin, Ireland (2014)
6. Ishida, T. (ed.): The Language Grid: Service-Oriented Collective Intelligence for Language Resource Interoperability. Springer, Heidelberg (2011). ISBN: 978-3-642-21177-5. Observation of strains. Infect Dis Ther. **3**(1), 35–43 (2011)
7. Phillips, A., Davis, M.: Tags for Identifying Languages. IETF Best Current Practice, September 2009. http://tools.ietf.org/html/bcp47

Service Platform and Service Management

The Language Application Grid

Nancy Ide[1]([✉]), James Pustejovsky[2], Christopher Cieri[3], Eric Nyberg[4],
Denise DiPersio[3], Chunqi Shi[2], Keith Suderman[1], Marc Verhagen[2],
Di Wang[4], and Jonathan Wright[3]

[1] Vassar College, Poughkeepsie, NY, USA
{ide,suderman}@cs.vassar.edu
[2] Brandeis University, Waltham, MA, USA
{jamesp,shicq,marc}@cs.brandeis.edu
[3] Linguistic Data Consortium, Philadelphia, PA, USA
{ccieri,dipersio,jdwright}@ldc.upenn.edu
[4] Carnegie-Mellon University, Pittsburgh, PA, USA
{ehn,diwang}@cs.cmu.edu

Abstract. The Language Application (LAPPS) Grid project is establishing a framework that enables language service discovery, composition, and reuse and promotes sustainability, manageability, usability, and interoperability of natural language Processing (NLP) components. It is based on the *service-oriented architecture* (SOA), a more recent, web-oriented version of the "pipeline" architecture that has long been used in NLP for sequencing loosely-coupled linguistic analyses. The LAPPS Grid provides access to basic NLP processing tools and resources and enables pipelining such tools to create custom NLP applications, as well as composite services such as question answering and machine translation together with language resources such as mono- and multi-lingual corpora and lexicons that support NLP. The transformative aspect of the LAPPS Grid is that it orchestrates access to and deployment of language resources and processing functions available from servers around the globe and enables users to add their own language resources, services, and even service grids to satisfy their particular needs.

Keywords: NLP frameworks · Web services · Service grids · Open advancement · Resource licensing

1   Introduction

The need for robust language processing capabilities across academic disciplines, education, and industry is without question of vital importance to national security, infrastructure development, and the competitiveness of American business. However, while the past two decades have produced reliable and accurate tools for the various linguistic analyses required by Natural Language Processing (NLP) applications, component interoperability–and hence, reusability–has remained a serious problem for the field. A few application frameworks have

© Springer International Publishing Switzerland 2016
Y. Murakami and D. Lin (Eds.): WLSI 2015, LNAI 9442, pp. 51–70, 2016.
DOI: 10.1007/978-3-319-31468-6_4

been recently developed for the integration and delivery of end-to-end language software (e.g., UIMA, GATE), but these frameworks provide for interoperability among tools and components only within the frameworks themselves. Additionally, while such frameworks provide for *syntactic interoperability* via internally-defined physical formats, *semantic interoperability* [11], even within a given framework, is still problematic because users must define their own type systems and ontologies, which vary widely. As a result, the field has remained relatively fragmented, characterized by a lack of standard practices, few widely usable and reusable tools and resources, and much redundancy of effort. Rapid development and deployment of NLP applications has also been hindered by the lack of ready-made, standardized evaluation mechanisms, especially those which enable evaluation of component performance in applications consisting of a pipeline of processing tools. This capability, coupled with access to a repository of interoperable NLP processing components and test data, will enable a major leap in productivity for researchers and developers alike.

To meet this need, the Language Application (LAPPS) Grid project is establishing a framework that enables language service discovery, composition, and reuse and promotes sustainability, manageability, usability, and interoperability of natural language Processing (NLP) components. It is based on the *service-oriented architecture* (SOA), a more recent, web-oriented version of the "pipeline" architecture that has long been used in NLP for sequencing loosely-coupled linguistic analyses. The LAPPS Grid provides a critical missing layer of functionality for NLP: although existing frameworks such as UIMA and GATE provide the capability to wrap, integrate, and deploy language services, they do not provide general support for service discovery, composition, and reuse.

The LAPPS Grid is a collaborative effort among US partners Brandeis University, Vassar College, Carnegie-Mellon University, and the Linguistic Data Consortium at the University of Pennsylvania, and is funded by the US National Science Foundation. The project is part of a larger multi-way international collaboration including key individuals and projects from the U.S., Europe, Australia, and Asia involved with language resource development and distribution and standards-making, who are creating the "Open Language Grid" federation [14], a multi-lingual, international network of web service grids and providers that integrates large-scale computing, high-speed networks, and massive data archives across the world to support the development and testing of integrated natural language applications. The key to the success of this federation is the *interoperability* among tools and services that is accomplished via the service-oriented architecture and the development of common vocabularies and multi-way mappings that have involved key researchers from around the world for over a decade, including members of the LAPPS Grid project[1].

---

[1] E.g., in the NSF-funded Sustainable Interoperability for Language Technology (SILT) project (NSF-INTEROP 0753069) [12], the EU-funded Fostering Language Resources Network (FLaReNet) project [1], the International Standards Organization (ISO) committee for Language Resource Management (ISO TC37 SC4), and parallel efforts in Asia and Australia, together with the LAPPS project and international collaborators.

These efforts laid the groundwork in terms of standards development, raising community awareness and buy-in, and proof-of-concept implementation upon which the creation of a comprehensive, international infrastructure supporting discovery and deployment of web services for language resources and processing components is now being built.

The development and deployment of the LAPPS Grid and its integration in the Open Language Grid has already demonstrated its potential to significantly transform the way language data is accessed, analyzed, and exploited across disciplines for diverse research and development needs, and to ultimately enable a major leap in language processing capabilities that can impact the way people use and interact with computers. The LAPPS Grid offers the following benefits:

- access to high-performance computing NLP facilities for members of the research and education communities who would otherwise have no such access, or who have little background in NLP, while reducing the often prohibitive overhead now required to adapt or develop new components;
- substantially increased access to resources for members of the NLP community as well as researchers in sociology, psychology, economics, education, linguistics, digital media, etc., including mono- and multi-lingual lexical, semantic, and ontological resources that provide information relevant to a wide range of sub-domains (e.g., speech, machine translation, information retrieval);
- means to address the current lack of interoperability among NLP components and data by negotiating across formats and categories;
- access to a state-of-the-art, sophisticated evaluation environment that facilitates assessment of component contribution to overall performance and iterative application development;
- capabilities for rapid development of resources for less-resourced and endangered languages, for which automatic language processing capabilities are only beginning or have yet to be developed;
- enhanced capability for state-of-the-art, "on-the-fly" stream processing of language by enabling NLP applications to call services and extract information from service resources;
- enhancement of research, development, and teaching of NLP by providing controlled access to resources that are otherwise too costly to acquire or restricted by intellectual property rights, as well as access to large-scale computing required to process massive language resources.

It is important to note that the transformative aspect of the LAPPS Grid is not the provision of a suite of web services and composite workflows, but rather that it orchestrates access to and deployment of language resources and processing functions available from servers around the globe and enables users to add their own language resources, services, and even service grids to satisfy their particular needs. As such, the LAPPS Grid is ultimately a community-based project, to which services will be contributed by members of the community and existing service repositories and grids can be federated to enable universal access.

In this paper we provide an overview of the LAPPS Grid and the technologies we are developing to support its use. Section 2 describes the overall architecture of the LAPPS Grid. In Sect. 3, the development of the LAPPS Web Service Exchange Vocabulary, which enables interoperability among services in the Grid, is described. Section 4 introduces the LAPPS/Galaxy interface for accessing and constructing atomic and composite web services, and in Sect. 5 we overview the open advancement evaluation capabilities that are being provided in the Grid. Section 6 discusses our approach to handling potentially divergent licensing constraints in web service pipelines. Finally, Sects. 7 and 8 discuss user-provided evaluation of the LAPPS Grid and the relation of this project to similar projects in Asia, Australia, and the European Union.

2   LAPPS Grid Design

The fundamental system architecture of the LAPPS Grid is based on the Open Service Grid Initiative's Service Grid Server Software developed by the National Institute of Information and Communications Technology (NICT) in Japan and used to implement Kyoto University's Language Grid, a service grid that supports multilingual communication and collaboration. Like the Language Grid, the LAPPS Grid provides three main functions: language service registration and deployment, language service search, and language service composition and execution. From the perspective of application developers, one of the intended audiences for the LAPPS Grid, several aspects of service deployment are important:

1. *Service Discovery.* An application designer can query for existing components and services that provide some desired functionality, and quickly identify elements in the repository that are suited to the task.
2. *Service Adaptation.* The LAPPS Grid supports straightforward customization and adaptation of each component or service (e.g., by exposing parameters, options, etc.).
3. *Service Composition.* New applications can be built from existing elements and tested on client data with a minimum amount of programming.
4. *Metrics and Measurement.* The LAPPS Grid is instrumented to provide relevant component-level measures for standard metrics, given gold-standard test data. New applications automatically include instrumentation for component-level and end-to-end measurement; intermediate (component-level) I/O is logged to support effective error analysis.

By opting to begin with the software supporting the Japanese grid, we have been able to deploy a new service grid hosted entirely within the United States, without incurring the very significant cost of an entirely new software development effort, although differences in local reality and implementation made it necessary to augment the service grid software in a number of ways. The LAPPS Grid extends the core functionality of the Service Grid Software by (1) further enabling composition of tool and resource chains as well as providing sophisticated evaluation services; (2) implementing a *dynamic licensing* system (see

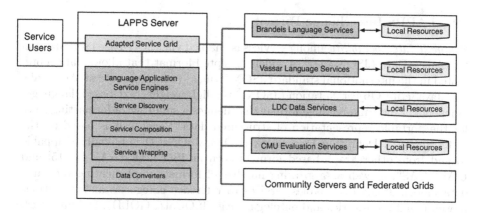

Fig. 1. LAPPS grid architecture

Sect. 6 for handling license agreements on the fly; (3) providing the option to run services locally, with high-security technology to protect sensitive information where required, improve data delivery services; and (4) enabling access to grids other than those based on the Service Grid technology. Also, because the LAPPS Grid is a community-based resource to which members of the community will increasingly contribute as well as use, we provide user-friendly, transparent facilities for wrapping user-provided services.

The basic components of the LAPPS Grid are presented in Fig. 1. The main LAPPS server maintains a workflow repository for composite linguistic services and is equipped with a workflow engine to enable users to develop their own composite (pipelined) services. It also contains modules for discovery, wrapping and conversion. LAPPS Grid nodes housed at Brandeis University and Vassar College maintain repositories of known atomic linguistic services and provide service discovery functionality to users and applications. The LDC node houses various data services, and the node at CMU provides services for automatic measurement and analysis of workflow components, including error analysis at the component and end-to-end application level.

3   Interoperability

Differing specifications of linguistic categories and typologies from application to application have posed a well-known obstacle to interoperability. We have worked with researchers, projects and standards-making bodies from around the world to develop common vocabularies and multi-way mappings, using as a basis the output of various international efforts undertaken over the previous decade[2]. Our developments address both *syntactic interoperability* among web services by providing an implementation of a well-established physical format for web service exchange, as well as *semantic interoperability* to enable services to mutually understand the "meaning" of exchanged objects.

---

[2] E.g., SILT [12], FLaReNet [1], ISO TC37 SC4, etc.

3.1 LAPPS Interchange Format

Syntactic interoperability among services is enabled via JSON-based serialization for Linked Data (JSON-LD)[3], a widely accepted format that allows data represented in the international standard JSON format[4] to interoperate at Web-scale. The JavaScript Object Notation (JSON)[5] is a lightweight, text-based, language-independent data interchange format that defines a small set of formatting rules for the portable representation of structured data. Because it is based on the W3C Resource Definition Framework (RDF), JSON-LD is trivially mappable to and from other graph-based formats such as ISO LAF/GrAF [13,15] and UIMA CAS[6], as well as a growing number of formats implementing the same data model. JSON-LD enables services to reference categories and definitions in web-based repositories and ontologies (e.g., ISOCat[7], GOLD[8], Dublin Core[9], OLiA[10]) or any suitably defined concept at a given URI.

We have designed the LAPPS Interchange Format (LIF) to represent linguistically annotated data in JSON-LD. Services that implement a linguistic application (or wrap an existing application) must consume LIF objects and are responsible for creating LIF objects. Each web service in the LAPPS Grid publishes metadata describing what it requires for input and what it produces as output. A process that is constructing a service pipeline can then query each service to determine compatibility. Where necessary, data converters included in the Language Application Service Engines (see Fig. 1) are automatically invoked map from commonly used formats to the JSON-LD interchange format. For a fuller description of LIF, see Verhagen *et al.*, "The LAPPS Interchange Format", in this volume.

3.2 Exchange Vocabulary

Semantic interoperability among web services is a far greater challenge. Although the pipeline architecture has been implemented in several NLP frameworks over the past two decades, including self-contained (non-service) frameworks such as GATE and UIMA, no accepted standard for module description or input/output interchange to support service discovery, composition, and reuse in the language application domain exists. To address this, we have worked closely with interested and invested groups and members of ISO TC 37 SC4 to develop a lightweight, web-accessible, and readily mappable hierarchy of concepts called the Web Service Exchange Vocabulary (WS-EV) that specifies a terminology for a

---

[3] http://json-ld.org.

[4] http://www.ecma-international.org/publications/files/ECMA-ST/ECMA-404.pdf.

[5] http://www.json.org and http://www.ietf.org/rfc/rfc4627.txt.

[6] The *Common Analysis Structure* (CAS) is the internal format for exchange among modules in the UIMA framework.

[7] http://www.isocat.org.

[8] http://linguistics-ontology.org.

[9] http://dublincore.org.

[10] http://nachhalt.sfb632.uni-potsdam.de/owl/.

core of linguistic objects and features exchanged among NLP tools that consume and produce linguistically annotated data. Development is further guided by collaboration with projects such as the CLARIN Data Concept Registry[11] and ISOcat[12], and integration with existing web service ontologies such as the Language Grid's Language Service Ontology [10]. The WS-EV addresses a need within the community to not only identify a readily usable set of terms, but also specify the relations among them. However, it is crucial to note that the goal of the WS-EV is not to provide a definitive set of terms and relations that will serve every purpose and satisfy every user, but rather to provide a base set of terms, trivially mappable from a substantial number of widely-used schemes, that can be used for exchanging linguistic data among web services. A fuller description of the WS-EV and the philosophy behind it are provided elsewhere in this volume.[13]

Our approach to development of the WS-EV is "bottom-up", in order to avoid a priori development of a comprehensive linguistic type system. To that end, we have adopted a "minimalist" strategy of providing a simple core set of objects and features. Where possible, the core is drawn from existing repositories such as ISOCat; however, because many categories and objects relevant for web service exchange are not included in such repositories, we have attempted to identify a set of (more or less) "universal" concepts by surveying existing type systems and schemas–for example, the Julie Lab and DARPA GALE UIMA type systems and the GATE schemas for linguistic phenomena–together with the I/O requirements of commonly used NLP software (e.g., the Stanford NLP tools, OpenNLP, etc.).[14]

We have established an Exchange Vocabulary Repository[15] similar to schema.org, in order to provide web-addressable terms and definitions for reference from annotations exchanged among web services for NLP tools and processes. Wherever possible, terms in the vocabulary are mapped to categories defined in other repositories, ontologies, registries, etc. (including mapping to multiple repositories when appropriate). For this purpose we utilize the taxonomy of relation types defined in RELcat [21], which accommodates multiple vocabularies for relation predicates including those from the Web Ontology Language (OWL) [19] and the Simple Knowledge Organization System (SKOS) [20].

Terms in the repository are organized in a shallow hierarchy, with inheritance of properties, as shown in Fig. 2. WS-EV development is undertaken in collaboration with a Working Group within ISO TC37 SC4, to guarantee substantial

---

[11] https://openskos.meertens.knaw.nl/ccr/browser/.

[12] http://www.isocat.org.

[13] See Ide et al., "The Language Application Grid Web Service Exchange Vocabulary", in this volume.

[14] The survey of basic linguistic objects was undertaken within a Working Group of ISO TC37 SC4. A working draft and an inventory of type systems are available at http://vocab.lappsgrid.org/EV/ev-draft.pdf and http://vocab.lappsgrid.org/EV/materials/.

[15] http://vocab.lappsgrid.org/.

community involvement and so that our results may ultimately become a part of the larger set of ISO standards for language resource management.

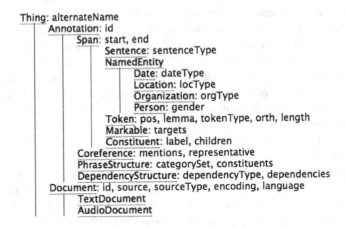

Fig. 2. Fragment of the WS-EV type hierarchy (associated properties in gray)

References in the LAPPS JSON-LD representation exchanged between web services point not only to definitions for specific linguistic categories, but also to documentation for processing software and "rules" for processes such as tokenization, entity recognition, etc. used to produce a set of annotations, which are often left unspecified in annotated resources, thus inhibiting replication of results (see for example [5]). While not required for web service exchange in the LAPPS Grid, the inclusion of such references can contribute to the better replication and evaluation of results in the field.

Figure 3 shows the information for *Token*, which defines the concept, identifies application types that produce objects of this type, cross-references a similar concept in ISOCat, and provides the URI for use in the JSON-LD representation. It also specifies the common properties that can be specified for a set of Token objects, and the individual properties that can be associated with a Token object.

The LAPPS WS-EV is intended to support URI-based references to basic concepts used in the description and processing of linguistically annotated corpora from JSON-LD and other linked data representations such as W3C RDF, or any linguistically annotated resource. There is no requirement to use any or all of the specified properties, and we foresee that many web services will require definition of objects and properties not included in the WS-EV or elsewhere. We therefore provide mechanisms for (principled) definition of objects and features beyond the WS-EV. Two options exist: users can provide a URI where a new term or other documentation is defined, or users may add a definition to the WS-EV. In the latter case, service providers use the name space automatically assigned to them at the time of registration, thereby avoiding name clashes and providing a distinction between general categories used across services and more idiosyncratic categories.

Thing > Annotation > Span > Token

Definition	A string of one or more characters that serves as an indivisible unit for the purposes of morpho–syntactic labeling (part of speech tagging).
Similar to	http://www.isocat.org/datcat/DC-1403
URI	http//vocab.lappsgrid.org/Token

Metadata

Metadata from Annotation

Properties	Type	Description
producer	List of URI	The software that produced the annotations.
rules	List of URI	The documentation (if any) for the rules that were used to identify the annotations.

Properties

Properties	Type	Description
pos	String or URI	Part-of-speech tag associated with the token.
lemma	String or URI	The root (base) form associated with the token. URI may point to a lexicon entry.
tokenType	String or URI	Sub-type such as word, punctuation, abbreviation, number, symbol, etc. Ideally a URI referencing a pre-defined descriptor.
orth	String or URI	Orthographic properties of the token such as LowerCase, UpperCase, UpperInitial, etc. Ideally a URI referencing a pre-defined descriptor.
length	Integer	The length of the token

Properties from Span

Properties	Type	Description
start	Integer	The starting offset (0–based) in the primary data.
end	Integer	The ending offset (0–based) in the primary data.

Properties from Annotation

Properties	Type	Description
id	String	A unique identifier associated with the annotation.

Properties from Thing

Properties	Type	Description
alternateName	String	An alias for the item.

Fig. 3. Token definition in the LAPPS WS-EV

4   LAPPS/Galaxy Workflow Engine

The Galaxy project[16] started in 2005 to create a system enabling biologists without informatics expertise to perform computational analysis through the web [7]. Galaxy is an open-source application[17] that includes tool integration and history capabilities together with a workflow system for building automated multi-step analyses, a visualization framework including visual analysis capabilities, and facilities for sharing and publishing analyses [8]. It is accessed through a graphical interface where data inputs and computational steps are selected from dynamic menus, and results are displayed in plots and summaries that encourage interactive workflows and the exploration of hypotheses.

Rather than duplicate the extensive work of the Galaxy project, we recently adopted it as the primary workflow management system for the LAPPS Grid.[18] We have worked with the Galaxy development team in order to adapt the system

---

[16] http://galaxyproject.org.

[17] Distributed under the terms of permissive Academic Free License; http://getgalaxy.org.

[18] http://galaxy.lappsgrid.org.

to our domain, and continue this collaboration to both enhance the capabilities we require as well as contribute to the expansion of Galaxy to domains outside the life sciences, which is a current goal of the Galaxy project.

We provide Galaxy wrappers to call all LAPPS web services to the Galaxy ToolShed[19]. This enables the creation of complex workflows involving standard NLP components and composite services from a wide range of sources from within an easy-to-use, intuitive workflow engine with capabilities to persist experiments and results. An additional, and potentially hugely significant, outcome of the LAPPS/Galaxy collaboration is that it enables the use of LAPPS Grid NLP services to extract information from repositories of biomedical publications such as PubMed[20] and passing it on to biomedical analysis and visualization tools available in Galaxy. The synergistic development of capabilities supporting both NLP and genomic analysis within the Galaxy framework can have a significant impact on work in both fields. For example, NLP researchers will benefit enormously from access to sophisticated visualization software for display and analysis of results common to research in the life sciences, but rarely used in NLP research. Similarly, biologists will be able to take advantage of bio-oriented NLP web services for text mining of bio-entities and relations from textual sources, and via capabilities already present in Galaxy, integrate them into existing bio-data resources and analysis tools. The integration of data, tools, as well as workflows and methods from previously distinct scientific communities can provide unprecedented capabilities for both the emerging field of BioNLP and biomedical and genomic science.

In addition to access to LAPPS Grid tools and data, we have developed and contributed the following capabilities of the LAPPS Grid for use in Galaxy in order to support NLP research and development within that platform, including (1) exploitation of our web service metadata to allow for automatic detection of input/output formats and requirements for modules in a workflow and subsequent automatic invocation of converters to make interoperability seamless and invisible to the user, and (2) incorporation of authentication procedures for protected data using the open standard OAuth[21], which specifies a process for resource owners to authorize third-party access to their server resources without sharing their credentials. We also have contributed a "Galaxy Flavor" for LAPPS, which is effectively a pre-configured virtual machine (VM) that can be run in any of several VMS (e.g., VirtualBox, AmazonEC2, Google, Microsoft Azure, VMWare, OpenStack, etc.). This enables users to download a galaxy-stable image and run it locally. This capability is ideal for class work, workshops, and presentations as it allows full-blown installations to be easily shared and run. In addition, if the images are downloaded ahead of time, no network connection is required.

Figures 4 and 5 show a simple workflow configuration and a visualization of named entity annotation over a document.

---

[19] https://toolshed.g2.bx.psu.edu.
[20] http://www.ncbi.nlm.nih.gov/pubmed.
[21] http://oauth.net.

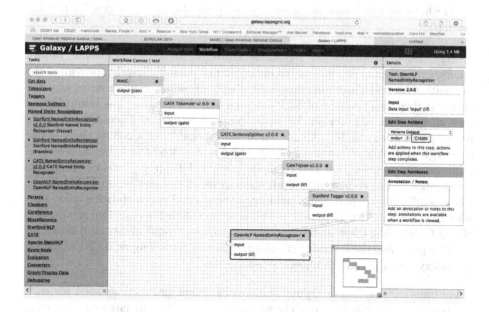

Fig. 4. The LAPPS/Galaxy interface: workflow configuration

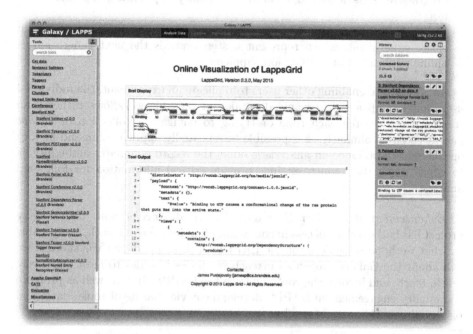

Fig. 5. Visualization of a named entity annotation using LAPPS/Galaxy

We have adopted and, as necessary, adapted Galaxy strategies for the following:

1. Replication of Experiments, Pervasive Sharing of Methods and Results. Reproducing experimental results is an essential part of scientific inquiry, providing the foundation for understanding, integrating, and extending results toward new discoveries. However, the field of NLP research and development has been plagued by a chronic lack of potential for replicability of results, as discussed in several recent publications [5,17]), blogs[22], and workshops[23]. As a result, there is not only a great deal of re-inventing of the wheel and wasted effort, but also serious inhibition to progress that can be made possible by tapping into the collective intelligence of the community. Evaluation of results is also seriously hampered when details of an experiment (including versions and parameters for data, software) are not included in papers, which is all too often the case. Our adaptation of the Galaxy workflow system enables us to foster replicability and reuse for NLP by providing the following capabilities (see [9] for a comprehensive overview of Galaxy's sharing and publication capabilities):

- automatic recording of inputs, tools, parameters and settings used for each step in an analysis in a publicly viewable history, thereby ensuring that each result can be exactly reproduced and reviewed later;
- provisions for sharing datasets, histories, and workflows via web links, with progressive levels of sharing including the ability to publish in a public repository;
- ability to create custom web-based documents to communicate about an entire experiment, which represent a step towards the next generation of online publication or publication supplement.

In addition to enabling other users to replicate an experiment, the individual user can develop a rich, organized catalog of reusable workflows rather than starting from scratch each time or trying to navigate a collection of *ad hoc* analysis scripts. Similarly, it is possible to repeatedly apply a command history on different data. Once an analysis is done, the record eliminates ambiguity as to which result used which settings provide critical information for follow-up analysis.

2. Enhancement of the User Base and Community Involvement. The Galaxy project has had notable success in community building and outreach, comparable to what we hope to achieve for the LAPPS Grid. Inspired by their success, we will adopt the Galaxy project's outreach strategies in order to most effectively reach, teach, and involve the community in the LAPPS Grid, as well as promote community engagement in LAPPS development via sharing of tools, data, and (especially) workflows and results.

---

[22] E.g., http://nlpers.blogspot.com/2006/11/reproducible-results.html.
[23] E.g., Replicability and Reusability in Natural Language Processing: from Data to Software Sharing: http://nl.ijs.si/rrnlp2015/.

5 Open Advancement

CMU has provided the tooling and infrastructure for two major services, based in part on the existing OAQA framework developed at CMU and deployed on a service node housed at CMU. The availability of this type of evaluation service, which implements state-of-the-art Open Advancement techniques, provides an unprecedented tool for NLP development that could, in itself, take the field to a new level of productivity. The open advancement (OA) approach for component- and application-based evaluation has been successful in enabling rapid identification of frequent error categories within modules and documents, together with an indication of which module(s) and error type(s) have the greatest impact on overall performance, thus contributing to more effective investment of resources in both research and application assembly [3, 22]. The OA approach was used in the development of IBM's Watson to achieve steady performance gains over the four years of its development [4]. More recently, the open-source OAQA project has released software frameworks which provide general support for open advancement of information systems [6, 22]; the OAQA software has been used to rapidly develop information retrieval and question answering systems for bioinformatics [16, 22].

A fundamental element of open advancement involves evaluating multiple possible solutions to a given problem, to find the optimal solution available using given components, resources and evaluation data. The output of the optimal solution is then subjected to error analysis, to identify the most frequent errors with the highest impact on system output quality. Possible enhancements to the system are then considered, with an eye toward achieving the largest possible reduction in error rate by addressing the most frequent error types. The performance of each new configuration is evaluated to determine whether a significant improvement has been achieved in comparison with prior baselines or best known configurations. When multiple teams collaborate to implement this process across several sites, types of components, etc. it is possible to make rapid progress in improving solution quality, as measured by the chosen metrics and evaluation dataset [3, 22]. To support rapid, open advancement, a developer can add new components to the system and test them in the context of existing pipelines by "plugging them in" to existing solutions. We also provide capabilities for parallel exploration of alternative workflows, evaluation of module-by-module results, and "best path" analysis to determine the optimal workflow.

The LAPPS/Galaxy workflow engine described in the previous section provides easy configuration and re-configuration of pipelines, and represents the first step in supporting open advancement by allowing users to rapidly configure and evaluate a new, single pipeline on a chosen dataset and metrics. In addition, the user can specify an entire range of pipeline configurations for comparative evaluation; the system evaluates each possible pipeline configuration and generate metrics measurements, plus variance and statistical significance calculations. We are working to extend the LAPPS/Galaxy interface to allow easy specification of configuration descriptors (ECD); [22] that define a space of possible pipelines, where each step in the pipeline might be achieved by multiple components or

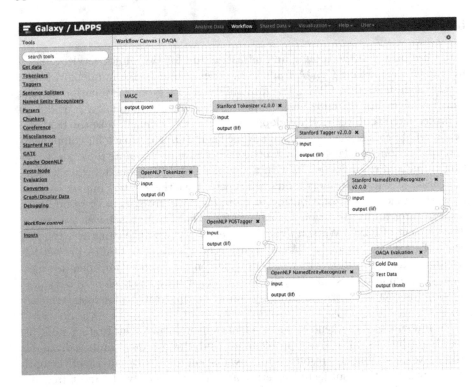

Fig. 6. The LAPPS/Galaxy interface: evaluation configuration for two workflows

services; each component or service may also have configuration parameters with more than one possible value to be tested. We are also extending the system to support automatic evaluation of each configuration so specified, by implementing a service-oriented version of the Configuration Space Exploration (CSE) algorithm [22].

Figure 6 shows a simple evaluation configuration in LAPPS/Galaxy, which compares evaluative statistics for two parallel pipelines performing named entity identification.

6   Resource Access

LDC's contributions to the multi-site LAPPS Grid focus naturally on data. LDC is creating services that provide grid access to the contents of its LDC Online service: multilingual newswire and transcribed conversational telephone speech in English, as well as to lexical databases. The challenges of this work lie in developing useful and efficient service interfaces to these data. In each case, we envision the interface as containing a number of simple operations: requests to retrieve the features of the supplied data, queries into the data using those features that return identifiers and requests to fetch data elements by identifier, via iteration or randomly. LDC already deploys data services, both internal and external, so our Grid work emphasizes enclosing those services in a thin wrapper within a Grid node that we host. Using the data source API developed by the LAPPS project, we pass on Grid requests to LDC services. Some LDC services, including the Grid node, run on virtual machines, allowing us to easily adjust system resources to match changing demand. LDC's infrastructure also includes a Solr[24] server for searching text, including some of the content available to the Grid.

Along with the flexibility the LAPPS Grid offers to users seeking to create service pipelines comes an increase in the complexity of intellectual property arrangements. We anticipate two major pipeline types. In the first, users request language resources from a given source (or supply their own) and route them through a workflow of multiple grid services with the final result returned to the user. In the second type, language resources are routed through a single service and then back to the user before being routed along to the next service. The difference between these user case types has implications for licensing and constraints imposed on grid users, services and operators. Moreover, within those cases, one must consider constraints imposed by the language resources, data and software enabling the web services.

At each point in either pipeline above, constraints depend upon the language resources or resulting services, processing and user. Resources may be constrained or unconstrained. Constraints may be imposed by legal principles such as copyright or by contract. Constraints may prohibit commercial use, derivative works or re-distribution or insist upon attribution or in-kind sharing of the user's intellectual products. Resources may be constrained as to user, typically forbidding use by commercial organizations, or as to use, whether for education, basic research, applied research, technology development, evaluation and deployment or resale. Processing may also be constrained, for example, ruling out derivative works and only permitting so-called transformative works. Users may be licensed or not. Their licensing may be defined by enumeration or by user features, for example whether they work in an academic, non-academic, not-for-profit, government, pre-commercial or commercial environments.

We manage this complexity by identifying the licenses associated with each Grid service and analyzing them into their component constraints. Those constraints are accumulated as the service pipeline is constructed, and users are notified about them before the pipeline is executed. Constraints are of two types, requirement and notification. Required constraints block the pipeline until the constraint is removed. Examples include cases where users must pay a fee or sign a specific agreement in order to access the desired resource or service. Other constraints, such as redistribution, commercial/non-commercial use, use of derivatives and so on are presented as conditions which users must acknowledge before the pipeline will be executed. Figure 7 summarizes that process.

Variation in license terms notwithstanding, the human language technology community has for some time envisioned open source-based models for language

---

[24] https://lucene.apache.org/solr/.

Constraint	Action
Redistribution	Notify
Use	Notify
Derivatives Use	Notify
Attribution	Notify
Share Alike	Notify
Fee	Require
Other Specific License	Require
Other Specific Constraint	?

Fig. 7. LAPPS grid license constraint enforcement

resource development and distribution. Most recently, META-SHARE proposes a network of distributed repositories that license resources from a single platform via open source agreements (META-SHARE Commons licenses) as well as more restrictive arrangements [18]. Although all levels of licensing complexity are acknowledged in the LAPPS Grid, the LAPPS license scheme depends on the utilization of open source software and resource licenses to the greatest extent possible. By limiting distribution and processing constraints, we aim to promote the project goal of community engagement through sharing, federation and other means. By developing a comprehensive model for addressing constraints on the intellectual property used in the Grid we hope to create a resource that is maximally open to users ranging from open source developers to commercial users of languages services.

7   User Evaluation

To a large extent, the measure of success for LAPPS is a matter of the ease with which the user community–both NLP researchers and developers and those with little knowledge of the field–can use the infrastructure to serve their needs. The project therefore includes an on-going user-evaluation component involving a range of user types, including those whose computational expertise may be limited, who provide periodic feedback concerning Grid access, adding applications to the Grid, using external applications or services in combination with the Grid, etc. In the spirit of open advancement, we measure the total time and effort required to determine the optimal configuration of existing components for a given problem and use these measures to improve the system's design.

To support community use, we regularly offer tutorials and training workshops on LAPPS Grid use at major conferences in the field[25], including venues associated with other disciplines, with the goal of introducing scientists and

---

[25] E.g., *Web Services for Effective NLP Application Development and Evaluation: Using and Contributing to the Language Application (LAPPS) Grid*, offered at LREC 2014.

engineers from diverse disciplines to a broad-based and integrated set of NLP services that has the potential to impact their research and development needs. We envision that research from sociology, psychology, economics, education, linguistics, digital media, as well as engineering, can be impacted by the ability to manipulate and process diverse data sources in multiple languages.

Another major effort aimed toward both development of the LAPPS Grid and user evaluation is inclusion of LAPPS use in courses offered at Carnegie-Mellon University and Brandeis University. At Carnegie-Mellon, two courses will use the LAPPS framework: a master's level seminar course including a project on "automatically building customized search engines with LAPPS", and a Question Answering course including development of a world history question-answering pipeline. At Brandeis, the LAPPS Grid will be deployed as the development, testing, and evaluation platform for several projects in a course on Fundamentals in Computational Linguistics course. We are also pursuing the development of courses relying on the LAPPS Grid for use in US Government agencies. Feedback from these courses on all aspects of the LAPPS Grid–configuration, availability of relevant services, usability of interfaces, etc.–will provide valuable input to iterative development of the LAPPS Grid.

8   Relation to Other Projects

The LAPPS Grid effort builds on the foundation laid in several recent U.S., European, and Asian projects, including the NSF-funded Sustainable Interoperability for Language Technology (SILT) project [12] and the EU-funded Fostering Language Resources Network (FLaReNet) project [1]. At the same time, the International Standards Organization (ISO) committee for Language Resource Management (ISO TC37 SC4)[26] has addressed the need for standards for linguistic data. Through these and other projects and parallel efforts in Asia and Australia, substantial groundwork—in terms of standards development, raising community awareness and buy-in, and proof-of-concept implementation—has been laid to turn existing, fragmented NLP technologies and data into web-accessible, stable, and interoperable resources that can be readily reused across several fields. As a result, existing and potential projects across the globe are beginning to converge on common data models, best practices, and standards, and the vision of a comprehensive infrastructure supporting discovery and deployment of web services that deliver language resources and processing components is an increasingly achievable goal.

Our vision is therefore not for a monolithic grid, but rather a heterogeneous configuration of federated grids that implement a set of best practices for managing and interchanging linguistic information, so that services on all of these grids are mutually accessible. To that end, the LAPPS Grid project has entered into a multi-way international collaboration among the US partners and institutions in Asia and Europe. The basis of the collaboration is the federation of the LAPPS Grid, the Language Grid (Kyoto University, Japan), NECTEC

---

[26] ISO/TC 37/SC4, Language Resources Management, http://www.tc37sc4.org.

(Thailand)[27], grids operated by the University of Indonesia[28] and Xinjiang University (China)[29], and LinguaGrid[30], to be formally as the "Open Language Grid" announced in January 2016.[31] The connection of these six grids into a single federated entity will enable access to all services and resources on any of these grids by users of any one of them and, perhaps most importantly, facilitate adding additional grids and service platforms to the federation in the future. Currently, the European MetaNet/Meta-Share[32] initiative is committed to joining the federation in the near future, which will provide access to the substantial resource holding of the European Language Resources Association (ELRA) as well as web services developed in the EU project PANACEA. We are also working with the EU CLARIN initiative[33], a large-scale pan-European collaborative effort aimed at making language resources and technology readily available for the whole European Humanities (and Social Sciences) communities, as well as the LINDAT-CLARIN Centre for Language Research Infrastructure's open digital repository of tools and data (Charles University, Prague), and the Australian Alveo Virtual Laboratory [2] to similarly share access to services and resources in the near future

One goal of our work is to ensure that all relevant parties can provide input to the development and/or refinement of standards and practices that promote increased interoperability among web service platforms. Therefore, we continue to reach out to other projects to join the collaboration and, where appropriate, grid federation, including EU projects such as KYOTO[34] as well as large projects developing NLP components and data such as the Global WordNet Grid[35] and U-Compare[36], which provides an interface to UIMA-based components primarily for the Biomedical domain. We are also pursuing potentially fruitful uni-directional federations, in which other grids and service nodes are one-way users of the LAPPS Grid; for example, users of an e-Learning Grid could be users of the LAPPS Grid in order to develop e-learning resources, but the LAPPS Grid need not be a user of the e-Learning Grid.

9   Conclusion

The LAPPS Grid project is currently in its third year and has so far provided the basic functionality of the framework. The next steps include expanding the range

---

[27] http://langrid.servicegrid-bangkok.org/en/overview.php.

[28] http://langrid.portal.cs.ui.ac.id/langrid/.

[29] Under development.

[30] http://www.linguagrid.org/.

[31] Funding for the LAPPS Grid involvement in the federation has awarded as a supplement to the NSF SI^2 grants ACI-1147912 and ACI-1147944.

[32] http://www.meta-net.eu/.

[33] http://eudat.eu/communities/clarin-common-language-resources-and-technology-infrastructure.

[34] http://www.kyoto-project.eu/.

[35] http://www.globalwordnet.org/gwa/gwa_grid.html.

[36] http://u-compare.org/.

of services offered and enhancing the integration with Galaxy. As noted above in Sect. 7, another important activity is the evaluation of current LAPPS Grid capabilities on the basis its use in several graduate-level courses in computational linguistics at major U.S. universities, which we hope will lead to significant enhancements of its usability as well as the range of available services. Another focus of activity will be to adapt the LAPPS Grid in order to empower users to carry out computational analyses without having to be an expert in computer science, so that users can focus on scientific rather than technical questions.

As our intention is to provide one piece of what is envisioned to become a global network of federated grids and services for NLP, another important activity is to pursue additional collaborations with similar projects around the world and work to ensure the maximal involvement of the community in the development of exchange mechanisms. We are also seeking means to incorporate individual services and composite service pipelines into the LAPPS Grid (either via direct inclusion or federation with grids that provide these services) for tasks relevant for research in areas such as digital humanities and bioinformatics, and in general to better accommodate the non-technical user.

Acknowledgements. This work was supported by National Science Foundation grants NSF-ACI 1147944 and NSF-ACI 1147912.

References

1. Calzolari, N., Baroni, P., Bel, N., Budin, G., Choukri, K., Goggi, S., Mariani, J., Monachini, M., Odijk, J., Piperidis, S., Quochi, V., Soria, C., Toral, A. (eds.) Proceedings of The European Language Resources and Technologies Forum: Shaping the Future of the Multilingual Digital Europe. ILC-CNR (2009)
2. Cassidy, S., Estival, D., Jones, T., Burnham, D., Burghold, J.: The alveo virtual laboratory: a web based repository API. In: Proceedings of the Ninth International Conference on Language Resources and Evaluation (LREC 2014). European Language Resources Association (ELRA), Reykjavik, May 2014
3. Ferrucci, D., Nyberg, E., Allan, J., Barker, K., Brown, E., Chu-Carroll, J., Ciccolo, A., Duboue, P., Fan, J., Gondek, D., Hovy, E., Katz, B., Lally, A., McCord, M., Morarescu, P., Murdock, B., Porter, B., Prager, J., Strzalkowski, T., Welty, C., Zadrozny, W.: Towards the open advancement of question answering systems. Technical report, IBM Research, Armonk (2009)
4. Ferrucci, D.A., Brown, E.W., Chu-Carroll, J., Fan, J., Gondek, D., Kalyanpur, A., Lally, A., Murdock, J.W., Nyberg, E., Prager, J.M., Schlaefer, N., Welty, C.A.: Building Watson: an overview of the DeepQA project. AI Mag. **31**(3), 59–79 (2010)
5. Fokkens, A., van Erp, M., Postma, M., Pedersen, T., Vossen, P., Freire, N.: Offspring from reproduction problems: what replication failure teaches us. In: Proceedings of the Conference of The Association for Computational Linguistics, pp. 1691–1701. The Association for Computational Linguistics (2013)
6. Garduno, E., Yang, Z., Maiberg, A., McCormack, C., Fang, Y., Nyberg, E.: CSE Framework: a UIMA-based distributed system for configuration space exploration unstructured information management architecture. In: Klgl, P., de Castilho, R.E., Tomanek, K. (eds.) UIMA@GSCL, pp. 14–17 (2013). Proceedings of the CEUR Workshop, CEUR-WS.org

7. Giardine, B., Riemer, C., Hardison, R.C., Burhans, R., Elnitski, L., Shah, P., Zhang, Y., Blankenberg, D., Albert, I., Taylor, J., Miller, W., Kent, W.J., Nekrutenko, A.: Galaxy: a platform for interactive large-scale genome analysis. Genome Res. **15**(10), 1451–55 (2005)

8. Goecks, J., Coraor, N., Team, T.G., Nekrutenko, A., Taylor, J.: NGS analyses by visualization with trackster. Nat. Biotechnol. **30**(11), 1036–1039 (2012)

9. Goecks, J., Nekrutenko, A., Taylor, J.: Galaxy: a comprehensive approach for supporting accessible, reproducible, and transparent computational research in the life sciences. Genome Biol. **11**, R86 (2010)

10. Hayashi, Y., Declerck, T., Calzolari, N., Monachini, M., Soria, C., Buitelaar, P.: Language service ontology. In: Ishida, T. (ed.) The Language Grid - Service-Oriented Collective Intelligence for Language Resource Interoperability, pp. 85–100. Springer, Heidelberg (2011)

11. Ide, N., Pustejovsky, J.: What does interoperability mean, anyway? toward an operational definition of interoperability. In: Proceedings of the Second International Conference on Global Interoperability for Language Resources (ICGL 2010), Hong Kong, China (2010)

12. Ide, N., Pustejovsky, J., Calzolari, N., Soria, C.: The SILT and FlaReNet international collaboration for interoperability. In: Proceedings of the Third Linguistic Annotation Workshop, ACL-IJCNLP, August 2009

13. Ide, N., Suderman, K.: The linguistic annotation framework: a standard for annotation interchange and merging. Lang. Resour. Eval. **48**, 395–418 (2014)

14. Ishida, T., Murakami, Y., Lin, D., Nakaguchi, T., Otani, M.: Open language grid-towards a global language service infrastructure. In: The Third ASE International Conference on Social Informatics (SocialInformatics 2014). Cambridge, Massachusetts, USA (2014)

15. ISO-24612: Language Resource Management - Linguistic Annotation Framework. ISO 24612 (2012)

16. Patel, A., Yang, Z., Nyberg, E., Mitamura, T.: Building an optimal QA system automatically using configuration space exploration for QA4MRE'13 tasks. In: Proceedings of CLEF 2013 (2013)

17. Pedersen, T.: Empiricism is not a matter of faith. Comput. Linguist. **34**(3), 465–470 (2008)

18. Piperdis, S.: The META-SHARE language resources sharing infrastructure: principles, challenges, solutions. In: Proceedings of the Eighth International Language Resources and Evaluation (LREC12). European Language Resources Association (ELRA), Istanbul (2012)

19. W3C OWL Working Group: OWL 2 Web Ontology Language: Document Overview. W3C Recommendation (2012)

20. W3C SKOS Working Group: SKOS Simple Knowledge Organization System Reference. W3C Recommendation (2009)

21. Windhouwer, M.: RELcat: a Relation Registry for ISOcat data categories. In: Calzolari, N., Choukri, K., Declerck, T., Dogan, M.U., Maegaard, B., Mariani, J., Odijk, J., Piperidis, S. (eds.) LREC 2012, pp. 3661–3664. European Language Resources Association (ELRA), Istanbul (2012)

22. Yang, Z., Garduno, E., Fang, Y., Maiberg, A., McCormack, C., Nyberg, E.: Building optimal information systems automatically: configuration space exploration for biomedical information systems. In: Proceedings of the CIKM 2013 (2013)

A Policy-Aware Parallel Execution Control Mechanism for Language Application

Mai Xuan Trang[1]([✉]), Yohei Murakami[2], and Toru Ishida[1]

[1] Department of Social Informatics, Kyoto University, Kyoto, Japan
trangmx@ai.soc.i.kyoto-u.ac.jp, ishida@i.kyoto-u.ac.jp
[2] Unit of Design, Kyoto University, Kyoto, Japan
yohei@i.kyoto-u.ac.jp

Abstract. Many language resources have been shared as web services to process data on the internet. As data sets keep growing, language services are experiencing more big data problems, such as challenging demands on storage and processing caused by very large data sets such as huge amounts of multilingual texts. Handling big data volumes like this requires parallel computing architectures. Parallel execution is one way to improve performance of language services when processing huge amounts of data. The large data set is partitioned and multiples processes of the language service are executed concurrently. However, due to limitation of computing resources, service providers employ policies to limit number of concurrent processes that their services could serve. In an advanced language application, several language services, provided by different providers with different policies, are combined in a composite service to handle complex tasks. If parallel execution is used for greater efficiency of a language application we need to optimize the parallel configuration by working with the language service policies of all participating providers. We propose a model that considers the atomic language service policies when predicting composite service performance. Based on this model, we design a mechanism that adapts parallel execution setting of a composite service to atomic services' policies in order to attain optimal performance for the language application.

Keywords: Language service composition · Big data · Parallel execution · Adaptation mechanism

1 Introduction

Rapid advance in data observation, collection and analysis technologies has led to a tremendous growth in the amount of data. Examples including tremendous size of multilingual data such as a very large-scale multilingual text published on Wikipedia[1]. There are more than 288 languages supported in Wikipedia, in each language there are millions of articles have been published, for example

---

[1] https://www.wikipedia.org/.

© Springer International Publishing Switzerland 2016
Y. Murakami and D. Lin (Eds.): WLSI 2015, LNAI 9442, pp. 71–85, 2016.
DOI: 10.1007/978-3-319-31468-6_5

currently there are almost 5 million articles in English, 2 million articles in Swedish, and the number of data sets keep growing approximately. With this large-scale of data, the challenge now is how to make applications effectively and efficiently process the large-scale data, so scientists and developers must rely on distributed and parallel processing methodologies (e.g. Hadoop MapReduce [5]) for comprehensive data analysis.

As success has been achieved in adding encapsulation and data integration to service oriented computing and Web service, the academic world and industry have started to adopt Web service and SOA (Service Oriented Architecture) to manage and process data on the Internet. This is promoting the development, operation and management of data-intensive applications. Many linguistic tools have been shared as language service such as translation services, parallel text services, etc. The performance or execution time of language services when processing huge datasets is a major concern. Many studies in the field of data-intensive services have been conducted. Technologies such as data-intensive computing [18], and scientific workflows [17] have the potential to enable rapid data analysis in many linguistic and scientific problems, however, they failed to consider parallel execution policies when composing language services, let alone consider how the policies of language services being executed affects overall efficiency of the composite service.

A common technique to improve performance of a language service when working with large-scale data is parallel execution. The large data is split into small independent portions that are executed in parallel by multiple processes of the language service. This should decrease the overall execution time of the service. However, the service providers will not have uniform computing resources. If a provider is rich in computing resources, he may ready to accept large numbers of concurrent requests. However, all computing resources are bounded and each service provider will limit the number of concurrent processes to maintain performance of currently provided language services. This parallel execution limitation becomes the policy of the service provider. Language service users should not violate this policy. In some cases, if the policy is violated the invocation of the service may fail or performance of the service maybe degraded. Since different providers have different computing resources and current loads, the parallel execution policies will also be different. When composing composite services by combining different language services, a promising way to realize good performance of composite services when using parallel execution is to make a model that can find the optimal parallel execution setting for each composite service with consideration of the atomic language services' policies.

In advanced language applications, to handle complex linguistic tasks, users combine several language services to define a collaboration workflow or so called composite service. Composing a composite service can be divided into two steps. First, at design-time, developers need to design the orchestration by selecting appropriate set of service specifications (hereby referred to as *abstract services*) such that the final system meets its functional requirements. Second, at runtime, for each *abstract service*, a service that matches the specification (hereby referred to as *concrete services*) is selected and bound to the *abstract service*. The set of concrete services is called the *execution plan* of the composite service. Forming the optimal execution plan that maximizes the composition's QoS is a well-known problem called *QoS-aware service composition or selection*. Many methodologies have been proposed for this problem. [3,21] proposed approaches for QoS-aware composite service based on linear integer programming, while [2] proposed an approach based on Genetic Algorithms (GAs). Most of the proposed approaches lack consideration of determining parallel execution settings that ensure that the composite service can attain optimal performance.

Different from current approaches, this paper focuses on configuring the parallel execution setting of a composite service (associated with concrete language service policies) to optimize its performance. The configuration of composite service must conform to the policies of all language services in the execution plan if its performance is to be optimized. To this end, we set the following goals:

– Predicting the performance of a composite service under parallel execution given the policies of the language services.
– Designing a mechanism to control parallel execution of composite services. Based on the prediction, this mechanism adapts parallel execution setting of the composite service to language services' policies to create optimal configuration. A new workflow representation with optimal parallel execution setting of a composite service is generated.

The remainder of the paper is organized as follows. Section 2 presents a motivating example. In Sect. 3, we introduces a mechanism to control parallel execution of composite service. Section 4 describes parallel execution policies of language services. The parallel execution optimization is briefly described in Sect. 5. We give an evaluation of our model in Sect. 6. Section 7 introduces some related works. Finally, Sect. 8 concludes the paper.

2   Motivating Example

The Language Grid [6] provides an infrastructure for sharing and combining language services. Different groups or providers can join and share language services on the Language Grid. Currently, more than 140 organizations have joined the Language Grid to share over 170 language services. Different providers may employ different policies for their provided services. With the Language Grid, users can easily combine different atomic language services to define new composite service that meets their requirement.

We consider here an real task when a Japanese agriculture expert want to translate a japanese document which contains two parts, one is information about rice and the other is information about fertilizer. The former is intended to transfer information to Vietnamese farmers, while the latter is for French fertilizer suppliers. Assume that, there is no direct translation services from Japanese to Vietnamese and French. The Japanese expert does not want to translate the whole document into Vietnamese or French due to high cost of

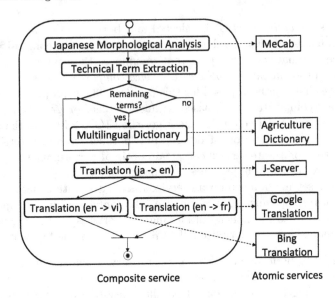

Fig. 1. An example of language service composition

the translation. In order to do this task, he use a composite service shown in Fig. 1. First, the document is translated from Japanese to English using J-Server translation service with a multilingual agriculture dictionary. A condition is used so that a part of the intermediate translated document is to be translated into Vietnamese by Google translation service and the other part into French by Bing translation service. J-Server and Bing translation services are not very fast, these slowdown the composite service. To improve performance of the composite service we use parallel execution.

Now, let us consider a scenario where the concrete atomic language services used in the composite service employ different policies for parallel execution. Lets say the dictionary service limits the maximum number of concurrent requests that they can serve to P_{dict}, while translation services J-Server, Google and Bing limit the maximum number concurrent requests that they can serve to $P_{jserver}$, P_{google} and P_{bing} respectively. The performance of J-Server or Bing exhibits no improvement when the number of concurrent requests sent to the services is larger than $P_{jserver}$ or P_{bing}, while performance of Google translation service becomes worse if more than P_{google} concurrent requests send to the service. In this scenario, when configuring parallel execution of the composite service we need to specify a suitable number of concurrent processes of the composite service to achieve optimal performance. Several questions to be asked here are (1) How can we model parallel execution policies of language services? (2) How to control parallel execution of a composite service with regard language services' policies in order to attain optimal performance? These issues are addressed in the next sessions.

3   System Architecture

In this section, we describe the system architecture of a policy-aware parallel execution control mechanism for composite language services. Figure 2 shows the overview of the system proposed in this paper. The system consists of the Workflow Execution Engine and Parallel Execution Setting Adapter.

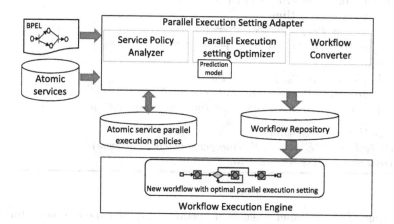

Fig. 2. Policy-aware parallel execution control framework

The input of our system is a composite service being executed. Assume that the composite service is described by WS-BPEL [10]. The Parallel Execution Setting Adapter converts the BPEL file to our workflow representation which provides parallel execution configuration for composite services, we call this representation is *parallel execution representation*. The Adapter also estimates the optimal case of parallel execution for the composite service based on atomic language services' policies and optimizes the new workflow representation with the optimal parallel execution setting. The Parallel Execution Setting Adapter consists of three components: Service Policy Analyzer, Parallel Execution Setting Optimizer and Workflow Converter.

- The Service Policy Analyser analyses parallel execution policy of atomic language service. From the endpoints of a composite services we can get information of language services. The Analyser invokes a language service with different parallel execution setting over a test data. Execution time of the service is recorded and analysed to determined parallel execution policy of the service. This policy is stored into a database for reused purpose.
- Based on the policies of atomic language services, the Parallel Execution Setting Optimizer estimates an optimal setting for a composite service where the composite service may have the best performance.
- The Workflow Converter converts BPEL workflow file to parallel execution representation and adds optimal parallel execution setting to create a new workflow representation.

Algorithm 1. Parallel Execution Optimization

Input: An execution plan of a composite service: TheExecutionPlan
Output: Recommended parallel execution setting for the execution plan

1 $concreteServiceList \leftarrow getServiceEndPoints(TheExecutionPlan)$
2 $performancePatterns \leftarrow \emptyset$
3 $parallelExecutionSetting \leftarrow \emptyset$
4 **foreach** s **in** $concreteServiceList$ **do**
5   **if** $isAnalysed(s)$ **then**
6          $p \leftarrow getPerformancePattern(s)$
7          $performancePatterns \leftarrow performancePatterns \cup p$
8   **else**
9          $p \leftarrow analysePerformancePattern(s)$
10         $insertintoPerformancePatternDB(p)$
11         $performancePatterns \leftarrow performancePatterns \cup p$

12 $parallelExecutionSetting \leftarrow$
   $optimizeParallelExecutionSetting(performancePatterns)$
13 **return** $parallelExecutionSetting$

Output of the Parallel Execution Setting Adapter is new representation of the composite service with an optimal parallel execution setting. The steps of optimizing parallel execution setting for a concrete composite service are shown in Algorithm 1. List of atomic language services is retrieved from the composite service representation. If a language service is already analysed, function *getPerformancePattern* gets policy of this service from the database. Otherwise, performance of the language service is analysed by function *analysePerformancePattern* to determine policy of the service. Function *optimizeParallelExecutionSetting()* uses language services' policies and a prediction model to produces the optimal parallel execution setting for the concrete composite service.

We adopt the integrated engine proposed in previous work [15] to be the Workflow Execution Engine to interpret and execute the new workflow representation. This engine enables parallel execution and pipelined execution when executing a composite service. Each atomic service in the composite service is invoked with multiple processes. Input data sets are streamingly sent to the service without waiting for the responses. This workflow execution engine helps to improve performance of a composite service significantly. However, due to parallel execution policies of atomic language services we need the Parallel Execution Setting Adapter to ensure the optimal performance of the composite service.

The main goal of our proposed mechanism is to create an optimal parallel execution setting for a composite service which conforms to policies of all participated providers. Our mechanism can be a middleware for a workflow system to make the system more efficiency when invoking composite services under parallel execution. A core issue is to predict the optimal parameter for composite service under parallel execution regarding atomic services' policies. We will briefly introduce the issue in the next sections.

4   Parallel Execution Policy of Language Services

Language services are designed to process huge amount of data sets. These services can benefit from the use of parallel execution to improve performance. That is, when a service processes large amounts of data, the data is separated and then each instance of the service will be applied over each partition in parallel. This process may significantly decrease execution time of the service. However, due to differences in computing resources, different providers set different parallel execution policies for their provided services. In this session we propose a model to describe parallel execution policies of language services.

Suppose that a language service processes a large dataset using parallel execution with n concurrent processes. This means that, the input data is split into M partitions and n processes of the language service are applied over n partitions in parallel. Execution time of the service depends on the number of concurrent processes, denoted by $f(n)$. Increasing n may help to decrease execution time of the service. However, this trend is not infinite, it will change when n reaches to a certain number which is specified by the service's policy, let's say this limitation number is P. Parallel execution policy of the language service is defined as following.

Definition (Parallel Execution Policy). *A parallel execution policy of an language service is a tuple of $(\alpha, \alpha^{\star}, \alpha', P)$. Where:*

- *α is execution time of the service when the M partitions are serially executed, i.e., $n = 1$: $f(1) = \alpha$.*
- *$\alpha^{\star}$ is execution time of the service to process M partitions with P concurrent processes, i.e., $n = P$: $f(P) = \alpha^{\star}$.*
- *α' is execution time of the service to process M partitions with M concurrent processes, i.e., $n = M$: $f(M) = \alpha'$.*

According to values of the above parameters we recognize three types of parallel execution policy: Slow-down policy, restriction policy, and penalty policy.

Slow-down Policy. The Slow-down policy throttles the performance improvement when number of concurrent processes exceeds specified number (P_s). This means that execution time of the service decreases as the number concurrent processes increases. When number of concurrent processes exceeds P_s speed-up of the execution time decrease is lower. The performance pattern, given by this policy, is depicted in Fig. 3a. The execution time of the service to process M partitions can be calculated by the following equation:

$$f(n) = \begin{cases} \alpha - \frac{\alpha - \alpha^{\star}}{P_s - 1}(n - 1), & \text{if } 1 \leq n < P_s \\ \alpha^{\star} - \frac{\alpha^{\star} - \alpha'}{M - P_s}(n - P_s), & \text{if } P_s \leq n \leq M \end{cases}$$

$$\text{with: } \alpha > \alpha^{\star} > \alpha', \text{ and } \frac{\alpha - \alpha^{\star}}{P_s - 1} > \frac{\alpha^{\star} - \alpha'}{M - P_s}$$

Restriction Policy. In this policy, service providers limit the maximum number of concurrent requests that their services can serve. Service performance has no improvement when number of concurrent processes exceeds a specified number (P_r). Performance of service remains the same when number of concurrent processes larger than P_r. This policy creates the service performance pattern shown in Fig. 3b. Execution time of the service to process M partitions can be calculated by the following equation:

$$f(n) = \begin{cases} \alpha - \frac{\alpha - \alpha^*}{P_r - 1}(n - 1), & \text{if } 1 \le n < P_r \\ \alpha^* = \alpha', & \text{if } P_r \le n \le M \end{cases}$$

$$\text{with: } \alpha^* < \alpha, \text{ and } \alpha' = \alpha^*$$

Penalty Policy. With this policy, service provider specifies a certain number of concurrent requests that yield good service performance. If number of concurrent requests send to the services exceeds specified number (P_p), service performance is reduced. The performance pattern of this policy is shown in Fig. 3c. The execution time of the service to process M partitions is calculated by the following equation:

$$f(n) = \begin{cases} \alpha - \frac{\alpha - \alpha^*}{P_p - 1}(n - 1), & \text{if } 1 \le n < P_p \\ \alpha^* + \frac{\alpha' - \alpha^*}{M - P_p}(n - P_p), & \text{if } P_p \le n \le M \end{cases}$$

$$\text{with: } \alpha > \alpha^*, \text{ and } \alpha' > \alpha^*$$

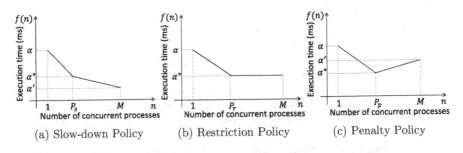

(a) Slow-down Policy   (b) Restriction Policy   (c) Penalty Policy

Fig. 3. Performance patterns of parallel execution policies

Using this model, when parallel execution policy of a language service is determined, we can predict execution time of the language service to process large data with different parallel execution setting. We use this prediction to predict performance of composite service when using parallel execution.

5   Optimizing Composite Service Parallel Execution

In the following sections we describe parallel execution of composite services and a model to predict performance of composite services considering parallel execution policies of atomic services. Based on the prediction the optimal parallel execution setting for the composite services is determined.

5.1 Parallel Execution of Composite Language Service

To build advanced language application, developers combine several atomic language services in a workflow. A service described by a workflow is called *composite service*. In order to improve performance of the applications when processing huge amounts of data, a promising way is to use parallel execution to execute workflows. We introduce two types of parallelism for executing a workflow: data parallelism and workflow pipeline execution.

Data Parallelism. Considering a workflow processes huge amounts of data sets. The data sets are split into independent portions, and several computing tasks of the composite are instantiated to process several portions in parallel.

Workflow Pipeline Execution. Input data sets are likely to be independent from each other, for instance when a single workflow is iterated in parallel on many input data sets. *Workflow pipeline execution* denotes that the processing of several independent input data sets by several instances of a language service are independent. This parallelism enables pipeline processing of a workflow. That is, when n concurrent requests are sent to a composite service, multiple instances of each atomic service are created to process the data partitions concurrently. The pooling technique is used such that when processing M data sets, n out of M data sets are streamingly sent to the composite service in parallel without waiting for responses. Since there are multiple instances of each atomic service, the execution of the composite service can be done in pipeline manner. Consider an example of a sequential composition of two services. This example yields the pipeline processing time-line shown in Fig. 4, where $L = \lceil M/n \rceil$ is number of time-steps needed to send M data sets, each time n data sets are sent in parallel, t_{ij}^n is the time that n concurrent processes of service s_i take to finish processing n data sets at time step j.

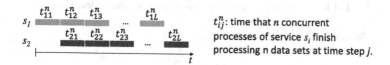

t_{ij}^n: time that n concurrent processes of service s_i finish processing n data sets at time step j.

Fig. 4. Pipeline processing time-line of composite services

Parallel execution of a composite service requires parallel invocation of each atomic language service in the composite service. However, as mentioned above, different language services employ different parallel execution policies. In order to achieve optimal performance of a composite service, the parallel execution setting needs to conform to the policies of the language services. There exist several workflow manager systems such as Kepler system [11], the Taverna workbench [12], and the Triana workflow manager [16]. These workflow managers support parallel execution of workflows, but none of them considers configuring optimal parallel execution setting for workflow with regard service policies. To control parallel execution, in Taverna users can limit number of parallel threads, however, users only care about their computing resources condition to set the limitation, the policies of each service in the workflow is not considered. A parallel execution control mechanism is needed that can control parallel execution setting of composite service based on language services' policies in order to attain optimal performance. This mechanism uses a prediction model that can predict composite service performance and estimate optimal parallel execution setting for the composite service regarding language services' policies.

5.2   Prediction of Composite Service Performance

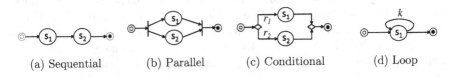

(a) Sequential   (b) Parallel   (c) Conditional   (d) Loop

Fig. 5. Four types of composite structures

There are four basic composite structures normally used to compose atomic services in a workflow: *Sequential, Parallel, Conditional* and *Loop*, see Fig. 5, where circles represent atomic services and arrows represent the transfer of data between services. QoS of a composite service is aggregate QoS of all atomic services. Existing QoS calculation methods can be classified into two categories: Reduction method with single QoS for service composition [3,8], and direct aggregation method with multiple QoSs for the service composition [1,20].

Table 1. Aggregation functions to predict execution time

Structure	Aggregate function
Sequential	$f_c(n) \approx \max\limits_{i=1}^{k} f_i(n) + \dfrac{\sum\limits_{i=1}^{k} f_i(n) - \max\limits_{i=1}^{k} f_i(n)}{\lceil M/n \rceil}$
Parallel	$f_c(n) \approx \max\limits_{i=1}^{k} f_i(n)$
Conditional	$f_c(1) \approx \sum\limits_{1}^{k} f_i(1)$ $f_c(n) \approx \max\limits_{i=1}^{k} f_i(r_i n)$, if $n > 1$
Loop	$f_c(n) \approx \dfrac{2 \sum\limits_{j=1}^{k-1} \max\limits_{i=1}^{j}(f(in))}{\lceil M/n \rceil} + (\lceil M/n \rceil - k + 1)\dfrac{\max\limits_{i=1}^{k} f(in)}{\lceil M/n \rceil}$

In this work we adapt the aggregation formulae, proposed in [3], to estimate execution time of composite service. We involved parallel execution policies and pipeline execution defined above to calculate execution time of a composite service. Given that a composite service C consists of k atomic services $C = \{s_1, s_2, \ldots, s_k\}$:

- Supposed that the input data of the composite service is split into M partitions.
- $(\alpha_i, \alpha_i^*, \alpha_i', P_i)$ is parallel execution policy of s_i.
- Execution time of s_i when processing M partitions with n concurrent processes is calculated by $f_i(n)$.
- Aggregate functions to calculate execution time of C for different structures are shown in Table 1. In the conditional structure, r_i denotes the probability with which service s_i is invoked, $\sum_{i=1}^{k} r_i = 1$. In the loop structure, k represents number of iteration of service s_1.

By using above equations, we can predict performance of a composite service with different parallel execution setting (number of concurrent processes of each atomic language service). From the prediction we are able to configure the composite service with optimal parallel execution setting.

6 Evaluation

In this evaluation we will evaluate accuracy of our prediction model and we will compare performance improvement of a composite service when using parallel execution in our workflow execution engine and a well-known workflow engine Taverna.

First, we evaluate how accurate is our prediction model, compared to the actual result. We invoke composite services with different settings and compare the actual performance results with our predictions. Consider the translation part of the composite service described in the motivating example. This part is combination of three translation services and uses two structures, i.e. *Sequential* structure and *Conditional* structure. This composite service translates a Japanese agriculture document containing 200 sentences. Firstly, the document is translated into English using J-Server translation service. Then, a part of translated document, containing information about rice (100 sentences), is translated into Vietnamese using Google translation service. The other part of, containing information about fertilizer (100 sentences), is translated into French using Bing translation service. After analysing performance of translation services, we observe that J-Server and Bing employ slow-down and restriction policies with $P_{sjserver} = 4$, $P_{rjserver} = 10$ and $P_{sbing} = 4$, $P_{rbing} = 14$, while Google employs slow-down and penalty policies with $P_{sgoogle} = 4$ and $P_{pgoogle} = 8$. Performance prediction of the composite service is shown in Fig. 6. We maximize the number of concurrent processes of service to 50, Google and Bing translation services are invoked in conditional structure with ratio of requests is $r = 0.5$, maximum concurrent requests of Google and Bing is 25. The green line is execution time of the composite service predicted by our model, while the purple line is the

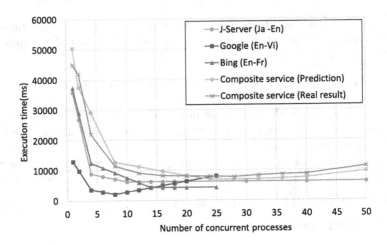

Fig. 6. Evaluation of a composite service (Color figure online)

real execution time. Our model predicts that the composite service attains best performance when number of concurrent processes is 28 (28 concurrent processes of J-Server, 14 concurrent processes of Google, and 14 concurrent processes of Bing) which matches the real result. However prediction of execution time is not so precise, the best execution time calculated by the model is 6811 milliseconds, while the real result is 7709 milliseconds. In the optimal case, execution time of the composite service decreases nearly 83 % compared to normal case (no parallel execution).

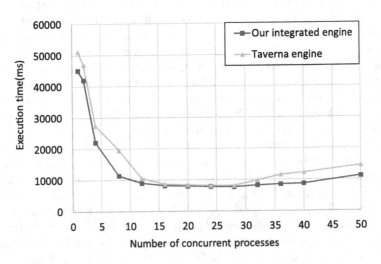

Fig. 7. Compare our workflow execution engine and Taverna engine

Secondly, we conduct an experiment to compare our workflow execution engine and Taverna engine. Taverna [12] is a well-known scientific workflow system, it offers a dataflow model to create and execute workflows. The second version Taverna 2 [14] enables pipeline execution and streaming of data. In this version, users can also number of parallel jobs for each service in a workflow, which is similar with in our integrated engine. Figure 7 shows performance of a composite service executed using parallel execution by our workflow execution engine and by Taverna. The result shows that parallel execution of our engine and Taverna's have similar performance improvement effect. With Taverna, the workflow has the best performance when number of concurrent processes is 28 which matches our prediction. Our prediction model can also be used for several popular workflow systems, which support parallel and pipelined execution, such as Taverna.

7 Related Work

Scientific workflows have emerged as an useful instrument to comprehensively design and sharethe best practices and create reproducible scientific experiment. Many Scientific Workflow Management Systems (SWMSs) have been developed, such as Taverna [12], Kepler [11], Triana [16] or WINGS/Pegasus [7] to enable graphical design, execution and monitoring of local or distributed scientific workflows. In the era of big data, workflow optimization has been an important. One of the common optimization targets is to improve the scientific workflow runtime performance. Scientific workflow runtime optimization is very heterogeneous as different criteria of the workflow can be taken into account. Typical criteria are the workflow structure, data processing or the component model. Whereas workflow structure optimization aims at clustering or dividing jobs, data processing tries to optimize the execution of jobs regarding their data usage and component model optimization schedules the single jobs regarding their task type.

Some of those solutions do not only support the optimization of execution time, but also other quality of service (QoS) parameters, such as cost, or reliability. The optimization extension for the WINGS/Pegasus SWSMS developed by Kuma et al. [9] focuses on the optimization of the runtime performance by modifying application parameters. The integrated framework takes quality of service requirements into account in order to adjust data dependent parameters so that, in a second step, the distributed data processing of applications can be improved.

Other proposed mechanisms apply heuristic-based optimization algorithms to manage the scheduling of large-scale scientific workflows such as Ant Colony Optimization [4], Multi-Objective Evolutionary Algorithms [19] or Genetic Algorithms [13]. These methods focus on user specified QoS constrains for certain applications. A threshold can be set and the method then tries to find a solution so that all constrains are met and optimized.

None of the existing work above take parallel execution policies of task providers into account in order to configure workflows with optimal parallel execution setting to attain the best performance as we do in this paper.

8   Conclusions

This paper proposed a prediction model that can predict performance of composite services that use parallel execution; the model well considers the policies of the language service providers. A mathematical model was proposed to categorize parallel execution policies of atomic services into three different types: Slow-down policy, Restriction policy, and Penalty policy. We have observed that several real-world web services (Google translation service, Baidu translation service, etc.) follow these types of parallel execution policies. Based on the prediction model we proposed a parallel execution control framework. The main contributions of this paper are:

- A prediction model that can predict the optimal parallel execution setting of a composite service which conforms to all atomic language services' policies.
- A parallel execution control mechanism for composite service. Using this mechanism, a workflow manager system (e.g. the Language Grid, Taverna) can dynamically adapts parallel execution of composite service to language service policies in order to attain best performance.

This mechanism is helpful for application based language service workflow to configure a best parallel execution setting regarding language service's policies. This is the first attempt to incorporate service providers' decisions into parallel computing for language application.

Our model is, however, not so accurate in predicting the execution time. Future work includes improving the model to increase prediction accuracy. Furthermore, we will consider the use of other QoS metrics such as cost and reputation.

Acknowledgments. This research was partly supported by a Grant-in-Aid for Scientific Research (S) (24220002, 2012–2016) from Japan Society for Promotion of Science (JSPS).

References

1. Ardagna, D., Pernici, B.: Adaptive service composition in flexible processes. IEEE Trans. Softw. Eng. **33**(6), 369–384 (2007)
2. Canfora, G., Di Penta, M., Esposito, R., Villani, M.L.: A framework for QoS-aware binding and re-binding of composite web services. J. Syst. Softw. **81**(10), 1754–1769 (2008)
3. Cardoso, J., Sheth, A., Miller, J., Arnold, J., Kochut, K.: Quality of service for workflows and web service processes. Web Semant. Sci. Serv. Agents World Wide Web **1**(3), 281–308 (2004)
4. Chen, W.N., Zhang, J.: An ant colony optimization approach to a grid workflow scheduling problem with various QoS requirements. IEEE Trans. Syst. Man Cybern. Part C Appl. Rev. **39**(1), 29–43 (2009)
5. Dean, J., Ghemawat, S.: MapReduce: a flexible data processing tool. Commun. ACM **53**(1), 72–77 (2010)

6. Ishida, T.: The Language Grid: Service-Oriented Collective Intelligence for Language Resource Interoperability. Springer Science & Business Media, Heidelberg (2011)
7. Gil, Y., Ratnakar, V., Kim, J., Gonzalez-Calero, P., Groth, P., Moody, J., Deelman, E.: Wings: Intelligent workflow-based design of computational experiments. IEEE Intell. Syst. **26**, 62–72 (2010)
8. Jaeger, M.C., Rojec-Goldmann, G., Muhl, G.: QoS aggregation for web service composition using workflow patterns. In: 8th IEEE International Enterprise Distributed Object Computing Conference, pp. 149–159. IEEE (2004)
9. Kumar, V.S., Kurc, T., Ratnakar, V., Kim, J., Mehta, G., Vahi, K., Saltz, J.: Parameterized specification, configuration and execution of data-intensive scientific workflows. Clust. Comput. **13**(3), 315–333 (2010)
10. Jordan, D., Evdemon, J., Alves, A., Arkin, A., Askary, S., Barreto, C., Bloch, B., Curbera, F., Ford, M., Goland, Y., et al.: Web services business process execution language version 2.0. OASIS standard, 11, 11 (2007)
11. Ludäscher, B., Altintas, I., Berkley, C., Higgins, D., Jaeger, E., Jones, M., Lee, E., Tao, J., Zhao, Y.: Scientific workflow management and the Kepler system. Concurrency Comput. Pract. Experience **18**(10), 1039–1065 (2006)
12. Oinn, T., Addis, M., Ferris, J., Marvin, D., Senger, M., Greenwood, M., Carver, T., Clover, K., Pocock, M.R., Wipat, A., Li, P.: Taverna: a tool for the composition and enactment of bioinformatics workflows. Bioinformatics **20**(17), 3045–3054 (2004)
13. Prodan, R., Fahringer, T.: Dynamic scheduling of scientific workflow applications on the grid: a case study. In: The 2005 ACM Symposium on Applied Computing, pp. 687–694. ACM (2005)
14. Sroka, J., Hidders, J., Missier, P., Goble, C.: A formal semantics for the Taverna 2 workflow model. J. Comput. Syst. Sci. **76**(6), 490–508 (2010)
15. Trang, M.X., Murakami, Y., Lin, D., Ishida, T.: Integration of workflow and pipeline for language service composition. In: Proceeding of the 9th International Conference on Language Resources and Evaluation Conference (LREC 2014), pp. 3829–3836
16. Taylor, I., Wang, I., Shields, M., Majithia, S.: Distributed computing with Triana on the Grid. Concurrency Comput. Pract. Experience **17**(9), 1197–1214 (2005)
17. Deelman, E., Gannon, D., Shields, M.: Workflows for e-Science. Springer, London (2007)
18. Williams, R., Gorton, I., Greenfield, P., Szalay, A.: Data-intensive computing in the 21st century. IEEE Comput. **41**(4), 0030–32 (2008)
19. Yu, J., Kirley, M., Buyya, R.: Multi-objective planning for workflow execution on grids. In: The 8th IEEE/ACM International Conference on Grid Computing, pp. 10–17. IEEE Computer Society (2007)
20. Yu, Q., Bouguettaya, A.: Framework for web service query algebra and optimization. ACM Trans. Web (TWEB) **2**(1), 6 (2008)
21. Zeng, L., Benatallah, B., Ngu, A.H., Dumas, M., Kalagnanam, J., Chang, H.: QoS-aware middleware for web services composition. IEEE Trans. Softw. Eng. **30**(5), 311–327 (2004)

A License Scheme for a Global Federated Language Service Infrastructure

Christopher Cieri and Denise DiPersio[✉]

Linguistic Data Consortium, 3600 Market Street, Philadelphia, PA 19104, USA
{ccieri, dipersio}@ldc.upenn.edu

Abstract. Language service infrastructures are an efficient means for hosting tools and services and processing data, but they can cause complications for licensing language resources. This paper describes the proposed license scheme for the US Language Application (LAPPS) Grid – an open grid incorporating diverse tools, services and resources – and suggests that the LAPPS Grid license approach can be extended to a global federated language service infrastructure.

1 Introduction

Language service infrastructures, often referred to as grids, have risen to prominence in the natural language processing and human language technology communities, capitalizing on the advantages of cloud computing for processing large amounts of data. The idea is that grids reduce the burden of tool acquisition, integration and hosting by presenting them as services and coordinating their input and output requirements, while the grid infrastructure rapidly builds and executes workflows and pipelines from resources and services. How that framework interacts with licensing constraints is a question that has received some attention and approaches vary across grids. As interest in a global language service infrastructure gains traction, the question becomes how license conditions on multiple resources and tools combined in complex workflows across different platforms can be rationalized to support grid interoperability on a large scale. Solving that problem requires the community to rethink traditional language resource and tool distribution schemes, some of which carry a host of use restrictions, in an environment based on open access and cross-platform integration.

Researchers and organizations that rely on language resources (LRs) are well acquainted with the class of use restrictions under a set of finite standard license arrangements. In that scenario, users take time to integrate the LR into a local workflow before acquiring the next resource. Unless grid developers create a mechanism that coordinates licensing issues while constructing workflows, they risk exacerbating intellectual property issues while they ameliorate tool integration problems. In the sections below, we present steps for handling licensing constraints within a language service grid with a proposal for implementation in a globally-federated language service infrastructure.

Y. Murakami and D. Lin (Eds.): WLSI 2015, LNAI 9442, pp. 86–98, 2016.
DOI: 10.1007/978-3-319-31468-6_6

2 Web Service Complexities

Web-based language services implement and combine data sets and tools in new ways that may not fit comfortably under established intellectual property law and existing contracts. In a traditional license model, a data center or data provider gives a user the right to process data, but prohibits the user from sharing the LR with others. To the extent that moving the resources over the web for processing could be considered a kind of "redistribution" – albeit not in the sense of the original license condition – it is not clear that all copyright holders would consider web processing a permitted use. Shared software in a service grid presents challenges as well. How will users know any license terms or that attribution is required when they are working in an organic grid pipeline where source code is not visible and the command line is not needed?

Add to this the fact that service grids are characterized by multiple stakeholders. *Grid operators* are responsible for the software and servers that support the infrastructure. *Service providers* control access to data and to software. *Users* avail themselves of grid services to access data and otherwise process it. Importantly, grid operators and service providers may or may not be the copyright holders of the software and data underlying the services they provide. Each stakeholder's view of intellectual property protection may vary depending on what is provided by whom to whom. Users generally favor less restrictions than providers do. Some operators and providers may be compensated. Operators will likely want to track user behavior. Service providers can impose multiple conditions including attribution and restricted use (e.g., research) and at the same time, use the data they process for their own research or system development purposes. Moreover, federated grids will have multiple grid operators each seeking to preserve the integrity of their particular infrastructure.

Furthermore, data and software are variously combined in these infrastructures in ways that produce varied effects on licensing. Examples follow in Figs. 1 and 2 below.

Figure 1 summarizes three simple grid use cases. The first example illustrates users directing their owned or controlled data through an external service controlled by a second party (Provider 2). In the second scenario, a single entity who is not the user (Provider 2) controls the data and the processing. In the third instance, one external

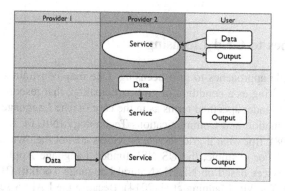

Fig. 1. Simple configurations of web services

party (Provider 1) controls the data while another controls the software (Provider 2). The presence of multiple parties and actions in each example has the potential to affect licensing depending on the constraints introduced by each.

Figure 2 sketches more complex use cases in which data passes through multiple services. The data may or may not be owned or controlled by the user, while the services are likely controlled by many separate parties as well. Examples of the first two use cases, which show data that is processed through multiple services, might have as its output translated speech that was first transcribed from audio and followed by translation of the transcribed text. The input speech can be controlled by the user (e.g., in voicemail transcription) or by an independent party (e.g., translated newswire). In the third case, multiple services operate on the same data that depend on inputs from other providers for operations on specific languages, such as language identification systems.

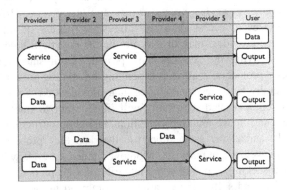

Fig. 2. More complex web service configurations

Moreover, the fact that no party controls the entire system adds another layer of complexity for licensing. Each stakeholder is likely distinct, there are many of them, and even more in a global federated grid, It is expected therefore that each may act in its own interest which probably does not align with the interests of others in the grid community.

3 Approaches to Grid Licensing

There are multiple approaches to grid licensing. One may constrain service and data providers by requiring as a condition of grid participation, that resources are available to particular users under specified terms as in the case of The Language Grid (National Institute of Information and Communications Technology (NICT), Kyoto University) (Ishida et al. 2008). But what if grid service providers are not the owners or developers of the resources? For example, the US NSF-funded Language Application (LAPPS) Grid contains services based on NLTK (Natural Language Toolkit) (Bird et al. 2009) and the Stanford Toolkit (Manning et al. 2014). Because the LAPPS service providers do not own those tools, they cannot directly license them to LAPPS users. A solution could be to provide the resources and their underlying agreements and constrain users to comply with the terms. A third alternative assumes that all parties are responsible for their actions during grid operations and no controls are imposed on providers or users. A fourth option restricts providers and users.

The licensing approaches used by existing grids are not easily discovered. They can be gleaned from the grids themselves in a few cases, from papers or web pages in others or by implication based on the licenses used. They are described below from available information.

META-SHARE is a membership-based infrastructure of networked repositories that contain language data and language processing tools. It does not provide grid services as they are described here. It is designed as an infrastructure for data providers and data users to promote resource description and sharing. Those language resources are available under three license types: all combinations of the Creative Commons licenses; META-SHARE Commons Licenses, based on the Creative Commons model, for resources available to META network members only; and "No Redistribution" licenses that prohibit users from redistributing a resource regardless of use, leaving control of distribution to the resource owner.[1] Its metadata catalog is publicly available under a Creative Commons license.

The META-SHARE license types permit a range of controls as seen above, some of which also include the payment of fees. META-SHARE presents the elements of each license group as a table of characteristics, in fact the model of our Table 2 below. The META-SHARE license scheme does not address cumulative rights, that is, what rights attach to any derivative works. Instead, members are asked to deposit any derivatives in the network under the same license as the original resource (Piperdis 2012).

PANACEA (Platform for Automatic, Normalized Annotation and Cost-Effective Acquisition of Language Resources for Human Language Technologies) was a European project whose object was to create an infrastructure to acquire, produce, update and maintain language resources needed for machine translation systems. Described as a factory, PANACEA acts like a grid in that it offers chained web services (workflows, tools) for processing data. A unique aspect of the platform is its capability to develop data sets on demand by crawling the web; those corpora can then in turn be processed through PANACEA's web services.[2]

The PANACEA licensing strategy is two-fold: (1) the cluster of open source tools comprising the web services are available under various open source software licenses (e.g., Apache 2.0, BSD, GPL); and (2) data sets developed on the platform or provided by users are governed by a non-commercial research only license. In both cases, it is the responsibility of the resource provider to "clear" intellectual property rights for tools and data even if the provider is not the owner of the resource. For the data sets developed by harvesting web sites, PANACEA consortium members undertook to obtain research rights to the source material; any materials for which permission was not obtained were not included among PANACEA resources.

---

[1] http://www.meta-net.eu/meta-share/licenses accessed 15 December 2014.

[2] http://panacea-lr.eu/en/project/ accessed 15 December 2014.

Users can try out the platform on an experimental basis but must register for extended access.[3] The PANACEA project ended in 2012, and the project consortium committed to operating the platform for an additional two years (Arranz et al. 2012).

The Language Grid developed by NICT is a closed system whose resources and services are available to members only under conditions established by the resource or service provider. There are three use categories: non-profit, research and commercial. License text appears in the resource description when available. When a workflow is executed, the licenses that pertain to the selected tools and data are displayed.[4] One can also browse the available language services which include for each service the "purpose of use," that is, research and/or non-profit.[5] The Language Grid has federated with like infrastructures in Thailand, Malaysia and China that operate under a common Service Grid Agreement (Ishida et al. 2011).

Bosca et al. (2012) describe **Linguagrid** as "open to different operators (Universities, Research institutes, Companies) with configurable service access policies: free, restricted to registered users, research or commercial licensing".[6] Linguagrid is administered by CELI, University of Trento (Italy). It is built on the Language Grid infrastructure and presumably employs that grid's license scheme.

CLARIN (the Common Language Resources and Technology Infrastructure) is a networked federation of European data repositories and service centers accessible to users in the participating countries.[7] Its diverse licensing options include those rooted in the Creative Commons licenses with clauses to constrain LRs by user group (e.g., META-SHARE members, academic users). For some resources, papers about them must be reported to the providers and in a variation on a share-alike condition, any derived resources are to be deposited in the CLARIN repository.

The LAPPS Grid model for license management is described in detail in Sect. 6. It is open to all users and accommodates a range of license types as well as fees. Since many licenses constrain behavior that occurs post-grid, the LAPPS license scheme is designed to block obvious and immediate violations of licenses, make users aware of constraints that affect future behavior and secure their agreement to relevant terms. Thus, constraints accumulate as the pipeline is constructed and are presented to users prior to the execution of the workflow. Most constraints are presented as notifications which users acknowledge before the workflow begins. A smaller set of constraints are presented as requirements and block the workflow until their conditions are satisfied (Cieri and DiPersio 2014).

---

[3] http://myexperiment.elda.org/ accessed 15 December 2014.

[4] http://langrid.org/en/index.html accessed 15 December 2014.

[5] http://langrid.org/operation/en/service_list.html accessed 15 December 2014.

[6] http://www.linguagrid.org/ accessed 15 December 2014.

[7] http://www.clarin.eu/ accessed 15 December 2014.

4 Dimensions of Constraints on Language Resource Use

License constraints vary along a number of aspects, starting with the object licensed. Software licenses generally pertain to using software and derivative works of the software, and data licenses regulate the use of the data and derivative works of the data. None of the software licenses reviewed for this paper placed limitations on the use of their output, which is often data. On the other hand, data licenses can and do impose restrictions on using processed data.

The LRs used in web services may be owned by the user, by someone else, or they may be in the public domain. Copyrighted LRs may carry various restrictions: on the use (commercial use, creating and using derivative works); on the user (research labs, non-profit organizations; commercial organizations); on sharing (with whom and how, including attribution and license requirements such as share-alike). There are less common restrictions as well. For instance, we are aware of at least one corpus that requires training in the treatment of human subjects prior to use.

An additional complexity lies in the fact that neither the law nor most licenses distinguish between derivative works (which are typically restricted) and transformative uses (which are typically not restricted). The difference can be illustrated with simple examples from human language technology and natural language processing tasks. Transcribing audio from a copyrighted news broadcast constitutes a derivative work subject, at least in the US, to copyright as well as any license restrictions on the source audio. In contrast, a unigram frequency list based on the transcript is deemed to be a highly transformed work not subject to such limitations.

Many licenses prevent commercial organizations from accessing an LR or using it to develop commercial technology. The motivation in some instances is to encourage direct negotiations with the provider for commercial access which can include a fee. User types typically distinguished by LR licenses include academic institutions, not-for-profit organizations, governments and commercial entities. Cases of pre-commercial technology development may receive different treatment. A licensing model must also recognize those organizations that have executed a required, specific license for a particular resource and those that have not executed the required agreement. Licenses can track users by enumeration or by features. The Linguistic Data Consortium (LDC) maintains databases of all users, all required licenses and the organizations that have executed each license. This is an example of licensing by enumeration. Tracking licenses by organization type (e.g., non-profit organizations) is an example of licensing by feature.

Existing grid licenses in general do not address the use case where service providers wish to benefit from user activity. For instance, a translation service that computes n-grams from processed text that are used to improve the provider's models – in addition to translating the input text as requested by the user – raises the question of whether the user can permit, or consent to, such use by the provider.

5 Combining Licensing Constraints

For some combinations of license constraints, users should be notified that a specific workflow is blocked or requires agreement to a set of conditions. Clear cases of the former are those in which some input data requires a specific license that the user had not executed or in which some processing service required a fee that the user had not yet paid. With respect to the latter, a commercial organization should be warned by the grid when it wants to use an LR with a non-commercial restriction and should be required to click-through its assent to that condition before activating the workflow.

In the United States (and likely elsewhere), copyright law and individual licenses commonly associated with LRs do not directly address questions relevant to web-based language services. For example, the notion of "fair use" under US copyright law is not defined, but rather depends on a case-specific analysis under the four-factor statutory criteria. Accordingly, it is expected that laws will be of little help in developing a way to assess the effect on any given workflow of a combination of constraints.

For example, what license attaches to the output of a workflow that uses two LRs, one which permits commercial use and another that does not? We posit a pipeline that consists of a language recognition service that identifies the language of the input and routes it to a machine translation service. If the language identification service relies on an LR that cannot be used commercially, can the resulting translation be sold if the input data and the translation system permit commercial applications? We may think this is acceptable, but would our thinking change if the data used by the translation engine was restricted to research purposes? Is the answer different if the input text cannot be used commercially but other components in the pipeline could?

Another thorny area is the derivative work-transformative work continuum. Should an LR with a no derivatives element in its licensing contract be blocked from further processing on the assumption that such processing might be a derivative use? As shown in Table 3 below, the LAPPS Grid license model does not block processing on those grounds, but provides the user with notifications about any conditions on derivative and transformative uses.

Of some comfort perhaps is the fact that grid licensing is not so different from traditional LR license schemes in that users agree to a set of conditions and providers are not generally informed about the planned use. The gaps in the law referred to above are present in both instances. And in both, users are expected to abide by any applicable agreements and conditions. From a data center perspective, we can say that the language research community generally acts responsibly in that regard. The noteworthy difference in the web language service environment is that the analysis of multiple license terms and users' acquiescence to them happen on the fly, raising the concern that some users may miss the import of the license. Hence the need for careful planning in the grid license infrastructure to include user-friendly license information and click-through options as well as any necessary authentication mechanisms.

6 The Language Application Grid

We now consider the resources implemented in the LAPPS Grid as a model for a license management solution.

To date, the LAPPS Grid has used 27 unique software packages (programs, toolkits, APIs, libraries) covered by the nine licenses summarized in Table 1.

Table 1. LAPPS grid software by license

License	Software
Apache 2.0	Language Grid, NLTK, ANC2G0, UIMA, OAQA, Uimafit, guava-libraries, ActiveMQ, AnyObject, Jaxws-maven-plug-in, Jetty, OpenNLP
BSD	Hamcrest, NERsuite, CRFsuite (in NERsuite)
CDDL 1.1	Jaxws-rt
CPL 1.0	MALLET, AGTK, JUnit
Eclipse 1.0	logback (v1.0), Jetty
HTK-Cambridge	HTK
MIT	Mockito, libLBFGS (in NERsuite), GIZA (v3)
Python	NLTK
WordNet	Genia tagger library (in NERsuite)

The LAPPS Grid includes a small number of data sets. Those include the Manually Annotated Sub-Corpus (MASC), an open resource that can be used by anyone for any purpose,[8] and portions of LDC's Gigaword corpora, distributed under LDC's standard license model.[9]

Many of the constraints imposed by those licenses fall into recognizable categories summarized in Table 2.

These many licenses have in common the constraints and values summarized in Table 3.

Grid operators have less flexibility with respect to licensing conditions than providers under the historical distribution model. In the latter case, any fees are generally required in advance and it is not unusual for providers to condition resource delivery on a signed license or click-through consent. Or users may receive the LR and its license on the understanding that the user's consent to license terms is deemed made when the resource is used. Also, as mentioned earlier, most licenses address future events, such as redistribution, derivative works, attribution and share-alike. Thus, a key consideration for a grid licensing model is for it to accommodate those kinds of license provisions in real time as a workflow is built and executed. We address this in the LAPPS Grid by establishing two classes of enforcement, **requirement** and **notification** (summarized in Table 4). For required actions, a pipeline is blocked until conditions are

---

[8] http://www.anc.org/data/masc/ accessed 9 January 2015.

[9] https://catalog.ldc.upenn.edu/LDC2011T07 accessed 9 January 2015.

Table 2. LAPPS grid licenses and common constraints

License	Redistribution	Use	Derivative use	Attribution	Share alike	$
Apache 2.0	Yes	Commercial	Commercial	Yes	No	N
BSD	Yes	Commercial	Commercial	No	No	N
CDDL 1.1	Yes	Commercial	Commercial	Yes	Yes	N
CPL 1.0	Yes	Commercial	Commercial	No	No	N
Eclipse 1.0	Yes	Commercial	Commercial	Yes	Yes	N
HTK-Cambridge	No	Commercial	Commercial	No	No	N
MIT	Yes	Commercial	Commercial	No	No	Y
Python	Yes	Commercial	Commercial	Yes	No	N
WordNet	Yes	Commercial	Commercial	Yes	No	N
LDCFP member	No	Commercial	Commercial	No	No	N
LDCNFP member	No	Research	Research	No	No	N
LDCNon-member	No	Research	Research	No	No	Y
CC-Zero	Yes	Commercial	Commercial	No	No	N
CC-BY	Yes	Commercial	Commercial	Yes	No	N
CC-BY-SA	Yes	Commercial	Commercial	Yes	Yes	N
CC-BY-ND	Yes	Commercial	None	Yes	No	N
CC-BY-NC	Yes	Research	Research	Yes	No	N
CC-BY-NC-SA	Yes	Research	Research	Yes	Yes	N
CC-BY-NC-ND	Yes	Research	None	Yes	No	N
GPL (v2,3)	Yes	Commercial	Commercial	Yes	Yes	N

Table 3. LAPPS grid common license constraints and values

Constraint	Values
Redistribution	Yes/No
Use	Commercial/Research only
Derivative use	Commercial/Research only/None
Transformative use	Commercial/Research only/None
Attribution	Yes/No
Share alike	Yes/No
Fee	Yes/No
Other constraint	–

met. Otherwise, users are presented with accumulated conditions before the pipeline is executed. Actual licenses must be made available as well since summarizing license terms is not a legal substitute for the subject license.

The two types of enforcement, requirement and notification, are naturally implemented differently in the LAPPS Grid. Notification is treated similarly to a click-through license. Specifically, the software used to build grid pipelines queries each service as it is added to the pipeline for any licensing constraints. Those constraints may include Creative Commons primitives or the requirement to agree on the

Table 4. LAPPS grid license constraint enforcement

Constraint	Action
Redistribution	Notify
Use	Notify
Derivatives use	Notify
Attribution	Notify
Share alike	Notify
Fee	Require
Other specific license	Require
Other specific constraint	?

fly to specific licenses such as those listed in Table 1. The user is offered the opportunity to review each of those licenses and is notified that continued execution of the pipeline signals agreement with their terms. Requirement is implemented through a special module that connects the user to the organization responsible for enforcing the relevant constraints. The module passes to the authorizing organization the identifier of the resource requested and a token uniquely identifying the session. The authorizing organization may require the user to present login credentials, make payment or otherwise demonstrate that he has satisfied the constraint, after which it returns an approval or rejection that causes the pipeline to be executed or blocked respectively.

7 A Federated Grid Licensing Model

We propose the framework in Fig. 3 for a federated grid licensing model.

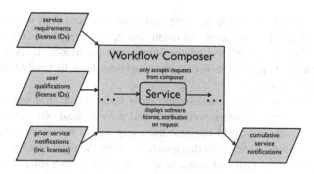

Fig. 3. Federated grid licensing model

Users initiate their sessions by authenticating themselves in one of the federated grid frameworks. Resources and services are requested from the workflow management tools. For instance, in the LAPPS Grid, the Composer (Ide et al. 2014, Ide and Suderman 2014) displays available tools and services which are selected by the user in their preferred order which can include multiple parallel operations on the same data.

The Composer directs resources to the appropriate service, taking into account varying tool input and output requirements. Using the LAPPS Grid Planner, users specify input and output requirements and a pipeline is then constructed.

Grid services are linked to the workflow managers, so users cannot implement in a pipeline any resources outside the grid. As the user builds a workflow, the management tools query license conditions from each requested resource or service; they may also query an API or data center regarding the user's satisfaction of license conditions. The pipeline is blocked if certain required conditions such as a fee or a signed license (Table 4) are not satisfied. If there are no required pre-conditions, a list of click-through licenses and their provisions are accumulated by the manger as the pipeline grows. The end result is a summary of restraints with links to the license texts with which the user must agree before processing can commence. Similarly, any service license conditions such as attribution or statements from a README file or in the command line are also displayed by the manager.

The success of this model depends on the existence of a closed grid system where few management programs control each process. Some problems cannot be resolved, such as the distinction between derivative and transformative uses. Our proposed licensing scheme utilizes a conservative legal approach in that case, issuing appropriate warnings about uses that might be considered derivative.

Where formerly independent service grids are federated, we must also address the question of managing the variation in practice related to intellectual property that arises from their separate evolutions. In Sect. 3, we provided examples of how several extant grids approach licensing. In subsequent sections, we proposed a model for managing agreements between software and data service providers, on the one hand, and users on the other. Here, we continue by discussing the kinds of agreements that must be coordinated across all stakeholders in federated grids. We will set aside differences in local law, which are beyond the scope of this paper, focusing instead on differences in agreements.

Federated grids must decide whether participants should sign agreements developed specifically for the federation. As noted above, existing grids seem to differ with respect to how "membership" and related agreements are treated. If there is no single federation agreement, it will be necessary to address how to resolve differences in pre-existing grid agreements.

Federated grids must also consider the basis upon which grid operators, service providers and copyright holders participate and how to deal with mismatches. For example, does a non-profit grid operator have any say as to whether providers may offer services for a fee? Along with that question comes the issue of what responsibility stakeholders assume by virtue of working together. If a service offered commercially becomes unavailable to the detriment of users, does the grid operator or service provider accept responsibility? Similarly, if any users, service providers, grid operators or software developers disrupt a grid, whether their home infrastructure or a federated grid, whether accidentally or intentionally, who assumes responsibility and what are the remedies? Finally, does any grid operator, service provider or copyright holder make any warranties of any kind relative to their offerings? Should disputes arise between grid users and providers, or between operators or federated grids, how are these disputes resolved and in which jurisdiction? This becomes especially important in the case of a dispute between a user and a remote grid operator.

Secondary issues include what information grid operators or service providers may collect from users and does that vary when the user comes from a remote grid? This will be particularly important in the case of unique, proprietary and business sensitive data. Also, in the event of changes to the grid or its hosted services, who is responsible for notification of the change and how does that information flow to other stakeholders? Finally, who decides whether a user is authorized to use the grid, does such authorization commute to federated grids, is it similarly revoked from all grids if revoked from any?

8 Conclusion

We discussed the challenges web language service infrastructures present for licensing language resources and how those challenges are addressed in the US LAPPS Grid. The LAPPS Grid license schema is based on a two-fold enforcement mechanism – requirement and notification. Under that model, most pipelines will be executed once a user agrees to the accumulated license provisions that attach to workflow components. A few pipelines that include resources with pre-use requirements such as a fee or signed license will be blocked until the condition is satisfied. This model protects intellectual property interests while permitting credentialed users to construct complex pipelines. Finally we proposed an extension of the LAPPS Grid license scheme to an open globally-federated language service infrastructure.

Acknowledgements. This work was supported by US National Science Foundation grants NSF-ACI 1147944 and NSF-ACI 1147912.

References

Arranz, V., Choukri, K., Hamon, O., Bel, N., Tsiavos, P.: PANACEA Project D2.4, Platform Software, Project Tools + Resources, Licensing Policy and Exploitation Plan (2012)

Bird, S., Klein, E., Loper, E.: Natural Language Processing with Python. O'Reilly Media, Sebastopol (2009)

Bosca, A., Dini, L., Kouylekov, M., Trevisan, M.: Linguagrid: a network of linguistic and semantic services for the Italian language. In: Proceedings of the Eighth International Language Resources and Evaluation (LREC 2012). European Language Resources Association (ELRA), Turkey (2012)

Cieri, C., DiPersio, D.: Intellectual property rights management with web service grids. In: OIAF4HLT Workshop: Open Infrastructures and Analysis Frameworks for HLT. The 25th International Conference on Computational Linguistics (COLING 2014), Dublin, Ireland (2014)

Ide, N., Pustejovsky, J., Cieri, C., Nyberg, E., DiPersio, D., Shi, C., Suderman, K., Verhagen, M., Wang, D., Wright, J.: The language application grid. In: Proceedings of the Ninth International Language Resources and Evaluation (LREC 2014). European Language Resources Association (ELRA), Reykjavik (2014)

Ide, N., Suderman, K.: The linguistic annotation framework: a standard for annotation interchange and merging. Lang. Resour. Eval. **48**(3), 395–418 (2014)

Ishida, T., Murakami, Y., Tsunokawa, E., Kubota, Y., Sornlertlamvanich, V.: Federated operation model for service grids. In: Ishida, T. (ed.) The Language Grid, pp. 279–298. Springer, Heidelberg (2011)

Ishida, T., Nadamotoa, A., Murakami, Y., Inaba, R., Shigenobu, T., Matsubara, S., Hattori, H., Kubota, Y., Nakaguchi, T., Tsunokawa, E.: A non-profit operation model for the language grid. In: International Conference on Global Interoperability for Language Resources, pp. 114–121 (2008)

Manning, C., Surdeanu, M., Bauer, J., Finkel, J., Bethard, S., McClosky, D.: The stanford CoreNLP natural language processing toolkit. In: Proceedings of 52nd Annual Meeting of the Association for Computational Linguistics: System Demonstrations, pp. 55–60 (2014)

Piperdis, S.: The META-SHARE language resources sharing infrastructure: principles, challenges, solutions. In: Proceedings of the Eighth International Language Resources and Evaluation (LREC 2012). European Language Resources Association (ELRA), Istanbul (2012)

Language Mashup: Personal Grid for Language Resources

Masayuki Otani[1]([✉]), Takao Nakaguchi[1], Donghui Lin[1],
Yohei Murakami[2], and Toru Ishida[1]

[1] Department of Social Informatics, Kyoto University, Kyoto, Japan
{m-otani,nakaguchi,lindh,ishida}@i.kyoto-u.ac.jp
[2] Unit of Design, Kyoto University, Kyoto, Japan
yohei.murakami@design.kyoto-u.ac.jp

Abstract. This paper proposes a language service infrastructure for personal use called Language Mashup. It enables users to develop domain-specific multilingual applications on their personal devices by combining various kinds of language services created from the language resources provided by both academia and industry. To discuss the potential of Language Mashup, this paper introduces two key communication problems, and then our solution of a multilingual application that supports international meetings whose participants come from various countries and communicate with each other in their own languages.

Keywords: Service infrastructure for personal use · Language service · Language resource · Machine translation · Services computing

1 Introduction

With the expansion of globalization, the communication environment has become more and more diversified. Not just the activities of companies and international NPO/NGO but also individual activities have become more frequent. Individual people traveling abroad for private trips or migration, or are making friends in foreign countries through online games or community sites on the Internet. The communication environment is becoming far more multi-faceted with such personal behavior. The changes in communication infrastructures are influencing this trend. Let us imagine the case of an international student. He may use Skype to communicate with the university friends who speak different languages. He also has to send e-mail about his research progress to his supervisor. He will talk with his host family during dinner time. Since the styles and backgrounds of communication are different in each case, the communication support tools should also be different. Even if a complete communication tool is prepared for this student, this is applicable to just him and people with identical behavior; actually there is no one else who has identical behavior.

To cope with the extremely diversified communication needs, it is necessary to build a communication environment that suits each individual. Unfortunately, existing language services suit only adapt general users. Although

Y. Murakami and D. Lin (Eds.): WLSI 2015, LNAI 9442, pp. 99–110, 2016.
DOI: 10.1007/978-3-319-31468-6_7

there are several sophisticated language resources whose performances have been improved year by year, we have to deal with the following problems. First, language resources, which include dictionaries, parallel texts, part-of-speech taggers, machine translators and so on, are often not accessible by end users because of intellectual property rights. Second, even if they are accessible, said language resources are often not easy to use because of nonstandard interfaces and quality glitches. Third, language resources are seldom customizable, i.e., machine translators do not allow users to modify them; it is often impossible to add new words to their dictionaries.

To overcome the language barrier, we have successfully operated the language service infrastructure called the Language Grid for seven years [4,5]. It enables users to develop new language services by sharing and combining language resources as language services. However, we also encountered difficulties in concluding contracts among service providers, service users, and grid operators. Legal issues have become one of the biggest problems facing the language service infrastructure. Furthermore, registration and invocation of services is allowed only to organization users, i.e., personal users cannot invoke services on the Language Grid directly. Personal users are able to use only the applications that have been developed and published non-commercially.

Given the above background, this paper proposes Language Mashup, which enables its users to combine the language services provided by academia, industry and other users on their own devices by using the language service platform called Open Language Grid which allows personal users to invoke its registered language services.

2   The Language Grid

2.1   Overview of Language Grid

Although there are many sophisticated language resources such as machine translators (Google translate, Bing translator, etc.) available on the Internet, it is still hard for ordinary people to develop multilingual environments that suit their problem domain by using those resources for the following reasons: (i) they cannot use the machine translators and domain-specific language resources (e.g., medical dictionaries, parallel corpora on disasters, etc.) until they negotiate with the companies or the research institutes that provide the machine translators, and make contracts with them; (ii) they cannot combine the language services provided by several organizations that have different specifications unless the interfaces of the language services are standardized [1].

To overcome these problems, we proposed and operated Language Grid; it allows language resources to be easily shared and combined by its users as language services wrapped with a standard interface. Language resource providers who join Language Grid as users can register their own language resources as language services by using the wrapper library provided by the Language Grid operation center. Services that are wrapped as the same service type are switchable since those services have the same interface.

Users also can create new services by combining services via the standard interface, which we call the composite language service. Figure 1 illustrates the process of composing a variety of atomic language services for Japanese agricultural experts to translate their knowledge for Vietnamese farmers. We first need to cascade Japanese-English and English-Vietnamese translators, because there is no available direct translator handling Japanese to Vietnamese with assured translation quality. To replace the words output by machine translators with the words in multilingual dictionaries for agriculture, part-of-speech taggers are necessary to divide the input sentences into parts. We can train example-based machine translators with Japanese-Vietnamese parallel texts. We then have different types of translators including example-based machine translators and will face the problem of determining which one is best: example-based machine translators can create high quality translation only when they trained with similar sentences. We may use back-translation, say Japanese-Vietnamese-Japanese translation, to compare original and back-translated Japanese sentences, and select the translator that produces back-translated sentences most similar to the originals. If the quality of translation is still not enough for the Vietnamese farmers to understand, however, Japanese experts may use human translation services.

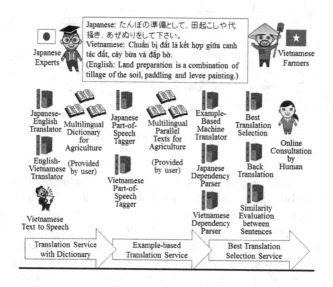

Fig. 1. Language service composition

The Language Grid is built on the Service Grid, which has been released as open source software and is being used by other initiatives as a service infrastructure [3]. Figure 2 shows details of the service grid architecture [6]. The Service Manager plays a front-end role for any functions other than service invocation. All of the management information (i.e., domain definition, grid information,

node information, user information, service information and resource information) are registered through it. It also controls service validation according to
providers' policies. The Grid Composer connects its service grid to others. The
Service Database is a repository to store various types of information registered
through the Service Manager and service invocation logs. The Composite Service
Container provides composite service deployment, composite service execution,
and dynamic service binding so that service users can customize services. In
developing and invoking a composite service, users can use Java coded workflows or the BPEL Engine.

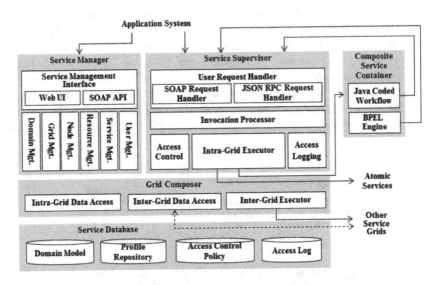

Fig. 2. Service grid architecture

The Language Grid employs federated operation [7] where multiple operator
organizations combine to globally disseminate the service grid which is centered
on non-profit organizations like universities and research institutes. The forces
driving federated operation include not only the limited number of users that a
single operator can handle, but also the locality caused by geographical conditions and application domains. Although we are able to solve such problems by
using federated operation, sometimes it is impossible for different service grids
to use exactly the same agreements. A typical problem is the governing law.
For international affiliation, a possible idea is to adopt a common law like New
York State law, but operators may wish to adopt the governing law of their own
locations. In such a case, operators will use the same agreements except for the
governing law. In that case, the service providers would need to accept the use
of the different governing law to handle the affiliated users in that location.

2.2   Uncovered Problems

After designing an institutional framework for a public service grid operated by non-profit organizations such as universities and research institutes, we found several hidden problems that hindered personal users from using this framework to develop specific multilingual environments.

To promote the provision of language services from a range of providers, the Language Grid employs strict agreements to protect intellectual property rights, and requires that agreement be reached between organizations not individuals, and prohibits commercial use of the language services. However, these limitations resulted in the participation of only a few users, such as universities and non-profit organizations. The agreement excluded companies who were interested in commercial use of the language services, and individuals who wanted to use them for their personal use.

Moreover, the current operation model of Language Grid assumes that language grid operators reach agreement with each other for the federated operation, and language grid users register their language services into the servers so that the third parties can use them. Server software was implemented to realize this operation model, but the software based on this operation model interfered with access to free commercial language services for personal use. This is because access from the Language Grid is regarded as invocations for third party use not personal use. Also, this operation model demands that service providers operate their services stably.

3   Mobile Mashup Framework

As elucidated in the previous section, the following problems should be solved to develop the multilingual applications available on personal devices by using both commercial and non-commercial services.

- Since registration and invocation of the services on Language Grid is allowed only to organizations, personal users cannot invoke its services directly.
- Although the services which can be registered to Language Grid have to be non-profit use, many services are provided for commercial use and allowed only for personal users.

To overcome these problems, this paper proposes a language platform for personal users, which is called Language Mashup. It enables personal users to develop multilingual communication environments that suit their problem domain by combining commercial language services which are installed in their own devices and language services which are registered on the language platform for open access called Open Language Grid, wherein personal users can invoke services usually developed as open source resources by research institutes.

This section starts with an overview of Open Language Grid. Next, Language Mashup is described.

3.1 Open Language Grid

To remove the limitations pointed out in the previous section and involve more potential users like individuals and companies, we introduce a different language grid and propose its coordination with the existing one: Open Language Grid allows individuals to participate, to use language services for commercial purpose, to easily start operation of grid servers, and to freely connect their servers to other servers. Hereafter, to explicitly distinguish it from the existing one, we call the existing one a *contractual grid*, and the Open Language Grid an *open grid*.

These changes mainly impact the legal agreement and the registered language services. In terms of agreement, this new policy is not compliant with any existing agreement. Language services on the contractual grid cannot be accessed from the open grid but the reverse is allowed.

In terms of available language resources, the open grid permits users to register only the language resources that can be freely provided to the other users as services, such as open-source language resources. Accordingly, we have registered open-source language resources into the Open Language Grid, such as Stanford POS Tagger for English, SVMTool for Spanish, and MeCab, ChaSen, and Juman for Japanese. These freely available language resources are published by academic communities. They are easily found using LRE Map [2], which provides the possibility of search based on a fixed set of metadata and to view the details of found resources.

In terms of available language resources, the open grid permits users to register only those language resources that can be freely provided to the other users as services, such as open-source language resources. Open-source language resources registered with the Open Language Grid so far include Stanford POS Tagger for English, SVMTool for Spanish, and MeCab, ChaSen, and Juman for Japanese. These freely available language resources are published by academic communities. They are easily found using LRE Map [2], which provides the possibility of search based on a fixed set of metadata and to view the details of found resources.

3.2 Language Mashup

The operation models of both the contractual grid and open grid assume that users register their language services with servers so that the third parties can use them. Unfortunately, free commercial language services permit only personal use and access to said services from either grid is regarded as invocation for third party use not personal use. To solve this problem, we introduced Language Mashup (hereafter referred to as mashup). The rest of this section details mashup, and how to coordinate both grids and mashup. The purpose of mashup is to combine useful commercial language resources that are open to the public but limited to just personal use. There are many such language resources on the Web, for example, Bing Translator, Google Translate, Baidu Translation, and SYSTRANet. They often provide high-quality services if users pay for them.

However, even if the users pay for them, they cannot register the services with either the contractual or the open grid unless permission is explicitly given by the providers. To solve this intellectual property right problem, we normally need to spend a long time in negotiation, and implement some special functionality to control access in a more secure manner. It is not realistic to deal with each case by working with this type of language resource.

The design philosophy of mashup is to operate a grid server on the user's smart device(s) for his/her personal use and register the language resources necessary to implement his/her environment by himself/herself. Figure 3 shows the concept of mashup. By invoking mashup on the user's smart device, the user can form a composite language service by invoking language services that are located on the users' device, the remote servers, or contractual/open grids, without considering where the service is located and what kind of device the service is installed. To realize the framework whereby users can invoke a service without notifying the location of the service or the device in which the service is installed, mashup implements the following functions.

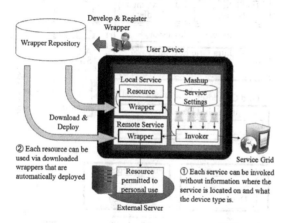

Fig. 3. The concept of Language Mashup

Virtualization of language resources by managing service setting which includes information of location and device. Mashup manages the settings of service invocation and handles invocation requests from users' applications to combine services which are located on remote servers, installed in users' device, and registered with contractual/open grids. Concretely, it manages the following settings: setting name, device information (on user's device, on contractual/open grid), and service location. The user applications can invoke one or more services by setting name and parameters without its location and device. This framework for controlling service invocation allows other invocation methods to be implemented as long as these methods become components which mediate between the invocation component of mashup and composite/atomic services by employing the invocation interface of mashup.

Automatic wrapping of local resources by using wrapper repository. To apply wrappers to language resources accessible for only personal use and located on user's device or remote servers, we developed a framework for downloading and deploying wrappers, where wrappers can be uploaded or downloaded from a wrapper repository and are installed in the users' devices as services which can be invoked via mashup.

Furthermore, we developed a miniaturized composite service engine suitable for mobile devices by removing the components of federation, from the existing service grid. Finally, we downsized the software to 1 MB. Figure 4 shows the system architecture of mashup.

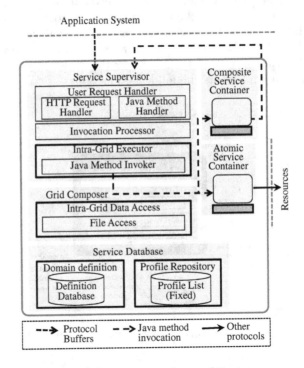

Fig. 4. Language mashup architecture

The mashup framework where users can form composite language services by invoking services regardless of their location or device type is also applicable to the Internet of Things (IoT) because it can combine personal and community services. For example, a user whose name is Ken can turn on the light of his room by saying "Turn on Ken's room", i.e., this user combined speech recognition, text-to-speech, and translation services with the family's dictionary where the word of his room is registered as "Ken's room". Thus, mashup can be expected as the useful interface to IoT devices by providing domain-specific communication.

Table 1 compares the features of each grid server including mashup. This shows they can complement each other in dealing with various situations.

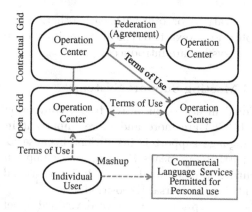

Fig. 5. Coordination among contractual grid, open grid, and mashup

In particular, the ranges of available language resources differ with grid server type. The contractual grid can make various language resources available if their providers reach agreement. The open grid can provide only open-source language resources to avoid complex legal negotiations. Mashup can combine free commercial language resources with academic language resources for the userfs personal access.

Table 1. Comparisons between three kinds of grid servers

	Agreement	Operator/User	Purpose	Language Resources (LRs)
Contractual grid	Strict	Organization/Organization	Non-profit, Research	LRs provided under the agreement
Open Grid	Relaxed	Organization/Individuals	Non-profit, Research, Profit	Open-source LRs (e.g. MeCab, Stanford POS Tagger)
Language Mashup	None	Individuals/Individuals	Only personal use	LRs permitted for personal use (e.g. Bing Trans.)

By coordinating the three kinds of grid servers, we can create multilingual environments to suit various situations. Figure 5 indicates how to coordinate them. Each arrow represents the direction of a service invocation. Users of the contractual grid can combine language services on both grids. On the other hand, mashup users can combine commercial language services on mashup and academic language services on open grid by registering the former with the mashup server.

4   Potential of Language Mashup

To show the potential of mashup, this paper describes an application that was developed to support multilingual meetings where the people from several countries make presentations or talk with each other. This section starts by overviewing the application. Next, two typical examples of the multilingual meetings supported by the system are introduced.

4.1 Multilingual Meeting Support System

Although international meetings, incentive tours, conventions or conferences, exhibitions (called MICE) are more and more important in the increasingly globalized world, language support is insufficient because its major activities assume that every participant speaks English, an assumption that is not warranted. This is a current problem and is seen in international festivals such as the Olympics, World Cup, Universal Exposition, etc.

To overcome the above problem, we have developed a web system for supporting multilingual meetings that allows users to communicate with each other through their mobile devices in real time. Figure 6 provides a conceptual overview of this system. This system is constructed as a web application that the users are able to browse via their mobile devices. When the participants submit texts written in their language, the system translates it into other languages through the contractual/open grid. The translated texts are not only shown in the reading area of the web system but are also published to social networking services such as Twitter so that the participants are able to receive the translated texts more easily. The participants are also able to select text-based or speech-based input/output methods, i.e., they can use a text-based machine translation service, speech recognition service, speech synthesis service, etc. Some users who have installed mashup on their mobile device are able to improve the translation results by using the language services which are already installed on their devices.

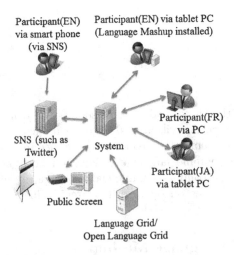

Fig. 6. Overview of multilingual meeting support system

4.2   Y's Men International Convention

We will support Y's Men International 26th Asia Area Convention[1] which will be held in 2015 and have approximately 1,000 participants from around the world. Major Asian languages will be supported in addition to English in this convention, i.e., Japanese, Chinese, and Korean. In the presentation sessions, the conference room will be separated into four areas (Japanese, English, Chinese, and Korean); a screen is placed at the front of each area. The presenters give their presentations in English on the front screen, and the speeches are transcribed by a note-talker in real time. The audiences are able to see the transcribed speeches translated into their own languages on their screens during the presentation.

  To enable the participants to understand the presentations more easily, the translated texts are shown on not only the front screen of each language group but also on user mobile devices such as smartphones, laptop, or tablet PCs. Since many commercial machine translation services are not available on the current contractual grid, it is difficult to provide optimal translation services for those personal users from different countries with different languages. However, mashup makes it possible for personal users to mashup commercial services that are only available for personal use, and so participants can form various machine translation services on their mobile devices for better translation quality during the convention.

4.3   Communication Support in Enokojima Art, Culture and Creative Center

We will also support communication in the Enokojima Art, Culture and Creative Center (Enoco[2]), which encourages the activities of artists from all over the world. Although the artists need the help of volunteers, they have difficulty in communicating with the volunteers who are usually not good at English since they are local Japanese people.

  We will solve the communication problem in Enoco by applying mashup and our developed application. Since we assume oral communication between artists and volunteers, the system will be configured around speech recognition and speech synthesis. Even if the participants find translation errors during a discussion, they can improve service quality by editing the dictionaries or changing translators through their mobile devices.

5   Conclusion

This paper proposed a language platform for personal devices called Language Mashup. It represents a new solution where everyone can solve diversified communication problems in their domain since it provides the following attributes.

---

[1] Web site of Y's Men International 26th Asia Area Convention: http://aac2015.jp/en/.

[2] Web site of Enokojima Art, Culture and Creative Center (in Japanese): http://www.enokojima-art.jp/.

– Allows users to instantiate language service servers on an open grid, where users employ a simple open source Terms of Use instead of concluding legal agreements among providers, users and operators. By avoiding legal negotiations, usability of language services is significantly improved.
– Allows users to mashup commercial language services and services registered with the open grid. Since commercial services are often free for personal use, users can compose various language services on their mobile devices.

Two typical examples of the use of our web application based on Language Mashup showed that the language platforms we propose have potential for solving a lot of communication problems existing all over the world by establishing cooperation among the platforms. We believe that our proposal will contribute to the construction of a new communication environment where everyone can communicate each other regardless of distance and language in the near future.

Acknowledgments. The project was carried through the collaboration of many people in various organizations. We acknowledge the considerable support of the user community of Language Grid. This research is supported by a Grant-in-Aid for Scientific Research (S) (24220002, 2012–2016) from Japan Society for the Promotion of Science (JSPS).

References

1. Calzolari, N., Zampolli, A., Lenci, A.: Towards a standard for a multilingual lexical entry: the EAGLES/ISLE initiative. In: Gelbukh, A. (ed.) CICLing 2002. LNCS, vol. 2276, pp. 264–279. Springer, Heidelberg (2002)
2. Calzolari, N., Gratta, R.D., Francopoulo, G., Mariani, J., Rubino, F., Russo, I., Soria, C.: The LRE map. Harmonising community descriptions of resources. In: Eighth Language Resources and Evaluation Conference (LREC 2012), pp. 1084–1089 (2012)
3. Ide, N., Pustejovsky, J., Cieri, C., Nyberg, E., DiPersio, D., Shi, C., Suderman, K., Verhagen, M., Wang, D., Wright, J.: The language application grid. In: Ninth Language Resources and Evaluation Conference (LREC 2014), pp. 22–30 (2014)
4. Ishida, T.: Language grid: an infrastructure for intercultural collaboration. In: IEEE/IPSJ Symposium on Applications and the Internet (SAINT 2006), keynote address, pp. 96–100 (2006)
5. Ishida, T., Murakami, Y., Lin, D., Tanaka, M., Inaba, R.: Language grid revisited: an infrastructure for intercultural collaboration. In: Demazeau, Y., Müller, J.P., Rodríguez, J.M.C., Pérez, J.B. (eds.) Advances on PAAMS. AISC, vol. 155, pp. 1–16. Springer, Heidelberg (2012)
6. Murakami, Y., Lin, D., Ishida, T.: Service-oriented architecture for interoperability of multilanguage services. In: Buitelaar, P., Cimiano, P. (eds.) Towards the Multilingual Semantic Web. Springer, Heidelberg (2014)
7. Murakami, Y., Tanaka, M., Lin, D., Ishida, T.: Service grid federation architecture for heterogeneous domain. In: 9th IEEE International Conference on Services Computing (SCC 2012), pp. 539–546 (2012)

Developing Language Resources and Services

Building Indonesian Local Language Detection Tools Using Wikipedia Data

Puji Martadinata[✉], Bayu Distiawan Trisedya, Hisar Maruli Manurung,
and Mirna Adriani

Faculty of Computer Science, Universitas Indonesia, Depok, Indonesia
{puji.martadinata,b.distiawan,maruli,mirna}@cs.ui.ac.id

Abstract. The widespread use of social media today has generated lots of research interest towards information retrieval, natural language processing, and also machine learning. The vast diversity of languages used on social media creates the need for accurate automated language identification tools. In this research, we develop a language identification tool that can help automatically identify social media posts in Indonesian, Javanese, Sundanese, and Minangkabau. The latter three are some of the most widely spoken regional languages in Indonesia. We conducted experiments to compare three popular methods used to develop language identification tools, namely *N*-grams, statistical models, and the Small Words technique. Our experiments conducted using articles on internet for training and tested using social media data that we constructed, show that the statistical method obtains the best result among all the methods used.

Keywords: Language identification · Language model · N-gram · Wikipedia · Twitter · Statistical method

1 Introduction

Nowadays, language identification has become an important pre-processing task for various applications, e.g. information retrieval, machine translation and natural language processing. This is due to the fact that we can find so many documents on the Internet, where the languages of the text are so diverse. Documents are written in English, Spanish, Japanese, Chinese or local language such as Sundanese and Javanese. Thus, even though language identification has been researched for a long time, both in text domain and in the speech domain [1] and is a much studied task, one still needs to study the various methods and factors that can increase the accuracy and efficacy, particularly when considering identification of languages that have previously not been handled.

The challenge faced by language technology researchers in Indonesia is quite large. Indonesia has 746 [2] active local languages, although not all of these languages have many speakers. Another problem faced is the lack of resources for such local languages, as many local languages in Indonesia are not well documented.

These two problems have led us to conduct initial research to develop language identification tools for several Indonesian local languages. The purpose of the development of language identification tool is to automate the process of filtering in order to

Y. Murakami and D. Lin (Eds.): WLSI 2015, LNAI 9442, pp. 113–123, 2016.
DOI: 10.1007/978-3-319-31468-6_8

collect data for research that requires local language corpora. The data we want to collect is social media data that is written using local languages. With limited data available, the idea that we propose is to utilize online resources available, one of which is Wikipedia[1]. We use Wikipedia as a training data corpus and testing data. We also interested on testing the language identification model on social media data like Twitter[2]. Contribution of this research is to provide tools for research in IR and NLP especially research that utilizes the twitter data.

2   Literature Review

2.1   Language Identification

In this experiment, we use three methods for language identification. All of them will be trained with the Wikipedia Corpus and tested with a Twitter corpus. These methods are: N-grams with rank order statistic, statistical method and small word technique. These three methods use the same general system architecture for identifying the language of a text.

Figure 1 shows the general architecture of the method that we use in this experiment. The system first needs a corpus for building the language model. The language model will be used as the basis of the language identification. When a text needs to be classified, the system will consult the language model and compute some type of distance or probability and choose the closest language as the text language. The three methods differ on how the language is modeled and how the computation is carried out.

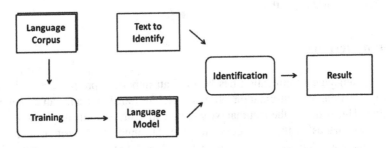

Fig. 1. The system general architecture

2.2   N-Grams with Rank Order Statistic

N-grams are substrings of a word that depends on the size of n. In this method we assume a blank character at the beginning and end of a word, signified below with a "_" character. It aims to make it easier to determine the beginning of a word or the end of a word. Examples of n-grams for the word "TASK" are:

---

[1] www.wikipedia.com.
[2] twitter.com.

- Uni-gram: T, A, S, K
- Bi-grams: _T, TA, AS, SK, K_
- Tri-grams: _TA, TAS, ASK, SK_

This technique was implemented by Cavnar and Trenkle [3]. In our experiments we use TextCat[3] for the method implementation. The system will create a language model based on n-gram frequency. According to Kranig [4], unigrams can be ignored because they do not account too much for the language information. The language model will be consists of the n-gram profile and the n-gram frequency. The profile will be sorted in decreasing frequency order.

The identification phase also constructs a language model based on the text that we want to classify. After we obtain the language model, the system will compute a distance between all the language models that the system has and the language model of the given text. The computation will be based on the position of the language model. We can see the computation illustration on Fig. 2. After the system computes the distance, the system will choose the language that gives the smallest distance.

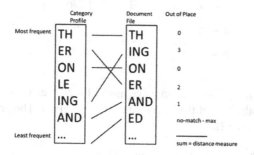

Fig. 2. The computation process of N-grams from Cavnar and Trenkle (1994)

2.3 Statistical Method

This technique was implemented by Ted Dunning [5]. This experiment use lingua::ident[4] which is a CPAN module for the implementation. The systems will divide into two phases, training phase and identification phase. The training phase will make a language model based on Markov process with length k characters. The Markov process; that already counted when the training phase takes place; will be converted into probabilities using Eq. (1).

$$p\left(w_1 \dots w_{k+1}\right) = \frac{T\left(w_1 \dots w_{k+1}\right) + 1}{T\left(w_1 \dots w_k\right) + |A|} \tag{1}$$

---

[3] http://odur.let.rug.nl/~vannoord/TextCat/.
[4] http://search.cpan.org/~mpiotr/Lingua-Ident-1.7/Ident.pm.

Where $|A|$ is the size of alphabet, $T(w_1...w_k)$ is number of occurrences of Markov process prefix, $T(w_1...w_{k+1})$ is number of occurrences of the whole Markov process and $p(w_1...w_{k+1})$ is computed probabilities.

Examples in the processing of a text "abracadabra" in a Markov process with order $k = 1$ can be seen in Table 1, c is the number of occurrences of a Markov process and p is the probability of the calculation using Formula 1.

Table 1. Example of Markov model calculation

Prediction	C	P
a → b	2	3/10
a → c	1	2/10
a → d	1	2/10
b → r	2	3/7
c → a	1	2/6
d → a	1	2/6
b → a	2	3/7

In the identification phase, the language model for all the language will be used for computing the probabilities of the language of the text given. The probabilities will be computed based on Eq. (2).

$$\log p = \sum\nolimits_{w1....wk+1} T\left(w_1 \ldots .w_{k+1}\right) \log p(w_{k+1}, w_1 \ldots .w_k) \tag{2}$$

$T(w_1...w_{k+1})$ is the number of occurrences of all Markov process in the text. $p(w_{k+1}, w_1...w_k)$ is computed probabilities that stored on a particular model for each Markov process. After the system get all the language probability the probability that closest to zero is the best fitting language.

2.4   Small Word Technique

This technique was implemented by Grefenstette [6]. This experiment use lingua::identify[5] which is a CPAN module for the implementation. This method main idea is to store all the high frequencies word for every language. The word such as preposition, conjunction, and other is a good pointer to identify a language. Every document that needs to be classified will be compared with all the word on database. After we have all the frequencies, the frequency will be converted into probabilities. The probabilities are based on the number of occurrences of the word divide with the number occurrence of all word that occurs on the corpus.

---

[5] http://search.cpan.org/~ambs/Lingua-Identify-0.56/lib/Lingua/Identify.pm.

When we need to identified a sentence, the sentence will be divided into words. Then the words need to be compared with the words in our database, if the word from the sentence does not match the words from the database then that word will be given a minimum score from existed probabilities. The language probabilities for the sentence are the sum of all probability on every word.

3   Methodology

3.1   Data and Corpus

On our experiment, we use Wikipedia article as training and testing data. Wikipedia is an encyclopedia that is derived from a global collective intelligence; the content of Wikipedia can be altered or created by any internet users [8]. Wikipedia is a multilingual encyclopedia that has 287 languages and has 31 million articles with 1.7 billion times the conversion is done by 45 million contributors. In Wikipedia there are 337 thousand Indonesian articles, 220 thousand Minangkabau language (Minangnese) articles, 47 thousand articles written in Javanese and 17 thousand Sundanese articles. The data continues to increase every day. Besides being freely modified, Wikipedia articles are also freely distributed and also edited [10]. All articles on Wikipedia can be downloaded via the Wikimedia dumps.

Besides Wikipedia, we also used social media data as testing data. On our experiment we collect tweets that written in Indonesian local language. In a tweet, there are various textual features such as hashtags, mentions, retweets and links. If a tweet is a retweet it typically contains a marker signified by the string "RT" in the tweet. In a tweet we can also mention another user using the "@" character, if the tweet is a retweet, after the user name that is retweeted typically there is the ":" character. Hashtag features are marked with the character "#". These features are used to indicate that a tweet has relevance to a topic. The last feature is the link. These features are often used to display photos or shared URLs sent by the user.

3.2   Data Preparation

In this experiment we will use Wikipedia data dump for the training phase. The data dump will be in XML format and contain every article in a language that exists in Wikipedia. The language that we use for this experiment is Bahasa, Javanese, Sundanese and Minangnese. The Wikipedia data dump will be processed using the pre-processing process for deleting all noise. After we get the pre-processed corpus, we will make four different corpuses with different size for making the language corpus. The size will be 2 MB, 4 MB, 6 MB and the actual size. The process for making the language corpus is by sampling the article in processed Wikipedia data dump. The sampling will randomize the article until we get the size that needed for the experiment.

The testing phase will use four different language collection of tweet from Twitter. Every collection consist 200 tweets which maintain the element of a tweet such as username, hashtag or retweet.

3.3 Pre-processing

The pre-processing step in this experiment will be divided into three phases. The first is XML extraction which processes the Wikipedia data dump. The data dump will be extracted with WikiExtractor.py that erases tags, references, tables, and lists. The tool will give us the article title and body that needed for the next process.

The second phase is language filtering. In Wikipedia article, we found out that many article still include another language that can disturb the quality of language model. We also found that Sundanese article had so many English sentences and English language articles. So, for eliminate that problem we will filter all English sentence in every corpus using lingua::ident tools for identified English language.

The last phase is deleting all the non-alphabet character and every character that is not used in those four languages. Every character such as !, #, $, &, Japanese alphabet, Arabian alphabet and numbers will be deleted because that character is not needed for making the language model and not represent the language. But there is exception for character "é" that widely used in Javanese and Sundanese, that character will be replaced with character "e" because of they have the same meaning but different pronunciation.

3.4 Experimental Design

The language corpus will be processed by the tool for creating the language model. After the language model was created, we can start to identify the tweet. The tweet will be processed first for deleting the unnecessary sentences or words such as non-alphabetic characters, other kind of alphabets, links, retweet and username.

The experiment will be divided into four stages. For the first stage, we will compare the corpus size to get the optimal corpus for making the language model. In this stage, each language corpus with different size will be processed for creating the language model. Each language model will be used for every method and tested with tweet data for acquiring the precision percentages.

The second stage will use the experimental result from the first stage. The two most optimum corpuses will be used to assess the language identification method in which the n-gram and Markov method will be divided into three types. The Markov process will use the 2 + 1 g, 3 + 1 g and 4 + 1 g and for the n-gram method will use 3 g, 4 g and 5 g. So, we will have seven methods to be experimented. Every method will be tested by tweet data in which the hashtag removed for acquiring the precision percentages.

The experimental result from the second stage will be used for the third stage. The most optimum method will be used for this experiment. In this stage we will examine the number of the language factor. We will make three language groups for this experiment. The first is Bahasa and Javanese, the second is Bahasa, Javanese and Sundanese and the last group is Bahasa, Javanese, Sundanese and Minangnese.

For the last stage, we will examine the hashtag feature in Twitter. This stage will show us about the correlation between the language model with or without hashtag. For the first experiment we will delete the hashtag in every tweet that contains it and for the second experiment we will preserve the hashtag.

4   Experiments and Results

This experiment is focused on four factors that can affect the language identification system accuracy. The factors are corpus size, language identification method, the language that the system can choose, and Twitter feature especially hashtag.

4.1   Corpus Size

The first stage experiment is focused on corpus size factor. We can see that when the corpus size is 2 MB the total accuracy is the best than the others size with the highest accuracy is obtained by Markov method. The second highest accuracy can be obtained when the corpus size is the whole text. Both corpuses will be experimented in the second

Table 2. First stage results

Corpus size	Percentage (%)			
	Language	Markov	N-gram	Small words
2 MB	Bahasa	91.0	90.0	57.0
	Javanese	94.5	86.0	46.5
	Minangnese	4.0	20.0	43.0
	Sundanese	91.5	81.5	67.5
	Total	70.25	69.375	53.5
4 MB	Bahasa	90.5	91.0	52.5
	Javanese	94.0	86.5	48.0
	Minangnese	5.0	19.5	43.0
	Sundanese	92.0	81.5	67.5
	Total	70.375	69.625	52.75
6 MB	Bahasa	89.5	90.0	53.0
	Javanese	94.0	86.0	46.5
	Minangnese	5.5	18.5	43.0
	Sundanese	93.0	83.0	67.5
	Total	70.5	69.375	52.5
Whole text	Bahasa	90.0	89.5	54.0
	Javanese	94.5	86.0	46.5
	Minangnese	5.0	19.0	43.0
	Sundanese	92.5	83.5	67.5
	Total	70.5	69.5	52.75

stage. Whereas, the Table 2 show us that there is a bias regarding identification the Minangnese. Every method and corpus that identified the Minangnese are always under 50 % accuracy. When we study the language model and language corpus of Minangnese, we found out that there are so many repetitions in their article. Almost 90 % of the corpus is repetition that decreases the quality of the language model.

4.2 Language Identification Method

This stage is focused on language identification method. We use three type of Markov and N-gram method.

Table 3 shows us about the accuracy that every method gives with the whole text corpus. We can see that the highest accuracy is Markov method with 5 g and the lowest is the small word methods. This case happens because of small word method just need small amount of words that are not necessary contains in a tweet, but for Markov method which use Markov model to create the probabilities of a language will use entire tweet text for determine the tweet language.

Table 3. The whole text results

Method	Percentage (%)					
	Type	Bahasa	Javanese	Minangnese	Sundanese	Total
Markov	3 g	90.0	94.5	5.0	92.5	70.5
	4 g	95.0	96.5	1.0	96.0	72.125
	5 g	95.5	97.5	6.0	98.0	74.25
N-gram	3 g	91.0	79.0	30.5	87.5	72.0
	4 g	91.5	84.5	22.5	85.5	71.0
	5 g	89.5	86.0	19.0	83.5	69.5
Small word	*Default*	54.0	46.5	43.0	67.5	52.75

Table 4 contains data about the language identification method which using 2 MB text for the data training. In this experiments, we can see that the 3-g method have the highest accuracy. This is quite different from the results shown in Table 3, which the Markov method is a method that has the highest accuracy. This is because by using 2 MB as a corpus, the Markov method cannot capture Markov models well enough because only given a small training corpus. This makes the n-gram method is much better than the Markov method, this happens because the n-gram method does not use the Markov models and only take into account the number of n-grams. So, we can state that n-gram method is more robust while using a small data train.

Table 4. 2 MB text results

Method	Percentage (%)					
	Type	Bahasa	Javanese	Minangnese	Sundanese	Total
Markov	3 g	91.0	94.5	4.0	91.5	70.25
	4 g	94.5	94.5	0.5	95.5	71.25
	5 g	93.5	97.0	0.5	97.5	72.125
N-gram	3 g	92.5	78.0	32.0	87.5	72.5
	4 g	91.0	84.5	22.0	85.0	70.625
	5 g	90.0	86.0	20.0	81.5	69.375
Small word	*Default*	57.0	46.5	43.0	67.5	53.5

Accuracy is given by the 3-g is not greater than the accuracy given by Markov 5 g by using the whole corpus. So Markov 5 g will be used in subsequent experiments.

4.3 Variety of Languages

This stage will focus on the number of languages used. Table 5 shows that more language used will be smaller than the accuracy will be given. This is in accordance with the experiments carried out by Muantsa Padró [7]. However it appears that the reduction that occurred not too large so that the use of four languages in one machine can still be done without having to revere the decline in accuracy.

Table 5. Third stage results

Language	Percentage (%)		
	2 Lang	3 Lang	4 Lang
Bahasa	96.0	95.5	95.0
Javanese	99.0	97.5	96.5
Total	97.5	96.5	95.75

4.4 Twitter-Specific Features

In the fourth stage we conduct an experiment that focuses on the effect of hashtag usage in the language identification tools. This is an additional experiment that aims to identify whether hashtag feature has an effect on language detection accuracy or not. The result of this experiment is only intended for language detection using twitter data instead of general language detection. Table 5 shows that the accuracy when we didn't remove the hashtag is lower compared with accuracy when we remove the hashtag. This happens because the hashtag used in a tweet often use foreign languages. However, given the difference was not significant (Table 6).

Table 6. Fourth stage results

Language	Percentage (%)	
	Hashtag	No hashtag
Bahasa	95.5	95.5
Javanese	97.0	97.5
Minangnese	6.0	6.0
Sundanese	98.0	98.0
Total	74.125	74.25

5 Conclusion

In this research we have successfully implemented a language identification tools that employ the usage of existing online resource. The training data corpus used in this research is derived from the Wikipedia corpus and testing data corpus used is the data tweets from Twitter. We build three models using different method, namely: small word technique, n-gram model, and markov model. From our experiment, we can see that markov model give the best result among them. We also try these methods on social media data using specific feature like hashtag on a tweet, but unfortunately it does not give significant result.

We also compare some parameters that need to be considered to build another language identification tools, such as: the technique, size of corpus, and also the number of language included in the language identification tools. This research has a good impact because, the tool developed on this research can be a solution for another research that needs local languages are recognized in Indonesia, especially Javanese, and Sundanese.

References

1. House, A.S., Neuburg, E.P.: Toward automatic identification of the language of an utterance. I. Preliminary methodological considerations. J. Acoust. Soc. Am. **62**(3), 708–713 (1977)
2. Ruslan, H.: Bahasa Daerah di Indonesia Terancam Punah (2013). Retrieved from Republika: http://www.republika.co.id/berita/nasional/umum/13/06/12/moa5s5-bahasa-daerah-di-indonesia-terancam-punah
3. Cavnar, W.B., Trenkle, J.M.: N-gram based text categorization. In: Proceedings of SDAIR 1994, pp. 161–175 (1994)
4. Kranig, S.: Evaluation of Language Identification Method. Bakalárska práca. Universität Tübingen, Nemecko (2005)
5. Dunning, T.: Statistical identification of language. Technical report MCCS-94-273, Computing Research Lab, New Mexico State University (1994)

6. Grefenstette, G.: Comparing two language identification schemes. In: Proceedings of JADT 1995, 3rd International Conference on Statistical Analysis of Textual Data (1995)
7. Padró, M., Padró, L.: Comparing methods for language identification. Procesamiento del Lenguaje Nat. **33**, 155–162 (2004)
8. Wilkinson, D., Huberman, B.: Cooperation and quality in Wikipedia. In: Proceedings of the 2007 International Symposium on Wikis, pp. 157–164 (2007)
9. Adafre, S.F., De Rijke, M.: Finding similar sentences across multiple languages in Wikipedia. In: Proceedings of the 11th Conference of the European Chapter of the Association for Computational Linguistics, pp. 62–69 (2006)
10. Tyers, F.M., Pienaar, J.: Extracting bilingual word pairs from Wikipedia. In: Proceedings of the SALTMIL Workshop at the Language Resources and Evaluation Conference, LREC 2008, pp. 19–22 (2008)
11. Louvan, S., Ibrahim, M., Adriani, M., Vania, C., Trisedya, B.D., Wanagiri, M.Z.: University of Indonesia at TREC 2011 microblog track. In: Text Retrieval Conference Proceedings. NIST (2011)

Building Uyghur Dependency Treebank: Design Principles, Annotation Schema and Tools

Mairehaba Aili[1(✉)], Aziguli Xialifu[2], Maihefureti[1], and Saimaiti Maimaitimin[2]

[1] School of Information Science and Engineering, Xinjiang University, Urumqi, China
marhaba@xju.edu.cn
[2] School of Humanities, Xinjiang University, Urumqi, China
arzu221@sina.com, tilchin@162.com

Abstract. Treebank is a crucial source of information for NLP and linguistic researches. In this paper, we describe the process of building a Uyghur dependency treebank, including designing principles, annotation schemas and tools for corpus creation. The Uyghur Treebank is built from a public readings corpora, employed multi-tier representation for extending future use, and created about 23 dependency relations. This paper presents the preliminary results of this project and an overview of the new idea about combining this project with Language Grid.

Keywords: Dependency treebank · Annotation scheme · Uyghur language

1 Introduction

Treebanks are essential for many NLP tasks, such as evaluating linguistic theories, training and testing syntactic parsers. Currently, existing treebanks are mainly divided into two types according to grammatical formalism adopted. Dependency based formalism is assumed to suit better for representing syntactic structures of free order languages. Recently many dependency treebanks have been built especially for the rich inflectional languages. For example, Prague Dependency Treebank was developed for Czech [1], English-Czech dependency annotated parallel corpus [2, 3], and Dependency corpus for Arabic [4]. In addition to the above, dependency treebanks have already been developed for numerous European languages such as Swedish [5], Greek [6], Russian [7] and Slovenian [8]; and non-European languages such as Japanese [9] and Chinese [10]; and even for dead languages: e.g. a corpus for Latin [11]. Dependency-based parsing had been applied to 13 different languages in the shared task of the 10th Conference on Computational Natural Language Learning (CoNLL 2006) [12].

So far, there is no Treebank available for Uyghur language. Uyghur is one of the languages which still suffers from scarcity of annotated resources. The lack of such resources has become major limitation in developing NLP applications in Uyghur.

The research was supported by the National Natural Science Foundation of China (Grant No. 61262061) and Science & Technology Foundation of Xinjiang (Grant No. 201423120).

Developing a new annotated corpora becomes crucial, especially to lesser studied languages such as Uyghur, where we encounter difficulties in finding such data. To address this obvious problem, we have commenced an effort to develop the first Uyghur language treebank and, in this paper, we present the preliminary results of this project. With a set of future applications, we have undertaken the design of the Uyghur dependency treebank. In the future, it will include at least 20,000 sentences with morphological and syntactic annotations in Uyghur dependency treebank.

2 Uyghur Language

Uyghur is a Ural-Altaic language, and has rich and complex morphological structure. As a typical agglutinative language, Uyghur displays rather different characteristics compared to those more well-studied languages in the parsing literature. The word forms in Uyghur consist of morphemes concatenated to a root morpheme or other morphemes, which are much like beads on a string. The productive morphology of Uyghur implies potentially a very large vocabulary size. For example, Nouns in Uyghur can give rise to about 100 inflected forms, and verbs up to thousands.

Besides, Uyghur languages usually abide to phonetic harmony, which when concatenating an affixes to a root, some changes will occur to some vowels and/or consonant. Generally, there are 3 types of phonetic harmony: weakening, dropping and inserting. Sometimes dropping and weakening will occur simultaneously. For example:

mektep (school) + im (A3sg) = mektipim (his/her school)   (weakening)

burun (nose) + um (A3sg) = burnum (my nose)   (dropping)

arzu (wish) + ung (A2sg) = arzuyung (your wish)   (inserting)

Usually, one type of suffix in Uyghur has several variants, but only one of them would be selected according to phonetic harmony. As given in the following example, -da, -de, -ta, -te are the variants of locative case, but its concatenation to a word is determined by last vowel or consonant in root.

tam(wall) +da = tamda (on the wall)
öy(house) +de = öyde (in the house)
kitab (book) +ta = kitabta (in the book)
ishik (door) + te = ishikte (on the door)

In Uyghur, theoretically, one word can produce an infinite number of words by inserting some derivational suffixes like the causative suffix in a word multiple times. Sometimes, we can generate multi-layer suffix words as follows:

ölchemleshtürelmemsiler (couldn't you standardize it?)

We can break this word into morphemes as shown below:

ölchem + lesh + tür + ele +me + msiler?

On the syntactic side, Uyghur has SOV constituent order, and considered a free-constituent order language. However, the constituent order predominantly conforms to the SOV order in written texts, constituents may freely change their position depending on the requirements of the discourse context. Uyghur is also a pro-drop language, as the subject can be elided if necessary, and recovered from the agreement markers on the verb.

According to previous studies on similar languages such as Basque, Turkish, Finnish, Hungarian, and Japanese, the dependency grammar is better suited to model the various linguistic phenomena in Uyghur. It is the main reason why we choose dependency grammar as our treebank's theories.

3   Design Principle

We aim at building a dependency treebank to provide basic resources for future NLP researches. We expect the treebank users do not limit on computational linguists studies of language model and evaluating parsers, but include linguists investigating morphological structure, syntactic structure and other linguistic phenomenon. Therefore the method of representing the information is very important. Whereas many works on parsing have been mostly dedicated to languages with poor morphology, such as Penn Treebank in English [13], and there has been a growing interest to researches on agglutinative languages like Turkish, Basque, Finnish and Russian etc. [14] studied the use of several types of morphological information in Turkish, and showing that using morphemes as the unit of analysis (instead of words) has better performance. Similarly, other researchers have also verify this conclusion [15].

Uyghur has the same features with Turkish on the aspects of word structure— each word contains several morphemes that can be individually relevant to parsing. Words in Uyghur can be divided into a linear sequence of distinct morphemes or inflectional Groups (IG$_s$), each of which typically has a fairly consistent shape and a single consistent meaning or function. There are strong internal links among different annotation levels. The morphological annotation in an inflectional group can provide strong indicators for dependency relation identification and morphological word recognition. The following is an example that could explain the effect of suffix on syntactic relation.

In Fig. 1, the relation between *mektep + ke* (school + allative case) and *mang* (go) is labeled dative adjunction according to an allative case suffix *-ke*, and then *mang* becomes a modifier of *bala* (child) by adding *–ghan* (a suffix that forms adjective from verb).

As discussed above, morphological structure plays an important role in finding syntactic relations between words in Uyghur sentences. So all texts are morphologically

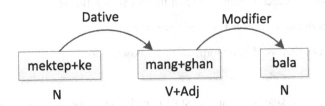

Fig. 1. Dependency relations in a Uyghur phrase

analyzed by Uyghur Morphological Analyzer (UMA) software [16]. Then, the results are corrected manually. There are 137 tags designed for POS tagging in our Treebank and 12 basic POS tags as shown in Table 1. Each category is also divided into several sub categories, for example, subcategory of Noun includes General Nouns (NG), Time Noun (NT), Locative Noun (NL), and Proper Noun (NP).

Table 1. Basic post tags in Uyghur languages

No	Tags	POS	No	Tags	POS
1	N	Noun	7	I	Imitative
2	A	Adjective	8	C	Conjunction
3	M	Numeral	9	T	Particle
4	Q	Quantifier	10	E	Exclamation
5	D	Adverb	11	V	Verb
6	P	Pronoun	12	R	Postposition

Inflected words in Uyghur either have derivational morphology or configuration suffixes such as causative and passive morphemes for verbs. However, the morphological structure of a word form can be quite complex when multiple derivations are involved. The information associated with a word form can be encoded using a finite number of tags, and it is also a common approach to deal with such phenomenon. But, using such a finite tagset approaches to Uyghur could easily lead to loss of information. The reason for this is that the morphological features of intermediate derivations can contain markers for syntactic relationships. Leaving out this information within a fixed-tagset scheme may prevent crucial syntactic information from being represented. For this reason, we have decided not to compress the morphological information associated with a Uyghur word in any way and represent such words as a sequence of inflectional groups (IGs), separated by ^DBs denoting derivation boundaries. In particular, we found that employing IGs, rather than a word form, as the basic parsing units improves the parsing accuracy. Thus a word can be represented in the following general form:

$$Root + Infl_1{}^{\wedge}DB + Infl_2{}^{\wedge}DB + \ldots. +^{\wedge}DB + Infl_n$$

Where the *Infl$_i$* denote relevant inflectional features including the POS for the root or any of the subsequent derived forms. Same work has been done to other languages such as Turkish [17], French [18] etc. But the work that tags the inflectional groups is not yet to be done in Uyghur because the morphological analyzer that we employed hasn't the function of tagging POS for inflectional groups, so we have just used simple form for inflectional groups. For example, *kitablirimizdiki* (in our books) can be annotated as following:

kitab + N^DB + lAr^DB + imiz^DB + Diki

4   Annotation Schema

4.1   Dependency Relations

As we discussed above, dependency relations between lexical items in Uyghur, are usually determined by inflectional groups (IGs), and they are represented by a simple dependency framework. Syntactic relation links only emanate from the last IG of a (dependent) word, and land on one of the IGs of the (head) word to the right (with minor exception) when a word is considered as a sequence of IGs. This feature of Uyghur dependency grammar is very similar to that of Turkish as exemplified in Fig. 2 [19]:

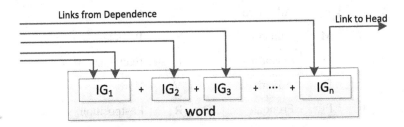

Fig. 2. Links and inflectional groups

Figure 3 shows a dependency tree for a Uyghur sentence *men alimning kitabini elip keldim* that means *I brought over Alim's book*. Note that, for the word *kitabini*, the previous word link to its second IG, while its third IG links to the verb *al* as object. For the word *al + ip*, its first IG, a verb, is the head of previous object while its second IG, a suffix that forms adverbials from verbs, links to final verb as modifier.

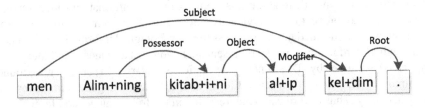

Fig. 3. Dependency structure for a sample Uyghur sentence

To choose a relationship for Uyghur dependency treebank, we employed a principle that it should be cover various linguistics phenomena, whereas too many relations will increase the difficulties of annotation and may result in the sparseness problem. Three factors are taken into consideration in decision making: (1) The broad coverage of syntactic relations; (2) Easily understanding by annotators; (3) Portability to and from other grammatical formalism. Considering above factors and syntactic features of Uyghur, we design a dependency relations scheme as general as possible. The schema adopts 23 dependency relation tags which are listed in Table 2.

Table 2. Dependency relation tags in Uyghur dependency treebank

No.	Label	Relations	No.	Label	Relations
1	ABL	Ablative adjunct	13	OBJ	Object
2	ATT	Attributive modifiers	14	POSS	Possessor
3	ADV	Adverbial modifier	15	POST	Postpositions
4	APPOS	Apposition	16	QUOT	Quotation
5	AUX	Auxiliary verb	17	ROOT	ROOT of sentence
6	CLAS	Classifier	18	PRED	predicate
7	COLL	Collocation	19	SUBJ	Subject
8	CONJ	Conjunction	20	CL	Clause
9	COORD	Coordination	21	IND	Independent component
10	DAT	Dative adjunct	22	COP	Copula
11	INST	Instrumental adjuncts	23	COMP	Comparison
12	LOC	Locative adjunct			

In which, some of the dependency relations need to be explained as follows:

- ABL: Ablative adjunct can be a reason, a source or a theme with ablative case suffix *–din/-tin*.
- ATT: Attributive modifiers is a modifier used for nominal, nominal phrases and adverbs alike. It is also possible for an adjective to take another adjective as a modifier dependency type.
- APPOS: Apposition is a noun which follows another noun or a pronoun and has the same reference as the first and they both have the same syntactic functions.
- AUX: Auxiliary Verb is a verb used to add functional or grammatical meaning to the clause in which it appears.
- CLAS: a classifier is a nominal modifier in nominative case (as in *book cover*).
- COLL: Collocations are idiomatic usages and word sequences with certain patterns.
- CONJ: Conjunction is linked to the conjunctive word with a head of another dependency.
- DAT: Dative Adjunct can be a goal, a destination, a beneficiary or a value carrier in a transaction, or a theme.
- POST: Postpositions is used to nominal complements of postpositions.

4.2 Special Cases

1. Coordination

The coordination has two types: direct (or conjunctionless) coordination and indirect coordination that syntactically linked via a conjunction. Uyghur is a pro-drop language and the subject may be elided on the surface. Such headless constructions as coordinating conjunctions have been one of the weaker points of dependency grammar approaches. Our solution for describing coordinate constructs essentially follows [20] solution. In our solution, the first member of the construction functions as the main element and the conjunction (if there is any) has to be linked to it with CONJ relation, then follow the other members of coordination linked to the preceding element with COORD relation. Figure 4 shows an example of that phenomena for a Uyghur sentence: *munewwer oqut-quchi we oqughuchilar* (excellent teachers and students):

2. Collocation

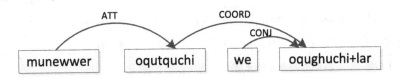

Fig. 4. Linking coordination

Collocation adjunction is used to mark stable construction word sequence like idioms, multi-word expressions, name entity etc. Such words had to be recognized at morphological analysis level to avoid worthless parsing for them. But some collocations are not recognized correctly, and some type of them are beyond the power of morphological analyzer software. So we need to mark them manually. For example, dependency parsing of a sentence ming minglighan kishiler (lots of people) are as follows:

3. Punctuations

Punctuation marks do not play a role in the dependency structure unless they participate in a relation. There are three conditions that punctuation acts as a part of dependency structure:

- The sentence final punctuation. The head of the sentence is linked to the final punctuation with relation ROOT as in Fig. 3;
- The use of comma in coordination. The comma plays a role of separating (or conjoins) the two conjunctions. We don't mark them to any, rather just linked the words before and after it.
- Punctuation marks can also have different roles such as marking the sentential complements. The head of sentential complement depends on the intervening punctuations which is a double-quote in this instance (Fig. 5).

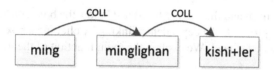

Fig. 5. Dependency relations of collocations

5   Annotation Tool

Constructing a treebank is a time-consuming and labor-intensive work. Efficient tools play a key role in lowering the costs of treebank development and enable creation of a larger and higher quality treebank. Both goals are crucial. A well-designed and well-implemented tool can aid the work of annotators considerably.

After a throughout study of existing annotation tools [21–23] which seem to be most suitable for our work, we found that none of them satisfied all our requirements (such as they do not have all the functions we required). Thus, a decision was made to design and implement an annotation tool. We aimed to speed up the annotation process by using graphical user-friendly interface and transforming the annotation process from a manual procedure into auto controlling and correcting procedure. The annotation tool has been implemented in c# programming language.

5.1   Framework

Uyghur dependency treebank annotation tool consists of three levels of annotation, including morphological analysis, morphological corrector and syntax analysis. Figure 6 shows the main data flow.

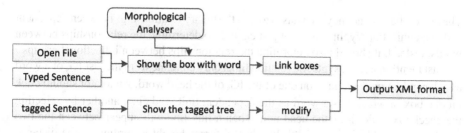

Fig. 6.   Main data flow

It takes raw sentences as an input and produces results in XML format. We have choose fiction and journalistic genre, with a smaller percentage of scientific and popular science texts as the source of corpus. The average length of sentences is bit shorter at the present stage in order to detect the core relations between words. In the future, the coverage of corpus would be extended.

After choosing one sentence (could type a sentence if necessary), it appears in a textbox with morphologically analyzed form. Then, annotator checks its validity by manually and corrects them if necessary. After that, each word in the sentence is shown in a box with word form and the IGs are listed just below the box with a checkbox form. The annotator then proceeds the dependency linking by clicking a box as a dependence and clicking another as a head. We explain the main function of the tool as follows.

5.2 Morphological Analysis

The most important characteristics of Uyghur is its very rich morphological structure. This structure has been represented by splitting the words into inflectional groups (IGs).

We have used Morphological Analyzer of Xinjiang University, which produces sequences of morphemes for each word in sentences (such as *Stem* + *suffix₁* + *suffix₂* ... + *suffixₙ* form) and tags. For example, the morphological form of a word *kitablirimizning* (*of our books*) is shown just as below.

Kitab/N +lar + imiz + ning

The morphological analysis stage is totally automatic except that the user can enter other analyses to each word if the correct one is not given or the analyzer couldn't suggest any analysis.

5.3 Morphological Correction

After automatic morphological analyses, the annotators are asked to verify the results and correct them if it is wrong. After correcting, the sentences will appear on screen, each word is in a box and being prepared for syntax analyses. This step is done by manually, and sentences could be recorrected if necessary.

5.4 Dependency Tagging

The aim of the dependency analysis is to find the binary relationships between dependent and head unit. For Uyghur, it is not just enough to determine the relationships between words, instead, it should also determine the relationships between inflectional groups.

Just mention above, syntactic relation links only emanate from the last IGs of a word as a dependent one, and land on one of the IGs of the head word. Annotator should click on one box in which has a word as the dependent unit, and click another by selecting the checkbox under it as the head unit. Then a link line will appear between the two words with the black color. Link line has different height according to the distance between two words. The further the distance between two units is, the higher the link line is. Then, relation type should be chosen. Each relation in scheme is specified in different color in order to distinguish the relation type from each other. After finishing the tagging work, the result is saved in XML format.

Another function of the tool is restore the saved result to the graphical form so that checking or modifying it if necessary.

5.5 XML File

The results of tagging are saved in XML form. Each sentence is bracketed with tags < s > and </s >. Each word in a sentence is represented by a sequence of the attribute lists of the words involved, bracketed by < w > and </w > tags. For example, *kitab oquchan qizchaq (the girl reading a book)* is shown as *kitab oqu + ghan qizchaq* after morphological analysis, the dependency relationship is shown as Fig. 7, so the result saved as XML form just shown as Table 3.

Table 3. The description of dependency unit attribution

w	ID	Lem	Morph	Inf	Rel
Kitab	1	kitab	kitab	kitab/N.	2,1,Subj
oqughan	2	oqu	oqu + ghan	oqu + ghan/V.	3,1,Det
qizchaq	3	qizchaq	qizchaq	Qizchaq/N.	

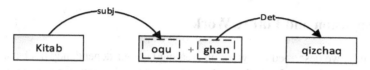

Fig. 7. An example for dependency parsing

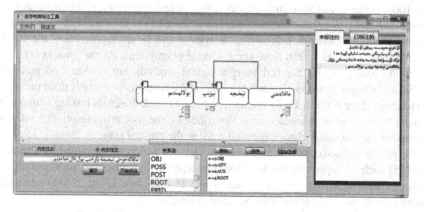

Fig. 8. The user interface of the treebank annotation tool

The attribute lists are including: (1) ID denotes the number or index of the word; (2) Lem denotes the lemma of the word, as one would find in a dictionary; (3) Morph indicates the morphological structure of the word as a sequence of morphemes, essentially corresponding to the lexical form. (4) Inf is a list of pairs of an integer and an inflectional group; (5) Rel denotes the relationship of these words, as indicated by its last inflection group, to an inflectional group of some other word. The form of Rel is a triplet form as $[N_1, N_2, R]$, in which N_1 is index of a word which current word dependent to, N_2 is the number of the inflection group in the N_1th word that the current word's last IG is linked to, and the R is a list of relation labels for any possible syntactic relationships between the IGs involved. Figures 8 and 9 show the tools interface and result of XML file of the senetence *Men maqalamni texiche yezip bolalmidim. (I have not finished my paper)* with Uyghur Arabic alphabet form.

```
⊟ S SentID=4
  <w ID=1 Lem="ماقاله" Morph="نی+م+ماقاله /N" Inf="(1، نی، 2)، (م)" Rel=<2,1,"OBJ">ماقالەمنی</w>
  <w ID=2 Lem="تېخىچه" Morph="تېخىچه/D" Inf="" Rel=<2,1,"ADV">تېخىچه</w>
  <w ID=3 Lem="ياز" Morph="ياز+پ/D" Inf=""Rel=<3,1,"AUX">يېزىپ</w>
  <w ID=4 Lem="بول" Morph="دىم+ما+ال+بول/V" Inf="(1، دىم، 3)، (ما، 2)، (ال)" Rel=<4,1,"ROOT">بولالمىدىم</w>
  <w ID=5 Lem="." Morph="." Inf="" Rel=<-1,1,"">.</w>
  </S.
```

Fig. 9. Sample treebank encoding a Uyghur sentence

6   Conclusion and Future Work

In this study, we described our work on creating Uyghur dependency treebank. To the best of our knowledge, this is the first effort to create a Uyghur dependency treebank. The project has begun from 2013 and the total number of annotated sentences is less than 1000, because our work to date has concentrated mainly on resolving annotation scheme for UDT. We have created the initial annotation schema and annotated the sentences with this schema. It is obvious that there will be some changes as the number of sentences increases which have some special phenomena. At the present stage, the annotation tool provides for full morphological analysis but couldn't do automatic parsing and suggest possible dependency link. The whole process is only done manually. The user interface is not friendly enough, and can't check the cross linking which is not allowed to occur in dependency tree. Nevertheless, the tool provides visible interface for annotating work and plays important roles at the present stage.

We plan to enhance its function with the services which are provided by Language Grid [25] such as improving the function of morphological analyzer, adding automatic parsing, checking wrong lines etc. and expect to complete about 20,000 annotating sentences with multiple annotators working in parallel.

References

1. Hajič, J., Pajas, P.: The Prague dependency treebank: annotation structure and support. In: Proceedings of the IRCS Workshop on Linguistic Databases, University of Pennsylvania, USA, pp. 105–114 (2001)
2. Čmejrek, M., Cuřín, J., Havelka, J.: Prague Czech-English dependecy treebank: any hopes for a common annotation scheme?. In: HLT/NAACL Workshop: Frontiers in Corpus Annotation, Boston, Massachusetts, pp. 47–54 (2004)

3. Čmejrek, M., Hajič, J., Kubo, V.: Prague Czech-English dependency treebank syntactically annotated resources for machine translation. In: Proceedings of EAMT 10th Annual Conference, pp. 1597–1600 (2004)
4. Hajič, J., Zemánek, P.: Prague Arabic dependency treebank: development in data and tools. In: Proceedings of the NEMLAR International Conference on Arabic Language Resources and Tools, pp. 110–114 (2004)
5. Nivre, J.: Theory-supporting treebanks. In: Nivre, J., Hinrichs, E. (Eds.) Proceedings of the Second Workshop on Treebanks and Linguistic Theories, Växjö University Press, pp. 117–128 (2003)
6. Prokopidis, S., Desipri, P., Koutsombogera, E., Papageorgiou, M., Piperidis, H.: Theoretical and practical issues in the construction of a Greek dependency corpus. In: Proceedings of the 4th Workshop on Treebanks and Linguistic Theories, Barcelona, pp. 149–160 (2005)
7. Boguslavsky, I., Grigorieva, S.: Dependency treebank for Russian: concept, tools, types of information. In: Proceedings of 18th International Conference on Computational Linguistics, pp. 987–991 (2000)
8. Džeroski, A., Erjavec, S., Ledinek, T., Pajas, N., Žabokrtský, P., Žele, Z.: Towards a Slovene dependency treebank. In: Proceedings of 5th International Conference on Language Resources and Evaluation (2006)
9. Lepage, I., Shin-Ichi, Y., Susumu, A., Hitoshi, A.: An annotated corpus in Japanese using Tesnière's structural syntax. In: Proceedings of COLING-ACL 1998 Workshop on the Processing of Dependency-Based Grammars, Montreal (1998)
10. Liu, H.: Building and using a Chinese dependency treebank. GrKG/Humankybernetik **48**(1), 3–14 (2007)
11. Bamman, D., Crane, G.: The design and use of a Latin dependency treebank. In: Proceedings of the TLT, pp. 67–78 (2006)
12. Buchholz, S., Marsi, E.: CoNLL-X shared task on multilingual dependency parsing. In: Proceedings of CONLL-X, New York, pp. 149–164 (2006)
13. Marcus, M.P., Santorini, B., Marcinkiewicz, M.A.: Building a large annotated corpus of English: The Penn Treebank. Comput. Linguist. **19**, 313–330 (1993)
14. Eryigit, G., Nivre, J., Oflazer, K.: Dependency parsing of Turkish. Comput. Linguist. **34**(3), 357–389 (2008)
15. Goldberg, Y., Tsarfaty, R.: A single generative model for joint morphological segmentation and syntactic parsing. In: Proceedings of ACLHLT Columbus, Ohio, USA (2008)
16. Aili, M., Wenbin, J., Zhiyang, W., Yibulayin, T., Qun, L.: Directed graph model of Uyghur morphological analysis. J. Softw. **23**(12), 3115–3129 (2012)
17. Oflazeri, K., Hakkani-Tiur, D., Tiur, G.: Design for a Turkish treebank. In: Linguistically Interpreted Corpora: EACL Post-Conference Workshop, pp. 1–9 (1999)
18. Abeillé, A., Clément, L., Toussenel, F.: Building a treebank for French. In: Abeillé, A. (ed.) Treebanks: Building and Using Parsed Corpora. Treebanks Text, Speech Language Technology, pp. 165–187. Springer, Netherlands (2003)
19. Oflazer, K.: Building a turkish treebank. In: Abeillé, A. (ed.) Treebanks: Building and Using Parsed Corpora, pp. 261–277. Springer, Netherlands (2003)
20. Mel'cuk, I.A.: Levels of dependency in linguistic description: concepts and problems. In: Dependency and Valency. An International Handbook of Contemporary Research, Vol. 1, pp. 188–229, Berlin-New York (2003)
21. Atalay, N.B., Oflazer, K., Say, B.: The annotation process in the Turkish treebank. In: Proceedings of the 4th International Workshop on Linguistically Interpreteted Corpora, pp. 33–38 (2003)

22. Kakkonen,T.: DepAnn - an annotation tool for dependency treebanks. In: Proceedings of the 11th ESSLLI Student Session, pp. 214–225 (2006)
23. Eryiğit, G.: ITU treebank annotation tool. In: Proceedings of the Linguistic Annotation Workshop, pp. 117–120 (2007)
24. Mamitimin, S., Ibrahim, T., Eli, M.: The annotation scheme for Uyghur dependency treebank. In: Proceedings of International Conference on Asian Language Processing, pp. 185–188 (2013)
25. Ishida, T.: The Language Grid: Service-Oriented Collective Intelligence for Language Resource Interoperability. Springer, Heidelberg (2011). ISBN 978-3-642-21177-5

Building Contemporary Uyghur Grammatical Information Dictionary

Jiamila Wushouer[1,2], Wayiti Abulizi[1,2], Kahaerjiang Abiderexiti[1,2],
Tuergen Yibulayin[1,2(✉)], Maierhaba Aili[1,2],
and Saimaiti Maimaitimin[2]

[1] School of Information Science and Engineering, Xinjiang University,
Urumqi, China
{jiamila,wayit,kaharjan,turgun,marhaba}@xju.edu.cn
[2] Xinjiang Laboratory of Multilanguage Information Technology,
Urumqi, China

Abstract. "Contemporary Uyghur Grammatical Information Dictionary" is the basic language knowledge base for the Uyghur information processing. It provides a large amount of grammatical information and collocation features for 49,072 words. The original intention of the development of Uyghur grammatical information dictionary is to provide basic resources for Natural Language Processing (NLP). Building information dictionary has far-reaching theoretical and practical value for Uyghur text retrieval, proofreading, machine translation, summary generation, linguistic knowledge acquisition, representation and usage, even allow the computer to "understand" language. In this paper, we use the methods of computational linguistics, corpus linguistics and NLP techniques to analyze Uyghur morphology, Uyghur syntax. On this basis, we study the grammatical features of Uyghur nouns, verbs, and adjectives and so on, and then establish classification system of part of speech of Uyghur. Guidance with this classification system, we use relational database technology to design structures of "Contemporary Uyghur Grammatical Information Dictionary". According to the principle of combining grammatical functions and meanings, using methods of corpus linguistics, we select words from contemporary balanced Uyghur corpus, and import them to the "Uyghur Grammatical Information Dictionary", then give each word's grammatical attributes. Finally we build "Uyghur Grammatical Information Dictionary" of practical value.

Keywords: Contemporary Uyghur language · Grammatical information dictionary · Uyghur morphology

1 Introduction

With "Grammatical Knowledge base of Contemporary Chinese" proposed and constructed [1, 2], in the field of minority language information processing such as Mongolian, Uyghur and Tibetan, researchers began to build the appropriate grammatical knowledge base. In terms of Uyghur information grammatical dictionary, researchers at the Xinjiang University and other research organization use "Grammatical Knowledge base of Contemporary Chinese" as a model, beginning to research related area of Uyghur information grammatical dictionary.

© Springer International Publishing Switzerland 2016
Y. Murakami and D. Lin (Eds.): WLSI 2015, LNAI 9442, pp. 137–144, 2016.
DOI: 10.1007/978-3-319-31468-6_10

In recent years, works of Uyghur information-processing is to deal with the development of the shallow sentence parsing, named entity identification, machine translation etc. Research and development of various applications in Uyghur information processing begin to come out [3]. Not only research of input methods, product localization but also other information processing area, such as NLP, has also been expanded for other aspects of Uyghur language. Xinjiang University, Xinjiang Normal University [4] and other universities have studied on the Uyghur language grammar, syntax [4], machine translation [5], and proofreading [6] and search engine. For example, Xinjiang Normal University professor Abdullah Yusuf research on Uyghur phrase tree. Xinjiang Laboratory of Multilanguage Information Technology (XJLMIT) lay the foundation for further research of Uyghur language processing by developing an automatic lexical analyzer, Uyghur text proofing system, bi-directional large-scale Chinese-English electronic dictionary [7].

Meanwhile, XJLMIT has also launched research on Uyghur sentence parser project that funded by the National Natural Science Foundation of China, mainly in the phrase structure grammar for parse system. But progress is slow, mainly because of lack of theoretical research and engineering support. For example, Uyghur character recognition, voice recognition, automatic proofreading, automatic transliteration of different Uyghur texts in various countries, intelligent information retrieval system must determine various properties of words in order to achieve full practical usages; machine translation needs every word's grammatical and semantic attributes to achieve the correct analysis and translation. In addition, the deep analyzing of the corpus, such as tagging and semantic annotation of phrases and other infrastructure work is also needed to do semantic analysis. Therefore, building of "Contemporary Uyghur Grammatical Information Dictionary" has a great importance for development of Uyghur information processing.

In the study of Uyghur language grammatical knowledge, many linguists have done a lot of research work and published grammar dictionary in Uyghur language. Unfortunately, these works suffer from three major limitations in NLP: (1) most of the research results are printed as a hard copy, electronic versions are not available. So they cannot be used in an information platform as a shared resource; (2) these works are for human use, without considering the needs of NLP, its scope of application has certain restrictions; (3) due to limited research conditions, grammar dictionary includes a limited amount of words, and their explanation and cited cases have some defects, especially the amount of information cannot be updated in time. Because of these deficiencies, resulting that value of existing grammatical information dictionary is not very high for NLP. In order to improve the utilization of the traditional Uyghur grammatical dictionary we need to design and develop electronic version of Uyghur grammatical information dictionary that can be used in NLP.

2   Establishing the Foundation of Dictionary

"Contemporary Uyghur Grammatical Information Dictionary" contains 49072 stemmed words with basic part of speech tag and additional part of speech tag annotated by manually. The dictionary consists of one general database, one auxiliary information database, 18 sub-database (see Fig. 1), each sub-database contains the words guaranteed to be unique (homograph words is distinguished by letters or numbers base on word formation. For example, نات (horse, nouns, homograph 1), نات (name, noun, homograph 2) and نات (throw, real verb). Each sub-database has different attributes according to their main features.

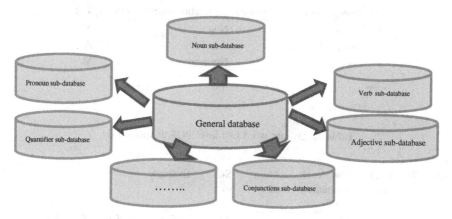

Fig. 1. Main structure of the contemporary Uyghur grammatical information dictionary

For the general database, Uyghur words and grammatical classification code representation (i.e. mark set) is of importance. Contemporary Uyghur language as an agglutinative language, there are plenty of inflections rules. Each class of words has its own word morphology (grammatical category, word formation etc.) and syntactic features (syntactic function, matching relationships). Determining the classification criteria, appropriate classification system and labeling set is an important basis for the dictionary. Choices of what kind of grammatical annotation system must be carefully considered. Therefore, we use "Uyghur POS Tag Annotation Set [3.0V] of Xinjiang Laboratory of Multilanguage Information Technology" as the reference to analyze and summarize various Uyghur grammatical rules and invite experts to discuss, and based on expert advices form a relatively complete system of formal description.

According to experts' opinions, the general database serves as a core syntax repository, which contains Uyghur words with its stem, grammatical information; each sub-database is constructed according to classification type of entries of total database; auxiliary information database consists of an additional component configuration sub-database, word-building additional component sub-database, punctuation and other non- lexical units of sub-database (see Fig. 2). The types of words are divided into two major categories: basic part of speech and additional classes. Among them, the basic parts of speech consists of a noun (N), adjective (A), verb (V), adverb (D), numeral (M), pronoun (P), conjunctions (C) etc.; additional classes consists of idiom (I), usage (U), punctuation (W), suffix (S), affixes (F) etc.

The word POS tags are divided into one level POS tags and two level POS tags (see Fig. 1). One level POS tags are divided into 18 categories (see Table 1), (where the verb is divided into real verbs and auxiliaries); Two level POS tags are divided into 72 categories (Table 2). For example, simple numerals points are classified as numerals, ordinal, cardinal etc.

Table 1. Uyghur word one level POS annotation set

ID	Annotation name (Uyghur)	Annotation name (English)	Tag
1	ئىسىم	Noun	N
2	سۈپەت	Adjective	A
3	سان	Numeral	M
...	...	...	...

Table 2. Uyghur word two level POS annotation set

Numeral سان					
ID	Two level annotation	Two level annotation tag	Main id	Sub id	Example
1	سۈپەت سان	MA	3	32	لىغان،لىگەن مىگلىغان،يوزلىگەن
2	مۆلچەر سان	MB	3	33	چە ياكى دەك،تەك، ئىككى سان قوشۇلۇش، سان +قانچە، نەچچە، سان+بىقىن، ئارتۇق،كۆپ، سان+لىغان، لىگەن
3	پەرتىب سان	MC	3	34	نچى، ئىنچى،تۆنجى،كەنجى

3   Database Structure of the Dictionary

In general, database design means that for a given application environment, construct optimal database model and its application to establish a database system to effectively store data to meet user's information requirements and processing requirements. On this basis, we design the dictionary's general database and its 18 sub-database. According to the different attributes of words, we design related field attributes for each sub-database. For example, the word in the general database treat stem as main unit to set up common attributes, such as, words (Word), part of speech tag (cl), phonetics (Latin), voice weakened, spelling variants, isomorphic, syllable types (open syllable/closed syllables), structure type, domain, sources, notes etc. (see Table 3), of all the words generated from this stem. In the same way the sub-database structure is shown in Table 4.

The general database and sub-databases are connected by keyword field (ID), and designed to various view to handle relationship between sub-databases. The relationship processing as shown in Fig. 2.

Table 3. General database structure

No	Field name	Data type	Field size	The annotation information or examples
1	ID	Automatic numbering	long	99000
2	IDS	Number	int	90000
3	Word	Text	100	نادەم
4	POS	Text	2	n; {n|v|a|d|q|m|n…}
5	Latin	Text	100	Adem
6	Char_len	Number	int	5
…	…	…	…	…

Table 4. Noun sub-database structure

No	Field name	Data type	Field size	The annotation information or examples
1	ID	Automatic numbering	Long	90000
2	Word	Text	100	نادەم
3	POS1	Text	2	NL\NP\NT\NB
4	Countable	Text	2	Y
…	…	…	…	…

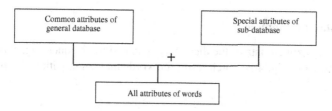

Fig. 2. Relationship between the general-database and sub-databases

In order to effectively manage, maintain and expand data in the dictionary, meanwhile allowing multiple users to easily use the dictionary in a network environment, we choose SQL Server database management system.

4 The Rules Adopted in the Dictionary

In the process of "Contemporary Uyghur Grammatical Information Dictionary" generation, about 70 % of the words in the dictionary comes from the *Uyghur tilining izahliq lughiti* (Contemporary Uyghur Detailed Dictionary), 30 % of the content (names, places, etc.) collected by manually. In the Dictionary, syllable segmentation, number of syllables, syllable types, weakening homograph, Latin transliteration, word suffix vowel variants and other grammar attributes automatically filled by related algorithms [8–10] according to the rules provided by grammarians.

5   Implementation of the Dictionary and Annotation Examples

The dictionary management platform consists of user management module, basic information system maintenance module, vocabulary maintenance module, annotation module, query statistics module etc. The overall system structure shown in Fig. 3.

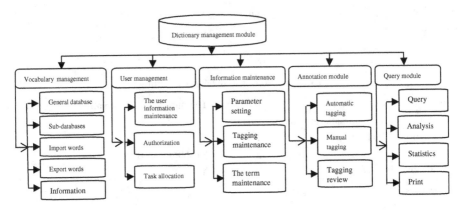

Fig. 3. The main function of dictionary management module

5.1   Annotation Examples

Figure 4 shows explicit data of the dictionary obtained by the querying. To be specific, the query shown in Fig. 4 is search result for words that begin with "تا", structures are

No	词语	词类	拉丁	长度	音节	音节数	弱化	变体	同形	兼类	词尾(元音)	词尾(元音2)	词尾(辅音)	开音节	结构	领域
7	تاتىراڭلىق	名词	tatiranqliq	10	تا+تى+راڭ+لىق	4				0	后元音	非圆唇元音	清辅音	0	合成词	
8	تاتىلغۇچ	名词	tatiliquč	9	تا+تى+لى+غۇچ	4	无			0	后元音	圆唇元音	清辅音	0	合成词	
9	تاجاۋۇزچى	名词	tajawuzči	9	تا+جا+ۋۇز+چى	4				0	后元音	非圆唇元音	浊辅音	1	合成词	
10	تاجاۋۇزچىلىق	名词	tajawuzčiliq	12	تا+جا+ۋۇز+چ...	5				0	后元音	非圆唇元音	清辅音	0	合成词	
11	تاختا	名词	taxta	5	تاخ+تا	2	تاختى			0	后元音	非圆唇元音	浊辅音	1	合成词	
12	تاختىپەر	名词	taxtipar	8	تاخ+تى+پەر	3				0	前元音	非圆唇元音	浊辅音	0	合成词	
13	تاخېئومېتىر	名词	taxɵometir	11	تا+خېئو+مې...	5				0	后元音	非圆唇元音	浊辅音	0	合成词	水务
14	تادانلىق	名词	tadanliq	8	تا+دان+لىق	3				0	后元音	非圆唇元音	清辅音	0	合成词	
15	تارازىچى	名词	taraziči	8	تا+را+زى+چى	4				0	后元音	非圆唇元音	浊辅音	1	合成词	
16	تاراش	名词	taraš	5	تا+راش	2	تارشى			0	后元音	非圆唇元音	清辅音	0	合成词	
17	تارتقۇ	名词	tartqu	6	تار+تقۇ	2	无	A		0	后元音	圆唇元音	清辅音	1	合成词	
18	تارتقۇ	名词	tartqu	6	تار+تقۇ	2	无	B		0	后元音	圆唇元音	浊辅音	1	合成词	
19	تارتقۇ	名词	tartqu	6	تار+تقۇ	2	无	C		0	后元音	圆唇元音	清辅音	1	合成词	
20	تارتقۇچ	名词	tartquč	7	تار+تقۇچ	2	无			0	后元音	圆唇元音	清辅音	0	合成词	
21	تارتقۇلۇق	名词	tartquluq	9	تار+تقۇ+لۇق	3	无			0	后元音	圆唇元音	清辅音	0	合成词	
22	تارتما	名词	tartma	6	تار+تما	2	تارتمى	A		0	后元音	非圆唇元音	浊辅音	1	合成词	
23	تارتىشىش	名词	tartišiš	8	تار+تى+شىش	3				0	后元音	非圆唇元音	清辅音	0	合成词	医学

Fig. 4. Annotation examples of the dictionary

compound words, and sources are from Uyghur noun. In Fig. 4, the search results consist of 17 columns, the name of each column expressed by Chinese because our dictionary interface language is in Chinese. The meaning of these 17 columns are follows: (1) sequence number of results; (2) searched word in Uyghur Arabic script (3) POS tag; (4) searched word in Uyghur Latin script (ULY); (5) word length; (6) syllable decomposition of word; (7) counts of syllable decomposition; (8) whether vowel weakening exist or not in the word; (9) variants of the word; (10) homonym; (11) is searched word belongs to multi-category words or not; (12) suffix (vowels 1, indicates whether back vowel or front vowel); (13) suffix (vowels 2, indicates whether round vowel or unrounded vowel); (14) suffix (types of consonants); (15) whether open syllable word or not; (16) structure of word; (17) domain of word.

6 Summary and Outlook

Building "Contemporary Uyghur Grammatical Information dictionary" is a huge project, and the annotation is one of the laborious and boring tasks. It requires a solid Uyghur grammar foundation. Until writing this paper the completed work as follows:

- Established a classification system and the Uyghur POS annotation set. The word attributes are divided into one level, two level and third level. One level word attributes are divided into 17 categories, two level word attributes are divided into 72 categories, and three level word attributes are divided into 52 categories.
- Designed a framework for the dictionary general database, sub-database and as well as attribute fields and each field's ranges.
- Implemented the dictionary management platform.
- Determined the dictionary grammatical information annotation specification.
- Completed 49,072 word's grammatical information annotation task.

There are several issues needs to be resolved:

- Improve two level word attribute annotation scheme.
- Determine classification standard after connection of words and affixes.
- Improve automatic tagging function of the platform.

Acknowledgments. This work has been supported as part of China National Fundamental Research Program (973) (2014cb340506), the NSFC (61331011, 61462083, 61463048), National Social Sciences Foundation of China (10AYY006), key projects of Xinjiang Education Department (XJEDU2011I08), as part of open project of Xinjiang laboratory of multi-language information technology (049807).

References

1. Yu, S., Zhu, X.: The Grammatical Knowledge-Base of Contemporary Chinese-A Complete Specification. Tsinghua University Press, Beijing (2003)
2. Wang, H., Yu, S.: The semantic knowledge-base of contemporary Chinese and its applications in WSD. In: Association for Computational Linguistics, pp. 112–118 (2003)
3. Kadir, A., Adir, K., Ibrahim, T.: Morphological analysis of Uighur noun for natural language information processing. J. Chin. Inf. Process. **20**(3), 43–48 (2006)
4. Ebeydulla, Y., Abliz, H., Yusup, A.: Research on the Uyghur information database for information processing. In: International Conference on Asian Language Processing, pp. 26–29 (2011)
5. Abiderexiti, K., Yao, T., Yibulayin, T., et al.: Implementation of Chinese-Uyghur bilateral EBMT system. In: International Conference on Asian Language Processing, pp. 87–90 (2013)
6. Maihefureti, A.W., Aili, M., et al.: Spelling check method of Uyghur languages based on dictionary and statistics. J. Chin. Inf. Process. **28**(02), 66–71 (2014)
7. Ibrahim, T., Baoshe, Y.: A survey on minority language information processing research and application in Xinjiang. J. Chin. Inf. Process. **25**(06), 149–156 (2011)
8. Wumaier, A., Tursun, P., Kadeer, Z., et al.: Uyghur noun suffix finite state machine for stemming. In: 2nd IEEE International Conference on Computer Science and Information Technology, pp. 161–164 (2009)
9. Aili, M., Jiang, W.B., Wang, Z.Y., et al.: Directed graph model of Uyghur morphological analysis. J. Softw. **23**(12), 3115–3129 (2012)
10. Kadeer, Z., Wumaier, A., Yibulayin, T., et al.: Uyghur noun stemming system based on hybrid method. Comput. Eng. Appl. **49**(01), 171–175 (2013)

Language Service Applications

Vietnamese Multimedia Agricultural Information Retrieval System as an Info Service

Thi H. Luong, Nhut M. Pham, and Quan H. Vu$^{(\boxtimes)}$

University of Science, VNU-HCM, Ho Chi Minh, Vietnam
vhquan@fit.hcmus.edu.vn

Abstract. Despite being crippled by a mandatory challenge, called "sematic gap," content-based information retrieval is still on the way of blooming. Its application can be seen across different domains, from several daily Google image-searches to an intense sport shot retrieval. Nonetheless, semantic agricultural information retrieval has been averted from the eyes of computer scientists. Meanwhile, farmer in the rural areas are suffering from the lack of information and guidance, resulting in poverty and low life-quality. Stemming from an agricultural country, it is our mission to put efforts on the field. There are two contributions in this work: (1) building a Vietnamese agricultural thesaurus, and (2) an agricultural multimedia retrieval system; putting together as an info service for farming guidance. We spring our thesaurus in 2 sub-boughs: the aquaculture ontology consists of 3455 concepts and 5396 terms, with 28 relationships, covering about 2200 fish species and their related terms; and the plant production ontology comprises of 3437 concepts and 6874 terms, with 5 relationships, covering farming, plant production, pests, etc. These ontologies serve as a global linkage between keywords, visual, and spoken features, as well as providing reinforcement for the system performances. On the other hand, constructing a semantic multimedia retrieval engine is a bit trickier. Automatic transcriptions of audio channels are marked as the anchor points for the collection of visual features. These features, in turn, got clustered based on the referenced thesauri, and ultimately tracking out missing info induced by the speech recognizer's word error rates. This compensation technique bought us back 16.2 % of loss recall and an increase of 9.4 % accuracy over the baseline system.

Keywords: Semantic information retrieval · Agriculture · Multimedia · Vietnamese · Info service · Language service · Agricultural ontology

1 Introduction

In Vietnam, agriculture plays an important part in the country's economic structure. In 2013, agriculture and forestry accounted for 18.4 percent of Vietnam's gross domestic product (GDP) [1]. As a result, information on agriculture comes out in large numbers and in different forms, from textual content to audio or videos. Farmers run into difficulties when searching for this kind of information, because of their lack of subject

© Springer International Publishing Switzerland 2016
Y. Murakami and D. Lin (Eds.): WLSI 2015, LNAI 9442, pp. 147–160, 2016.
DOI: 10.1007/978-3-319-31468-6_11

knowledge and most of the time novice users face insurmountable difficulty in for-mulating the right keyword queries [2], subsequently induces semantic mismatches between query intension and the fetched documents. Generic search engines such as Google or Bing can give decent results, but a carefully tailored search engine with specific domain knowledge and semantic retrieval techniques [6] can give a better performance. And hence it could bring out the possibilities for these novice seekers to be able to efficiently access to the vast multimedia resources available on the Web.

Multimedia resources, such as videos, are self-contained materials which carry a large amount of rich information. Researches [3–5] have been conducted in the field of video retrieval amongst which semantic or content-based (as compared to text- or tag-based) retrieval of video is an emerging research topic [6]. Figure 1 illustrates a full-fledged content-based video retrieval system which typically combines text, spo-ken words, and imagery. Such system would allow the retrieval of relevant clips, scenes, and shots based on queries which could include textual description, image, audio and/or video samples. Therefore, it involves automatic transcription of speech, multi-modal video and audio indexing, automatic learning of semantic concepts and their representation, advanced query interpretation and matching algorithms, which in turn impose many new challenges to research. All these topics are entangled in the name "semantic information retrieval" [3].

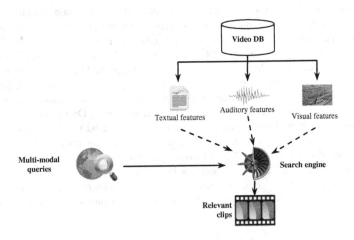

Fig. 1. A full-fledged content-based multimedia retrieval system.

Taking on semantic information retrieval requires works on both visual and audi-tory context of the media. This, however, is not a trivial task even with state-of-the-art approaches. Its mandatory challenge, called "sematic gap," [7] requires much more understanding of the way human perceive things (i.e., visual and auditory information). Computer scientists have spent thousands of hours seeking optimal solutions, only ended up falling in the bound of this gap for both visual and spoken contexts. In the spoken context, content-based retrievals are subjected to text-based retrievals by using an automatic speech recognition system to transcribe speech signal into text.

Referenced works from [8, 9] attained an average performance level around 76 % recall and 71 % precision, reasonable enough in academic but insufficient for field applications. Convictions are blamed on the erroneous generated transcription. On the other hand, pathways of visual information retrieval rely on low-level features for advancement, such as colors [10], textures [11], and sketches [12], etc. Nevertheless, these struggling efforts get us nowhere near human-level perceptions, but only the mediocre temporary solutions. Recent works [13, 14] also introduce a concept-based approach which makes use of ontology to expand user queries and knowledge indexing.

While an over-the-gap approach is unreachable, we insist on assembling current viable techniques from both contexts, aligned with a domain concept base (i.e., an ontology), to construct an info service for the retrieval of agricultural multimedia information. The development process spans over three packages: (1) building a Vietnamese agricultural thesaurus; (2) crafting a visual-auditory intertwined search engine; and (3) system deployment as an info service. Automatic transcriptions of audio channels are marked as the anchor points for the collection of visual features. These features, in turn, got clustered based on the referenced thesauri, and ultimately tracking out missing info induced by the speech recognizer's word error rates. Meanwhile, the domain ontologies serve as a global linkage between keywords, visual, and spoken features, as well as providing reinforcement for the system performances (e.g., through query expansion, knowledge indexing…).

The rest of this paper is organized as follows. Section 2 presents the ontology development process in full details. Section 3 covers our system's specification. Section 4 gives experimental results. And finally, Sect. 5 concludes the paper.

2 Ontology Development

Taking the same model as in [11], we divide the construction of the Vietnamese agricultural ontology into five stages: (1) Ontology specification, (2) Knowledge acquisition, (3) Conceptualization, (4) Formalization and (5) Implementation.

2.1 Ontology Specification

In this stage, we define the domain and scope of the ontology. The basic questions are what domain the ontology will cover and for what we are going to use the ontology. In our case, the interested domains are aquaculture and plant production, including their diseases, breeding and harvesting methods, etc. The main purpose of the ontology is to maintain and share knowledge in the field, increasing retrieval efficiency.

2.2 Knowledge Acquisition

The first step is to gather and extract as much as possible related knowledge resources from the literature, then categorize them systematically. Common groups of resources are ontology construction guidelines and criteria, related thesauri and dictionaries, and relationship guidelines. For this research, we follow general guidelines and criteria, for example, [16, 17]. Terms are collected from 5 Vietnamese textbooks. We also extract and translate terms from FishBase [18], a global species database of fish species, and the NAL Thesaurus [19]. Then we organize and summarize all of the related information.

2.3   Conceptualization

In this stage, a conceptual model of the ontology will be built, consisting of concepts in the domain and relationships among them. Concepts are organized in hierarchical structures; with each concept has its superclass and subclass concepts. Two main groups of relationships are hierarchical relationships and associative relationships. To identify concepts, we use both the top-down and bottom-up approaches [20]. The top-down approach can be used to identify hierarchical structures, while the bottom-up approach completes these structures by identifying bottom-level concepts and defining upper-class concepts until reaching the top. For hierarchical relationships, we use only one relation namely "hasSubclass". Concepts in different hierarchies that are related will be connected by associative relationships. Knowledge modelling tools, i.e., CmapTools [21], can be used for sketching the model. Figure 2 illustrates an example model in our aquaculture ontology.

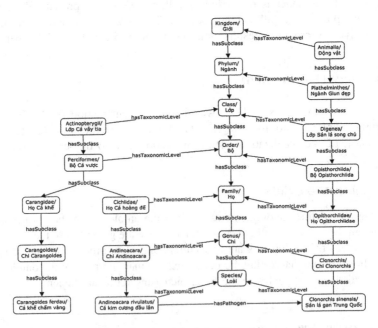

Fig. 2. An example conceptual model of the Vietnamese aquaculture ontology.

2.4   Formalization

The conceptual model from the previous stage is transformed into a formal model in this stage. We listed all the concepts and relationships in a data sheet. Then for each concept, we define a term representing the concept, which is called "preferred term". Synonym, or "non-preferred term", is a term in a same concept that is not selected to be the preferred term. Then we define the terminology relationships that are concept-to-term relationships, term-to-term relationships, and concept-to-concept relationships. The next step involves filling to formalize the concepts. There are three kinds of data sheet: data sheet for concept lexicalization, data sheet for formalizing concept and hierarchical relationship, and data sheet for formalizing concept and associative relationship.

2.5   Implementation

Finally, we can implement the ontology by using the Protégé tool [22]. Protégé is a feature rich ontology-editing environment with full support for the OWL 2 Web Ontology Language.

2.6   Results

Following the development process, we have developed two Vietnamese agricultural ontologies in two different sub-domains, namely aquaculture and plant production. Our ontologies come with two languages, Vietnamese and English. We also develop a simple web application for searching terms in the ontologies.

The aquaculture ontology consists of 3455 concepts and 5396 terms, with 28 relationships. It covers about 2200 fish species and their related terms. The plant production ontology comprises of 3437 concepts and 6874 terms, with 5 relationships, covering farming, plant production, pests, etc. The ontologies are categorized as classes to provide a comprehensive framework. The categories of the ontologies are summarized in Tables 1 and 2. The number of relationships is given in Tables 3 and 4. While being developed separately, the two ontologies share are a fair number of classes, so merging them could be seen in a near future.

There is difference in number of associative relationships between two ontologies because we used different relationship guidelines. The plant production ontology follows the NAL Thesaurus, which has only one associative relationship, namely "Related to." The aquaculture thesaurus, on the other hand, follows the AGROVOC ontology, where additional relationships are defined, for example, "hasInfectingProcess," "hasHost" or "hasNaturalEnemy."

A web-based application for searching terms in the ontology was also developed. It provides additional functions to enhance ontology browsing capability, for instance, bilingual searching (in English and Vietnamese), auto term completion, and external links to other resources. Some of the application's functions are illustrated in Fig. 3.

Table 1. Concepts of the aquaculture ontology

Object concept	Functional concept
Plant (weed, moss)/Thực vật (rong, cỏ dại)	Breeding process/Quá trình sinh sản
Animal (fish, mollusk, and amphibian)/Động vật (cá, giáp xác và lưỡng cư)	Pond preparation process/Quá trình chuẩn bị ao nuôi
Fungi/Nấm	Harvesting process/Phương pháp thu hoạch
Bacteria/Vi khuẩn	Protection and control process/Phương pháp kiểm soát và bảo vệ
Virus/Vi-rút	Cultivation process/Phương pháp nuôi trồng thủy sản
Chemical substance and element/Chất hóa học	
Fish anatomy/Giải phẫu học về cá	
Disease/Bệnh	
Environmental factor/Yếu tố môi trường	

Table 2. Concepts of the plant production ontology

Object concept	Functional concept
Plant (rice, fruit)/Thực vật (cây lúa, trái cây)	Plant genetic and breeding/Gen và nhân giống cây trồng
Animal (pest and natural enemy)/Động vật (sâu bệnh và thiên địch)	Soil preparation process/Quá trình chuẩn bị đất
Fungi/Nấm	Fertilizing process/Phương pháp bón phân
Bacteria/Vi khuẩn	Harvesting process/Phương pháp thu hoạch
Virus/Vi-rút	Protection and control process
Chemical substance and element/Chất hóa học	Cultivation process/Phương pháp nuôi trồng
Plant anatomy/Giải phẫu học về cây trồng	
Disease/Bệnh	
Environmental factor/Yếu tố môi trường Soil/Đất	

Table 3. Number of aquaculture ontology relationships

Relationship	Number
Equivalent relationship	2
Hierarchical relationship	1
Associative relationship	25
Total	28

Fig. 3. Ontology searching feature with auto term completion.

Table 4. Number of plant production ontology relationships

Relationship	Number
Equivalent relationship	3
Hierarchical relationship	1
Associative relationship	1
Total	5

3 Semantic Agricultural Information Retrieval System

The prominent concept of this work basically relies on the composition of visual and auditory (i.e., specifically speech) information, intertwining into each other by their ontology's keyword linkages. Figure 4 illustrates the construction of this idea – our proposed semantic information retrieval framework.

3.1 System Construction

For each video crawled from the online sources, we demux it into audio and visual channels, which are later segmented into a sequence of frames. The audio part got manually transcribed to serve as a training corpus for building the ASR module. This in turn, performs a force-alignment procedure on all video files, making them annotated with timestamps and keywords. Now, we define a concept shot F_k as follow:

$F_k(t, d) \sim$ derived frames clamped by keyword K begin at timestamp t and last for duration d

With the pre-built agricultural ontologies O, we then proceed to extract the concept shots F_{k-i} defined by all keywords $K-i$ existed in the ontologies, positioned by the timestamps generated from the ASR module. This way, our video database is now chopped down into segments – a set of concept-shots. We also keep track of their

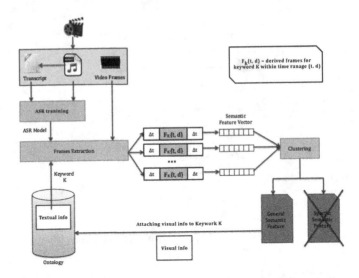

Fig. 4. Intertwined visual-spoken information retrieval framework.

contextual information by padding them with adjacent frames for a short leap Δt. F_k is then refined as:

$$F_{k-i}(t_i - \Delta t, d + 2\Delta t), \quad i \in [1...|O|], \ k_i \in O$$

Despite seeming scattered, concept-shots are closely related to each other, in term of concept relationships and inferring. Consider using a decision tree clustering technique [23], global shots would be divided into local groups where members share the same conceptual representation. HMM-GMM cluster-modeling is then taken place on the group's visual features. With the present of ontologies, specific semantic visual features are no longer required, and thus low-level features might be sufficient enough (i.e., ontologies take care of rendering the semantic layers). Here, we use a feature bag of Harris cues, edge, color, blob, and ridge. Figure 5 shows how concept-shots are shaped and clustered on each other through the linkage of ontologies.

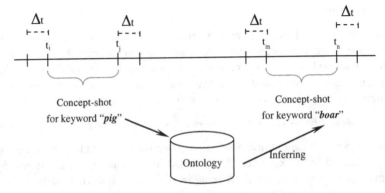

Fig. 5. Illustration of concept-shots and ontology-inferred clustering.

3.2   Building the ASR Engine

The speech recognition engine, serving as the system's kernel, needs to attain a certain level of performance as its outputs affect all other processes and outcomes. There are several techniques currently available for this task, such as the canonical HMM-GMM structure, its successor HMM-SGMM, or even a trendy Deep Neural Network (DNN), etc. Since our target data (i.e., broadcast agricultural videos) contain a massive amount of noise and spontaneous speech, DNN would be a rational choice. It provides an abstract level of representation for speech signals, just like the way human perceive things [24]. So noises and speaking styles would just blend in nicely, becoming parts of the acoustic information or what we called acoustic models.

In our framework, we take in HMM-DNN for acoustic modeling. 4397 tied-stated HMMs were derived in a typical manner, while DNN was setup with 11 context windows, 6 hidden layers, and an output layer representing context-dependent phonemes. This results in 429 input-nodes, 9000 hidden-nodes (i.e., 1500 nodes per hidden layer), and 4397 output-nodes. The training procedure then proceeded as described in [26].

3.3   Classification

Any future unseen media collected from the online sources will be auditorily transcribed and visually clustered into one of the available classes of our ontology (i.e., keywords or concept-shots). The classification of concept-shots would definitely compensate for word-error-rates of the transcriptions, and ultimately tracking out missing info potentially available in the media.

For example, in Fig. 5, if the feature bag of the "boar" shot is classified into the same group as "pig," then we would assume that there'd be some kind of pig in that shot (e.g., the wild boar for this case).

3.4   Deployment

To make the whole system a viable application, we've wrapped it into an info service, maintained as an AIS structure [25]. Our target audiences are the majority of farmers in developing countries, who are unable to reach modern farming information and knowledge. The info service is protocol- and platform- independent. It can be accessed by any front-end devices, from traditional mobile phones to PC, or smartphones, etc.

The service is being hosted in its beta stage at http://www.ailab.hcmus.edu.vn. Also, we would like to integrate our system with the language service to extend its reach across countries.

4 Experiment

This Section presents the results captured from our experimental procedure. Comparative analyses between a preset baseline and the proposed system are taken place to measure how well it performs. All of which are conducted in the corpus described below.

4.1 Datasets

Roughly 40 h of agricultural broadcast videos are collected from multiple broadcasting studios in Mekong Delta. We requested the original media instead of the recorded ones for their upper quality. Audio channels are sampled in 16 kHz, 16 bits, mono. And video channels are normalized in standard 480p. The corpus is then manually transcribed and divided into 3 subsets: training, development and test sets. Table 5 gives a detailed look into these subsets.

Table 5. Datasets

Corpus	Duration (hours)
Training set	20
Development set	1
Test set	19
Total	40

The training set is used for training ASR and building concept clusters, which are then verified and tuned by the development set. Retrieval performances are finally measure upon the test set.

4.2 Parameter Tuning

This experiment measures performances of the speech recognizer on the development set to further fine-tune system's parameters. We construct 2 ASR engines for comparative purposes: one by a traditional left-right tied-triphone HMM-GMM recipe, and the other by descriptions in Sect. 3.2. Recognition tasks include 412 utterances segmented from 1 h speech of agricultural conversation (i.e., the development set).

Figure 6 plots the performance function of the HMM-GMM engine. As the number of mixtures increases, accuracy acceleration slows down and reaches its limit eventually. In the best case, 78.14 % WAR (word accuracy rate) is achieved. This configuration was then taken to compare with the other engine – HMM-DNN. Details are shown in Table 6 with respect to the size of DNN's context windows.

An intuitive conclusion can be derived firsthand right from Table 6: the gain of DNN over GMM is almost entirely attributed to the context window range – the number of concatenated feature frames. It reflects the way we perceive speech: continuously and correlatively. And so on, independently from unseen data, we choose the

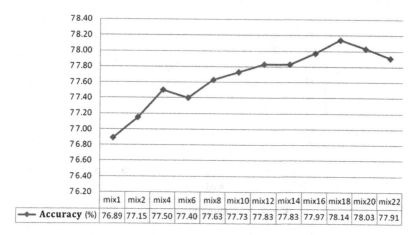

Fig. 6. GMM fine-tuning.

Table 6. Transcription performances

Context-window	HMM-GMM	HMM-DNN
1	78.1	75.3
3	–	79.5
5	–	81.8
7	–	82.4
9	–	83.2
11	–	83.7
13	–	83.1

best configuration of 11 context window DNN. Transcriptions generated by this one alone also serve as the indexed database for the baseline retrieval system.

The same routine applies for choosing a number of mixtures in each concept cluster-model. Feature bags extracted from 1-hour video are classified into one of 27 concept-classes found in the development set. With each model configuration, we logged down classification accuracy as in Fig. 7, leading to the selection of 32-mixutre candidate.

4.3   Retrieval Evaluations

Having set the ground for baseline system, ASR engine, and clustering models, we proceed to assess our proposed system upon the remaining 19-h test set. 500 pseudo test-queries are constructed to ensure the retrieved documents fall within the corpus's bound, thus making no false claim on missing retrievals.

Table 7 reports average recalls and precisions in a comparative manner for: speech-based system (baseline), vision-based system, and visual-auditory intertwined system. Since the semantic gap is too much for low-level features, vision-based system

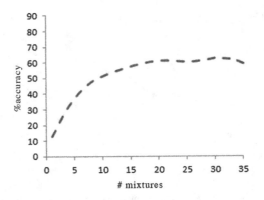

Fig. 7. Clustering performances.

seems falling back behind, while speech-based system renders recall closely to its transcription accuracy. False alarms did rise, because both system neglects the semantic layer. However, when combining spoken and visual features together under Ontology's linkages, we found the results shooting upward, attaining absolute increases of 16.2 % recall and 9.4 % precision over the baseline system.

Table 7. Retrieval performances

Metrics	Speech-based system	Vision-based system	Intertwined system
Recall	70.2 %	56.1 %	86.4 %
Precision	81.3 %	64.5 %	90.7 %

5   Conclusion

Not many achievements had been gained since our first approach of Vietnamese speech-based video retrieval in 2010. Our research on semantic information retrieval just lied dormant until the ICT torrent was brought to extension services. That's when we made an attempt to plan out a compensation technique that employs the use of visual features and Ontology together. Experimental results did confirm the hypothesis. Despite being a long way from human perceptions, the composite scheme surely shed light on applicable solutions for semantic information retrieval. We also deploy our system as an info service to support agricultural extension in Mekong Delta.

References

1. General Statistics Office: Thông cáo báo chí Tình hình kinh tế - xã hội năm 2013. http://www.gso.gov.vn/. Accessed 18 September 2014
2. Markey, K.: Twenty-five years of end-user searching, Part 2: future research directions. J. Am. Soc. Inf. Sci. Technol. **58**(8), 1123–1130 (2007)
3. Amir, A., et al.: A multi-modal system for the retrieval of semantic video events. Comput. Vis. Image Underst. **96**(2), 216–236 (2004)
4. Ballan, L., Bertini, M., Bimbo, A.D., Serra, G.: Semantic annotation of soccer videos by visual instance clustering and spatial/temporal reasoning in ontologies. Multimedia Tools Appl. **48**(2), 313–337 (2010)
5. Fujii, A., Itou, K., Ishikawa, T.: LODEM: a system for on-demand video lectures. Speech Commun. **48**(5), 516–531 (2006)
6. Hauptmann, A.G., Christel, M.G., Yan, R.: Video retrieval based on semantic concepts. Proc. IEEE **96**, 602–622 (2008)
7. Ekin, A., Tekalp, A.M.: Robust dominant color region detection and color-based applications for sports video. In: IEEE International Conference on Image Processing, Barcelona, Spain, vol. 1, pp. 21–24 (2003)
8. Brown, M.G., Foote, J.T., Jones, G.J., Sparck Jones, K., Young, S.J.: Automatic content-based retrieval of broadcast news. In: Proceedings of the 3rd ACM International Conference on Multimedia, pp. 35–43. ACM, January 1995
9. Adams, B., Iyengar, G., Neti, C., Nock, H.J., Amir, A., Permuter, H.H., Zhang, D.: IBM research TREC 2002 video retrieval system, In: TREC, November 2002
10. Gevers, T., Smeulders, A.W.: Pictoseek: Combining color and shape invariant features for image retrieval. IEEE Trans. Image Process. **9**(1), 102–119 (2000)
11. Ma, W.Y., Manjunath, B.S.: NeTra: a toolbox for navigating large image databases. Multimedia Syst. **7**(3), 184–198 (1999)
12. Del Bimbo, A., Pala, P.: Visual image retrieval by elastic matching of user sketches. IEEE Trans. Pattern Anal. Mach. Intell. **19**(2), 121–132 (1997)
13. Jaimes, A., Smith, J.R.: Semi-automatic, data-driven construction of multimedia ontologies. In: Proceedings of the 2003 International Conference on Multimedia and Expo, ICME 2003, vol. 1, pp. 1–781. IEEE, July 2003
14. Hollink, L., Worring, M., Schreiber, A.T.: Building a visual ontology for video retrieval. In: Proceedings of the 13th Annual ACM International Conference on Multimedia, pp. 479–482. ACM, November 2005
15. Thunkijjanukij, A.: Ontology development for agricultural research knowledge management: a case study for Thai rice. Ph.D. dissertation, Kasetsart University, Thailand (2009)
16. Noy, N.F., Mcguinness, D.L.: Ontology Development 101: A Guide to Creating Your First Ontology. Stanford University, Stanford (2001)
17. United States Department of Agriculture: Agricultural Thesaurus. http://agclass.nal.usda.gov. Accessed 18 September 2014
18. Uschold, M., Gruninger, M.: Ontologies: principles, methods and applications. Knowl. Eng. Rev. **11**(02), 93–136 (1996)
19. Froese, R.: FishBase. Oceanogr. Lit. Rev. **43**, 3 (1996)
20. Gruber, T.R.: Toward principles for the design of ontologies used for knowledge sharing? Int. J. Hum.-Comput. Stud. **43**(5), 907–928 (1995)

21. Cañas, A.J., Hill, G., Carff, R., Suri, N., Lott, J., Eskridge, T., Gómez, G., Arroyo, M., Carvajal, R.: CmapTools: a knowledge modeling and sharing environment. In: Proceedings of the 1st International Conference on Concept Mapping, Spain, vol. 1, September 2004
22. Knublauch, H., Fergerson, R.W., Noy, N.F., Musen, M.A.: The Protégé-OWL plugin: an open development environment for semantic web applications. In: Proceedings of the 3rd International Semantic Web Conference, Japan, November 2004
23. Vu, Q., et al.: A robust Vietnamese voice server for automated directory assistance application. In: VLSP (2012)
24. Abdel-Hamid, O., Mohamed, A., Jiang, H., Deng, L., Penn, G., Yu, D.: Convolutional neural networks for speech recognition. IEEE/ACM Trans. Audio Speech Lang. Process. 22(10), 1533–1545 (2014)
25. Hall, A.: Agricultural innovation systems: an introduction. Link-UNU-Merit
26. Dahl, G.E., Yu, D., Deng, L., Acero, A.: Context-dependent pre-trained deep neural networks for large vocabulary speech recognition. IEEE Trans. Audio Speech Lang. Process. (2011)

Mining Opinion Polarity from Multilingual Song Lyrics

Qian Liu[1,2]($\boxtimes$) and Zhiqiang Gao[1,2]

[1] School of Computer Science and Engineering, Southeast University,
Nanjing 210096, China
{qianliu,zqgao}@seu.edu.cn
[2] Key Laboratory of Computer Network and Information Integration
of Ministry of Education, Southeast University, Nanjing 210096, China

Abstract. Song opinion is an important criterion when people organize and access songs. The ever growing amount of song data in the Web, which includes multilingual songs, calls for the development of automatic tools in classifying songs by opinion polarity. Sony lyric is a critical resource for song opinion classification. In this paper, we propose an approach to mine the opinion polarity of songs based on song lyrics in a multilingual environment. This approach is based on classification and translation. Firstly, we build monolingual opinion classifiers using supervised learning techniques for resource-rich languages, i.e., languages that are rich of labeled training data. However, it is difficult to build a classifier for a resource-rare language. In this case, we employ Language Grid, which is an infrastructure that is built on the top of the Internet, and provides easy-to-use services for multilingual translation, to bridge the gap between the resources in different languages. Song lyrics are translated from resource-rare languages into resource-rich languages, then the pre-trained monolingual opinion classifiers can be used to classify the translated unseen lyrics. To build effective monolingual opinion classifiers, we employ statistical information of song lyrics as features rather than individual words in the song lyrics. Experiments show that, our proposed approach performs better than two typical baseline approaches.

Keywords: Opinion classification · Multilingual song lyrics · Language Grid

1 Introduction

Song opinion classification nowadays becomes a hot research topic due largely to the increasing demand of ubiquitous song access. Song digital libraries face the challenge of providing users with natural and diversified access points to songs. Song opinion (or mood, emotion) has been recognized as an important criterion when people organize and access songs [1]. The ever growing amount of song data in the Web calls for the development of automatic tools in classifying songs by opinion polarity.

© Springer International Publishing Switzerland 2016
Y. Murakami and D. Lin (Eds.): WLSI 2015, LNAI 9442, pp. 161–172, 2016.
DOI: 10.1007/978-3-319-31468-6_12

To date, most automatic song opinion classification algorithms and systems are solely based on the audio content of songs (as recorded in .wav, .mp3 or other popular formats) [2,3]. Recently, researchers have started to exploit song lyrics in opinion classification [4,5] and hypothesize that lyrics, which will be heard and understood by listeners, play an important role in determining the opinion polarity of songs. Therefore, detecting the opinion polarity of a song lyric effectively contributes to detecting the opinion polarity of the song. However, there is now comparatively less research done on methods for detecting the opinion polarity of songs based on lyrics. There has been indeed a very large literature already out there on opinion classification of traditional text. Song lyric opinion classification is more challenging than traditional text opinion classification, because songs can contain a series of negative lyrics but end with an uplifting, positive note, or vice versa. For example, love songs can be misleading because the lyrics often express how much the singer loves the other person, and then at the end of the song the singer expresses his sadness over a sudden breakup.

Most of the text opinion classification works are supervised learning techniques, which require training data annotated with the appropriate opinion polarity labels (e.g. document-level or sentence-level positive vs. negative polarity). However, labeled data is difficult and costly to obtain, especially for a multilingual text opinion classification system because the labeled data must be acquired separately for each language under consideration.

Previous works in multilingual opinion classification have focused on methods to adapt opinion resources (e.g. lexicons) from resource-rich languages (typically English) to other languages [6]. A monolingual opinion classifier is first constructed from a monolingual data. Opinion classifiers in target languages are then constructed using translation (of the classifier or source data). The learnt opinion classifiers are then used to classify data from their respective languages. In recent years, however, opinion-labeled data is gradually becoming available for languages other than English (e.g., [7–10]). In addition, there is still much room for improvement in existing monolingual opinion classifiers.

In this paper, we propose to classify opinion polarity of multilingual song lyrics using multilingual opinion classification techniques. There are two challenges in this work:

Challenge 1: The features used for training monolingual opinion classifiers are difficult to select. The classifiers which make use of all words in the song lyrics as features are proved to be ineffective [11] as many words in the song lyrics make little contribution to opinion expressing. The polarity of an opinion maybe inverted if negations and modifiers, which play a role to inverse or strengthen or weaken the opinions, are found around the opinion word. In addition, the overall opinion polarity maybe inverted by a sudden change at the end.

Challenge 2: The training data is difficult to obtain in resource-rare languages, and thus difficult to train classifiers based on supervised learning techniques in these languages directly. The human labeling work is difficult and time consuming in a monolingual domain, not to say a multilingual domain.

To address the aforementioned challenges, firstly, we train the monolingual opinion classifiers from resource-rich languages based on pre-defined statistical features instead of individual words. We use 10 features to represent the opinions expressed in a song lyric, these 10 features correspond to 10 equal size segments of the song lyric. In this way, we can represent and distinguish the opinions expressed in each segment, and it is helpful to handle the problem of a sudden inverse at the end of the lyric. Secondly, we translate the unlabeled data from resource-rare languages into resource-rich languages using a multilingual translator to adapt the pre-trained monolingual opinion classifiers.

The rest of this paper is laid out as follows: in Sect. 2 we present related work in multilingual opinion classification and how it has been extended to song lyrics. In Sect. 3, we introduce the methods used to classify the opinions of multilingual song lyrics. In Sect. 4, we discuss the experiment results. Finally, in Sect. 5, we conclude by discussing future work in song lyric analysis.

2 Related Work

2.1 Multilingual Opinion Classification

There is a growing body of work on multilingual opinion classification or sentiment analysis. Most approaches focus on resource adaptation from one language (usually English) to other languages with few sentiment resources [12]. For example, The work [13] generates subjectivity analysis resources in a new language from English sentiment resources by leveraging a bilingual dictionary or a parallel corpus. Instead, the works [14,15] automatically translate the English resources using automatic machine translation engines for subjectivity classification. The work [16] investigates cross-lingual opinion classification from the perspective of domain adaptation based on structural correspondence learning [17]. There are also works aim to build multilingual opinion lexicons to facilitate multilingual opinion classification, for example, the work [18] builds high-quality sentiment lexicons for 136 major languages.

2.2 Opinion Classification with Lyrics

Lyrical analysis for opinion classification is a relatively new area of research. Millions of lyrics are now available on the Internet to researchers in semi-structured formats. Lyrics are typically analyzed as part of a music classification task, where songs are classified by genre, mood, or emotion [19,20]. The work [21] uses lyrical features combined with audio, cultural, and symbolic features to classify songs by genre. They find that lyrics alone are poor indicators of a song's genre, but that when lyrical analysis is combined with other features, their system is able to achieve high genre classification accuracy.

Although lyrics are different from traditional text, traditional text opinion classification techniques can still be used for lyric opinion classification. Many literatures have been produced to address the opinion classification problem in natural language processing research. Three approaches are dominating, i.e. knowledge-based approach [22], information retrieval-based approach [23] and machine learning approach [24], in which the last approach is found very popular. For example, the work [24] adopts the VSM model to represent product reviews and apply text classification algorithms such as Naive Bayes, maximum entropy and support vector machines to predict sentiment polarity of given product review. However, the work [11] shows that song opinion classification with the VSM model, which considers all content words in the song lyric delivers disappointing quality because the VSM model is problematic in representing song lyric when the dimension of the vector space is too high. In this work, we also use VSM to represent song lyrics, however, we design new features to effectively represent the song lyrics.

3   Approach

We propose an approach for automatically mining opinion polarity from multilingual song lyrics. This approach is based on classification and translation technologies. We first give an overall introduction of the approach, and then introduce the classification and translation components in detail.

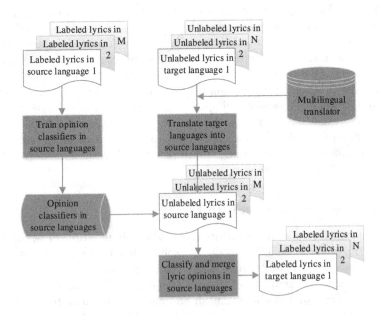

Fig. 1. Workflow of the proposed multilingual song lyric opinion classification approach.

In this paper, a set of song lyrics is called a labeled dataset if the opinion polarity of each song lyric in it is known and labeled. We refer to the languages which have labeled datasets for training classifiers as *source languages*, and refer to the languages which have only unlabeled datasets waiting to be classified as *target languages*. Our purpose is to predict the opinion polarity of each unlabeled song lyric in a target language by employing the labeled information in source languages.

Figure 1 presents the workflow of our proposed multilingual song lyric opinion polarity mining approach. Given labeled datasets $SD = \{sd_1, sd_2, ..., sd_M\}$ in source languages $S = \{s_1, s_2, ..., s_M\}$, and unlabeled datasets $TD = \{td_1, td_2, ..., td_N\}$ in target languages $T = \{t_1, t_2, ..., t_N\}$, this approach includes three steps:

- **Step 1:** For each source language $s_i \in S$ $(i = 1..M)$, train a monolingual opinion classifier c_i, then we get a set of classifiers $C = \{c_1, c_2, ..., c_M\}$ for S;
- **Step 2:** For each dataset $td_j \in TD$ $(j = 1..N)$ in target language t_j, translate td_j into source languages $s_1, s_2, ..., s_M$ using a multilingual machine translator, then we get a set of unlabeled datasets $std_j = \{td_{j1}, td_{j2}, ..., td_{jM}\}$ in source languages for td_j, and a set of unlabeled datasets $STD = \{std_1, std_2, ..., std_M\}$ in source languages for TD;
- **Step 3:** Classify the opinion polarity of each data in STD using the trained classifiers in C, and then merge the results from different classifiers to get the final class label for each data.

We give a detailed introduction of step 1 in Sect. 3.1, and introduce step 2 and step 3 in Sect. 3.2.

3.1 Building Monolingual Opinion Polarity Classifier

For the purposes of our studies, we limited opinion polarities of song lyrics to positive and negative. We use the vector space model (VSM) [25,26] as the document representation model, each song lyric is represented by a vector in VSM. [11] show that VSM-based text classification method is ineffective in song opinion classification if the model considers all content words within song lyric as features in classification since many words in song lyric actually make little contribution to opinion expressing. In addition, song lyrics are usually much shorter than traditional text, thus using individual words as features in VSM may suffer from serious sparse data problem, that is, most of words/features are not appeared in a song lyric.

To address the problem, we propose to utilize statistical information of a song lyric instead of individual words in it. For each song lyric, $f_i \in sd_j$, where $sd_j \in SD$ $(j = 1..M)$, we carry out the following process:

Part-of-speech Tagging. We extract tokens and their part-of-speech tags from f_i, and retain only whole words and remove all other noise (punctuation, parentheses, etc.). Also, the frequency of each token is calculated and stored along with f_i. We use Stanford Part-Of-Speech Tagger[1] for English part-of-speech tagging, and ICTCLAS[2] for Chinese part-of-speech tagging.

---

[1] http://nlp.stanford.edu/software/tagger.shtml.
[2] http://ictclas.org/ictclas_demo.html.

Stop-word Removal. Stop-words are the words that are of very little importance in the discrimination of documents in general. They can be specific to a dataset. In this paper, we assume that only nouns, verbs, adjectives and adverbs are useful for opinion classification, thus all words of other part-of-speech are treated as stop words and should be removed.

Morphological Analysis. The retained words are then analyzed in order to combine different words having the same root to a single one when necessary. For example, in English the words "love", "loved", "lover" and "loving" should be combined to form a single word, "love". This is logical because all such words convey the same (loosely) meaning. Also, it reduces the dimensionality of the resulting dataset. We use Porter Stemmer algorithm[3] for English morphological analysis.

Dictionary Matching and Weight Resetting. The final set of words are checked in the pre-defined opinion word dictionary, which contains opinion words such as "happy", "sad" and "love", etc., and a reverse word list, which contains words such as "not", "n't" and "never", etc. In this paper, we employ the bilingual HowNet sentiment word dictionary[4] as our opinion word dictionary. If a retained word w is matched with a positive word in the dictionary, then the weight of w equals to the frequency of w; if w is matched with a negative word in the dictionary or a word in the reverse word list, then the weight of w is set to $-fre_w$, where fre_w is the frequency of w; if w cannot be matched with any words in the dictionary, then the word is removed from the word set.

Opinion Representing. VSM is employed here to represent the opinion expressed in f_i, the vector for f_i is denoted by v_i. We use ten statistic scores as the features in v_i rather than individual opinion words for two reasons. Firstly, to avoid serious sparse data problem in VSM-based classification. Secondly, these features can represent and distinguish partial opinions expressed in the lyric and thus help to model a sudden inversion at the end of the lyric. To get the statistical features, the lyric f_i is divided into 10 equal segments according to the number of lines, and then a polarity score is computed for each part by adding the weights of all opinion words in this segment. The polarity score for each part of song lyric corresponds to a feature in v_i. The last, i.e., $11th$ dimension of v_i represents the opinion polarity of f_i, its value is "pos" if the polarity of f_i is positive, or "neg" if the polarity of f_i is negative.

Then we get a set of vectors for sd_i, the song lyric opinion classification can be viewed as a text classification task thus can be handled by standard classification algorithms. In this work, Support Vector Machines (SVM) [25,27] and Naive Bayes text classifiers [25] are chosen as our classifiers because of their strong performances in text classification.

---

[3] http://tartarus.org/martin/PorterStemmer/.

[4] This dictionary contains 17,887 entries, and consists of 12 subsets, i.e., Chinese/English positive/negative feeling, Chines/English positive/negative sentiment, Chinese/English opinion, and Chinese/English degree.

3.2   Multilingual Classification via Translation

After building monolingual opinion classifiers for the source languages, we can employ them to classify unlabeled datasets in target languages. A multilingual language translator is then needed to bridge the gap between the monolingual classifiers in source languages and unlabeled datasets in target languages. In this paper, we employ the Language Grid[5] [28] to translated song lyrics in target languages into source languages.

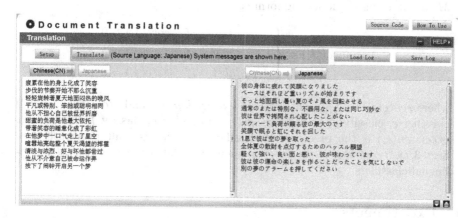

Fig. 2. Document translation service in Language Grid. The English translation of the song lyric is *"Tiredness on his body turned into a smile. The rhythm of his pace started not so heavy. The sultry summer night-wind is rotating gently. Ordinary or special, clumsy or smart is the same. He never worried about being tortured by the world. The sweet load is his biggest spiritual support. The sleepiness with a smile turned into a rainbow. He walked straight to the starry night sky in his dream. The noise light up the summer-long splurge desire. Light and strong, good and bad, he tasted them all. He never mind teased by his fate. Pressed the alarm clock, to open another dream."*

The Language Grid is an infrastructure that is built on the top of the Internet. It allows end users as well as professionals to conquer the language barriers by themselves. Users can combine existing language services provided by researchers and professionals, and create new language services for their own purposes by permitting them to add their own language resources. Since the Language Grid provides easy-to-use services for language translation as well as linguistic analysis such as morphological analysis and dependency analysis, etc., we use the language technologies it provides to facilitate our study. Figure 2 shows a screen shot of using Language Grid for document translation, the source language and target language can be changed at the end of the web page.

The process of classifying unlabeled datasets in target languages consists of three steps:

---

[5] http://langrid.org/en/index.html.

- **Step 1:** Translate each unlabeled lyric $f_i \in td_j$, where $j = 1..N$, $td_j \in TD$ in target language $t_j \in T$ into M source languages $s_1, s_2, ..., s_M$. This results in a new dataset with $M \times |TD|$ unlabeled lyrics in sources languages, where $|TD|$ is the number of song lyrics in TD;
- **Step 2:** Classify the translated lyrics using M monolingual classifiers trained on labeled datasets in source languages. For each unlabeled data, there are M labels predicted by M classifiers;
- **Step 3:** Determine the final class label $c\_label(f_i)$ for f_i data by merging the M results using the following formula:

$$c\_label(f_i) = \begin{cases} pos, & if \ \ score(f_i) > 0 \\ neg, & if \ \ score(f_i) < 0 \\ freq\_label, & if \ \ score(f_i) = 0 \end{cases}$$

where $score(f_i) = \sum_{i=1}^{M} polarity(c_i) \times precision(c_i)$, and $ploairty(c_i) = 1$ if classifier c_i classify f_i as positive, $polarity = -1$ if c_i classify f_i as negative, $precision(c_i)$ is the precision of classifier c_i, which is built previously (see Sect. 3.1). $freq\_label$ is the most frequent class label predicted by M monolingual classifiers.

4   Experiments

4.1   Data Acquisition

We use a dataset of 1,750 unique song lyrics, including 720 Chinese song lyrics, 730 English song lyrics and 300 Japanese song lyrics, divided equally between positive and negative opinion polarities (hereafter referred to as positive lyrics and negative lyrics).

To gather the ground truth opinion polarity labels for the song lyrics, we utilized Baidu Music's list of songs classified by mood, which includes sad, quiet, sweet, lonely, happy, delightful and romantic, etc[6]. Baidu Music is a music search engine, which provides comprehensive lists of popular Chinese music as well as music in other languages, such as English, Japanese, Korean, etc., it can also provide music, lyrics search and online music services. We assume that the mood label for each song in Baidu Music's list is labeled and checked manually, thus we use the collected dataset as our training set. We manually selected 360 Chinese, 365 English and 150 Japanese positive song lyrics from the song list with happy or delightful label, and selected 360 Chinese, 365 English and 150 Japanese negative song lyrics from the song list with sad or lonely label. In our experiments, we use Chinese and English song lyrics for training, and Japanese song lyrics for testing.

---

[6] http://music.baidu.com/tag.

4.2 Results and Analysis

We adopt the standard evaluation criteria in text classification, namely precision, recall and F_1-measure. For each class (positive and negative), precision, recall and F_1-measure are averaged over a 10-fold cross validation. We use the LIBSVM [29] implementation of SVM and Naive Bayes classifier in WEKA [30]. The default parameters of both LIBSVM and Naive Bayes classifiers are used for all the experiments.

To verify the effectiveness of our proposed monolingual opinion classifiers, we use two typical approaches for comparison.

Dictionary based approach. This approach also makes use of the bilingual HowNet sentiment word dictionary to detect opinion words and recognize the neighboring negations, and then compute the polarity scores of the opinion words in the song lyrics. The polarity of a lyric f is determined according to the following rules.

1. The opinion polarity of f is positive, if the final polarity score is positive after adding all the polarity scores of opinion words in f;
2. The opinion polarity of f is negative if the final polarity score is negative after adding all the polarity scores of opinion words in f;
3. If the final polarity score of f is 0, and if there are more positive opinion words than negative ones, then the opinion polarity of f is positive, otherwise, the opinion polarity of f is negative.

Table 1. Precision, recall and F_1-measure of the dictionary-based approach, opinion word based VSM approach and the proposed monolingual classification approaches.

Approach	Class	Chinese			English		
		Precision	Recall	F_1-measure	Precision	Recall	F_1-measure
Dictionary-based	positive	0.52	0.68	0.59	0.54	0.62	0.58
	negative	0.47	0.33	0.39	0.51	0.40	0.45
	Avg	0.50	0.51	0.49	0.53	0.51	0.51
Opinion word based VSM	positive	0.56	0.71	0.63	0.56	0.62	0.59
	negative	0.61	0.45	0.52	0.52	0.46	0.49
	Avg	0.59	0.58	0.57	0.54	0.54	0.54
Ours-SVM	positive	0.65	0.82	0.73	0.72	0.85	0.78
	negative	0.76	0.56	0.65	0.82	0.67	0.74
	Avg	0.71	0.69	0.69	0.77	0.76	0.76
Ours-NaiveBayes	positive	0.82	0.71	0.76	0.87	0.68	0.76
	negative	0.75	0.85	0.79	0.74	0.89	0.80
	Avg	**0.78**	**0.78**	**0.78**	**0.80**	**0.79**	**0.79**

VSM using opinion words as features. As in our approach, this approach uses VSM to represent a lyric as a vector. Each dimension in the vector corresponds to an opinion word in all the song lyrics under study, the value of each dimension is either the weight of the word if it appears in the lyric, or 0 if it does not appear in the lyric. The last dimension of the vector represents the opinion polarity of the lyric, its value is "pos" if the polarity is positive, or "neg" if the polarity is negative. Then LIBSVM is chosen to train the classifier as in our approach. The difference between opinion word based VSM and our proposed opinion statistical feature based VSM is the features used for training the classifiers.

Table 1 shows the precision, recall and F_1-measure of the dictionary-based approach, opinion word based VSM approach and ours on monolingual song lyrics. Opinion word based VSM approach performs better than the dictionary-based approach, and opinion statistical feature based VSM approaches, i.e., ours-SVM and ours-NaiveBayes, outperform the opinion word based VSM approach, ours-NaiveBayes is the best classifier of all. For dictionary-based approach, positive class gets higher F_1-measure than negative class in both Chinese and English classifiers, and it is the same case in opinion word based VSM approach and ours-SVM approach. That probably because song lyrics often express positive opinions at the beginning, and then inverted the opinion polarity at the end of the song, which is mentioned in the Sect. 1. In ours-NaiveBayes, negative class gets higher F_1-measure than positive class in both Chinese and English classifiers thanks to the statistical features used in the classifier.

Table 2. Precision, recall and F_1-measure of our proposed multilingual opinion polarity classifiers.

Translate Japanese	Class	Ours-SVM			Ours-NaiveBayes		
		Precision	Recall	F_1-measure	Precision	Recall	F_1-measure
To Chinese	positive	0.56	0.86	0.68	0.57	0.55	0.56
	negative	0.80	0.44	0.57	0.64	0.67	0.66
	Avg	0.69	0.63	0.62	0.61	0.61	0.61
To English	positive	0.54	0.68	0.60	0.57	0.55	0.56
	negative	0.67	0.52	0.58	0.64	0.67	0.66
	Avg	0.61	0.59	0.59	0.61	0.61	0.61
Combined	positive	0.56	0.86	0.68	0.57	0.55	0.56
	negative	0.80	0.44	0.57	0.64	0.67	0.66
	Avg	**0.69**	**0.63**	**0.62**	**0.61**	**0.61**	**0.61**

Table 2 shows the precision, recall and F_1-measure of our proposed multilingual opinion polarity classifiers. In average, ours-SVM performs better than ours-NaiveBayes, and Ours-SVM gets higher F_1-measure when translating Japanese into Chinese than into English. The performance of ours-NaiveBayes is stable when translating Japanese into both Chinese and English.

5   Conclusion

In this paper, we propose an approach for mining the opinion polarities in multilingual song lyrics based on classification and translation. Firstly, we train monolingual opinion classifiers in resource-rich languages, and then translate the unlabeled data into resource-rich languages to bridge the gap between the pre-trained monolingual opinion classifiers and the unlabeled data in resource-rare languages. After translation, the pre-trained monolingual opinion classifiers can be used to classify the unlabeled data in resource-rare languages. Experiments show that, our proposed approach is effective in classifying the opinion polarities in multilingual song lyrics.

In future work, we plan to explore more complicate features which can be used in the classifiers by analyzing the syntactic and semantic structures of the song lyrics.

Acknowledgments. This work was supported by the National Science Foundation of China under grant 61170165.

References

1. Vignoli, F.: Digital music interaction concepts: a user study. In: Proceedings of the 5th International Conference on Music Information Retrieval (2004)
2. Lu, L., Liu, D., Zhang, H.J.: Automatic mood detection and tracking of music audio signals. IEEE Trans. Audio Speech Lang. Process. **14**, 5–18 (2006)
3. Trohidis, K., Tsoumakas, G., Kalliris, G., Vlahavas, I.P.: Multi-label classification of music into emotions. In: ISMIR, pp. 325–330 (2008)
4. He, H., Jin, J., Xiong, Y., Chen, B., Sun, W., Zhao, L.: Language feature mining for music emotion classification via supervised learning from lyrics. In: Kang, L., Cai, Z., Yan, X., Liu, Y. (eds.) ISICA 2008. LNCS, vol. 5370, pp. 426–435. Springer, Heidelberg (2008)
5. Hu, Y., Chen, X., Yang, D.: Lyric-based song emotion detection with affective lexicon and fuzzy clustering method. In: ISMIR 2009, pp. 123–128 (2009)
6. Lu, B., Tan, C., Cardie, C., Tsou, B.K.: Joint bilingual sentiment classification with unlabeled parallel corpora. In: Proceedings of the 49th Annual Meeting of the Association for Computational Linguistics: Human Language Technologies, HLT 2011, vol. 1, pp. 320–330. Association for Computational Linguistics (2011)
7. Seki, Y., Evans, D.K., Ku, L.W., Chen, H.H., Kando, N., Lin, C.Y.: Overview of opinion analysis pilot task at NTCIR-6. In: Proceedings of NTICR-6 (2007)
8. Seki, Y., Evans, D.K., Ku, L.W., Sun, L., Chen, H.H., Kando, N.: Overview of multilingual opinion analysis task at NTCIR-7. In: Proceedings of NTCIR-7 (2008)
9. Nakagawa, T., Inui, K., Kurohashi, S.: Dependency tree-based sentiment classification using CRFs with hidden variables. In: Human Language Technologies: The 2010 Annual Conference of the North American Chapter of the Association for Computational Linguistics, pp. 786–794 (2010)
10. Schulz, J.M., Womser-Hacker, C., Mandl, T.: Multilingual corpus development for opinion mining. European Language Resources Association (2010)
11. Xia, Y., Wang, L., Wong, K.F.: Sentiment vector space model for lyric-based song sentiment classification. Int. J. Comput. Process. Lang. **21**(4), 309–330 (2008)
12. Balahur, A., Turchi, M.: Comparative experiments using supervised learning and machine translation for multilingual sentiment analysis. Comput. Speech Lang. **28**, 56–75 (2014)
13. Mihalcea, R., Banea, C., Wiebe, J.: Learning multilingual subjective language via cross-lingual projections. In: Proceedings of ACL (2007)

14. Banea, C., Mihalcea, R., Wiebe, J.: Multilingual subjectivity: are more languages better? In: Proceedings of the 23rd International Conference on Computational Linguistics, COLING 2010, pp. 28–36. Association for Computational Linguistics (2010)
15. Banea, C., Mihalcea, R., Wiebe, J., Hassan, S.: Multilingual subjectivity analysis using machine translation. In: Proceedings of the Conference on Empirical Methods in Natural Language Processing, EMNLP 2008, pp. 127–135. Association for Computational Linguistics (2008)
16. Prettenhofer, P., Stein, B.: Cross-language text classification using structural correspondence learning. In: Proceedings of the 48th Annual Meeting of the Association for Computational Linguistics, ACL 2010, pp. 1118–1127. Association for Computational Linguistics (2010)
17. Blitzer, J., McDonald, R., Pereira, F.: Domain adaptation with structural correspondence learning. In: Proceedings of the 2006 Conference on Empirical Methods in Natural Language Processing, EMNLP 2006, pp. 120–128. Association for Computational Linguistics (2006)
18. Chen, Y., Skiena, S.: Building sentiment lexicons for all major languages. In: Proceedings of the 52nd Annual Meeting of the Association for Computational Linguistics (Short Papers), vol. 2, pp. 383–389. Association for Computational Linguistics (2014)
19. Cho, Y.H., Lee, K.J.: Automatic affect recognition using natural language processing techniques and manually built affect lexicon. IEICE Trans. Inf. Syst. **E89–D**(12), 2964–2971 (2006)
20. Hu, X., Downie, J.S.: Improving mood classification in music digital libraries by combining lyrics and audio. In: Proceedings of the 10th Annual Joint Conference on Digital Libraries, JCDL 2010, pp. 159–168. ACM (2010)
21. McKay, C., Burgoyne, J.A., Hockman, J., Smith, J.B.L., Vigliensoni, G., Fujinaga, I.: Evaluating the genre classification performance of lyrical features relative to audio, symbolic and cultural features. In: ISMIR 2010, pp. 213–218 (2010)
22. Kim, S.M., Hovy, E.: Determining the sentiment of opinions. In: Proceedings of the 20th International Conference on Computational Linguistics, COLING 2004. Association for Computational Linguistics (2004)
23. Turney, P.D., Littman, M.L.: Measuring praise and criticism: inference of semantic orientation from association. ACM Trans. Inf. Syst. **21**, 315–346 (2003)
24. Pang, B., Lee, L., Vaithyanathan, S.: Thumbs up?: sentiment classification using machine learning techniques. In: Proceedings of the ACL-02 Conference on Empirical Methods in Natural Language Processing, EMNLP 2002, vol. 10, pp. 79–86. Association for Computational Linguistics (2002)
25. Manning, C.D., Raghavan, P., Schütze, H.: Introduction to Information Retrieval. Cambridge University Press, New York (2008)
26. Salton, G., Wong, A., Yang, C.S.: A vector space model for automatic indexing. Commun. ACM **18**, 613–620 (1975)
27. Joachims, T.: Learning to Classify Text Using Support Vector Machines: Methods, Theory and Algorithms. Kluwer Academic Publishers, Norwell (2002)
28. Ishida, T. (ed.): The Language Grid - Service-Oriented Collective Intelligence for Language Resource Interoperability. Cognitive Technologies. Springer, Heidelberg (2011)
29. Chang, C.C., Lin, C.J.: LIBSVM: a library for support vector machines. ACM Trans. Intell. Syst. Technol. **2**(3), 27: 1–27: 27 (2011)
30. Hall, M., Frank, E., Holmes, G., Pfahringer, B., Reutemann, P., Witten, I.H.: The weka data mining software: an update. SIGKDD Explor. Newsl. **11**, 10–18 (2009)

Cooperative Philology on the Way to Web Services: The Case of the CoPhiWordNet Platform

Riccardo Del Gratta$^{(\boxtimes)}$, Federico Boschetti, Angelo Del Grosso,
Fahad Khan, and Monica Monachini

Institute for Computational Linguistics "A. Zampolli",
Via Moruzzi 1, 56100 Pisa, Italy
{riccardo.delgratta,federico.boschetti,angelo.delgrosso,
fahad.khan,monica.monachini}@ilc.cnr.it
http://www.ilc.cnr.it

Abstract. In this paper we present ongoing research carried out at the Institute for Computational Linguistics "A. Zampolli" (ILC) in Pisa. The institute has been active since many years in the field of Digital Humanities providing resources, tools and solutions to address issues of the to digital humanists. Starting from those previous initiatives, we show how to re-engineer them as Web Services in order to make connections between lexicons, semantic resources and a fine grained text management. Linked Open Data is chosen as the paradigm used to link the different resources as well as the modality of data presentation.

Keywords: Cooperative philology · Web services · Linked open data · Canonical text services

1 Introduction

In this article we will describe ongoing research in the field of computationally assisted philology as carried out by two groups within the Institute for Computational Linguistics "A. Zampolli": the Laboratory of Cooperative Philology(CoPhiLab)[1] and the Language Resources and Infrastructures (LaRI) group, in close cooperation with various other national and international partners.[2] The extensive interaction between these two groups is motivated by the high levels of interdisciplinary collaboration demanded by the field of philology, with its focus on the evaluation of textual variants attested by different primary sources of the same work (for instance epigraphs, papyri or manuscripts), the reconstruction of

---

[1] http://www.cophilab.eu/CoPhiLabPortal.

[2] Musisque Deoque Project, http://mqdq.it
Open Philology Project, http://www.dh.uni-leipzig.de/wo/open-philology-project
Perseus Project, http://perseus.tufts.edu
Alpheios Project, http://alpheios.net.

© Springer International Publishing Switzerland 2016
Y. Murakami and D. Lin (Eds.): WLSI 2015, LNAI 9442, pp. 173–187, 2016.
DOI: 10.1007/978-3-319-31468-6_13

historical and cultural contexts relevant to the understanding of texts, and the interpretation of texts supported by stylistic and, above all, linguistic analyses.

Taking into account the fact that ILC is an active partner in both CLARIN- and DARIAH-ERIC initiatives, the presented work is part of a wider research program that is focused on models, resources, instruments and infrastructures for the Digital Humanities community.

With the overall program of research in Cooperative Philology proposed by the authors of the current paper, we wish to stress the importance of a library of components (CoPhiLib) to address issues pertaining to the philological domain [9]. The architecture and the implemented modules of CoPhiLib are the result of a continuous and fruitful interaction between experts in the domain of the Digital Humanities, software engineers, and software developers within the CoPhiLab and LaRI groups. This interaction aims at providing resources, tools and solutions to address the issues of the Digital Humanities community, causing a different method for approaching philological studies. The library is a work in progress, whose structure is described in [1]. By following a general trend, in the domain of Digital Humanities developers and engineers are progressively shifting from a *project-driven* approach to a *community-based* paradigm. This trend runs side by side with the shift from Collaborative to Cooperative Philology [18].

According to [28], collaboration requires direct interaction (i.e. negotiations, discussions, etc.) among individuals to create a product, whereas cooperation requires that all participants accomplish their assigned parts separately and share their results with the others. Thus, as pointed out in the aforementioned [18], Collaborative Philology produces Web applications and platforms, so that digital humanists, organized in communities, can work together with shared goals; on the other hand, Cooperative Philology produces libraries of components and Web Services that highly decouple their function from the overall goal they are designed for.

It is important that the design of single individual components take into consideration the principles of software engineering[3] by hiding all additional complexity from end users. In effect, users in Digital Humanities might be worried about the possible complexity that the use of software libraries could add to their routine activities. But such libraries are designed to decouple the activities of digital humanists from specific technologies.

Furthermore this work is ultimately directed towards the Web of Services[4] which is emerging as an important means for the Digital Humanities community to access new and existing instruments and resources.

1.1 Overview

In Sect. 2 we describe some of the most relevant models, resources and instruments for Cooperative Philology with regards to infrastructures for the wider

---

[3] For example bottom-up and top-down strategies, pattern programming, modularity, maintainability, performance, atomicity, strong user requirements ...

[4] http://www.w3.org/TR/ws-arch/.

Digital Humanities community. In Sect. 3 we present a high level description of the CoPhiLib library of components. Section 4 presents the Cooperative Philology WordNet Platform (CoPhiWordNet) as a case study to show the mutual benefits when Language Resource are enhanced with philological dimensions such as the interaction between linguistic and textual resources. The same section describes the implemented components of the library devoted to the management of the CoPhiWordNet. Finally Sect. 5 shows how the (Linguistic) Linked Open Data ((L)LOD) can serve as a paradigm used to link different resources as well as a modality of data presentation.

2 Background

Philology, as a historical discipline is language and culture dependent: Classical Philology, Germanic Philology, Romance Philology, etc. have different traditions and communities. Our attention is mainly focused on Classical Philology, even if several common methods and tools are exploited by other philological communities. As pointed out in Sect. 1, philological studies (in particular classical studies) are mainly based on texts, variant readings, the examination of primary sources, the evaluation of contextual information, stylistic and linguistic analyses. A general survey of digital and computational philology is provided by [4]. Here we wish to mention just a few initiatives, representative of different typologies of digital products.

Text Encoding Initiative (TEI)[5] suggests models, frameworks and guidelines for annotating digital texts and relevant textual phenomena, such as structural division in sections and subsections, gaps in the primary sources, variant readings, typographical rendering, etc. In order to overcome the scalability limitations of in-line annotation, citation schemes are provided by the Canonical Text Service (CTS) [7]. With CTS it is possible to associate an arbitrary number of annotations at any level of analysis to textual chunks (part of a word, word, phrase, etc.) that are uniquely identified. Given this machine actionable citation scheme and linguistic analyses that are arranged according to the *lemon* model,[6] the association between texts and related analyses can be easily expressed in RDF.

The largest collection of digital resources (texts) for Greek and Latin currently available under an open license is maintained by the Perseus Project and is continuously enhanced both by new OCR acquisitions and the integration of interchangeable sub-collections, such as the corpus of "Poeti d'Italia in Lingua Latina".[7] The Perseus Project also provides syntactically annotated corpora, the Greek and Latin Dependency Treebanks.[8] Furthermore, the Musisque Deoque and the Memorata Poetis[9] projects provide digital editions with critical apparatus and texts annotated with themes and motifs, respectively. [12] describes

---

[5] http://www.tei-c.org.
[6] http://lemon-model.net/.
[7] http://www.poetiditalia.it.
[8] http://nlp.perseus.tufts.edu/syntax/treebank.
[9] http://www.memoratapoetis.it.

computational instruments and linguistic tools for morphological analysis for Greek, and [35] for Latin. Syntactic parsers [30] and tools for Named Entity Recognitions [26] are currently under development. For lexico-semantic resources for classical languages it is worth mentioning Latin WordNet (LWN) [33,34] and the ongoing work on the Ancient Greek WordNet (AGWN) [5].

Finally, with regard to e-infrastructures we will mention the two largest European ERIC initiatives dedicated to the Digital Humanities communities, CLARIN[10] (focused on Language Resource) and DARIAH[11] (focused on cultural heritage). According to the manifesto of CLARIN, its mission is the setting-up of a "Common Language Resources and Technology Infrastructure, which aims to provide easy and sustainable access for scholars in the humanities and social sciences to digital language data …". CLARIN also offers humanists "advanced tools to discover, explore, exploit, annotate, analyse or combine them [i.e. the data], wherever they are located". The current status of the CLARIN infrastructure is described in [25]. The mission of DARIAH is to enhance and support digitally-enabled research across the humanities and arts. According to its manifesto DARIAH is "the Digital Research Infrastructure for the Arts and Humanities" which "aims to enhance and support digitally-enabled research and teaching across the humanities and arts. [. . .] DARIAH will develop, maintain and operate an infrastructure in support of ICT-based research practices".

The necessity of creating infrastructures to share Language Resources and Technologies (LRT) for the Digital Humanities community is an emerging research topic as demonstrated by initiatives such as InterEdition[12] and the aforementioned Open Philology and Perseus Projects.

3   CoPhilib: Analysis and Design

The library of components (CoPhiLib) which we describe here is strongly related to the identification of different roles within the Digital Humanities community at large. Digital and Traditional Humanists on the one side and software engineers and developers on the other provide us with the primary roles; but often a digital humanist may develop a software solution by him or herself and collapse two distinct roles into one. This mixed situation necessitates a deep analysis of the different user requirements of distinct actors. The more we aim at cooperation, the more evidently this need emerges.

Within the Language Resources and Technologies community, for example, the key role of user requirements has been clearly identified by META-SHARE,[13] the network of repositories of language data, tools and related Web Services implemented in META-NET.[14] In META-SHARE the different user

---

[10] http://clarin.eu.

[11] http://dariah.eu/.

[12] http://www.interedition.eu/.

[13] http://www.meta-share.eu/.

[14] Co-funded by the 7th Framework Programme of the European Commission through the grant agreement no. 249119.

requirements of various actors involved drive the design and the modeling of the infrastructures more than Information Technology, whose experts are asked to solve issues and provide solutions for the user requirements [19]. Also in CLARIN, a *user-driven* approach is clearly perceived as a need for the development of Digital Humanities Projects [27].

Along with the need for a *user-driven* approach, [24,31,40] many initiatives in the Digital Humanities community lack effective collections of reusable Abstract Data Types (ADTs) [10],[15] stable specifications of Application Programming Interfaces (APIs) [11,41], and essentially, suitable well-designed (software) libraries [2,38].

According to [16], this deficit occurs because communication between humanists and software engineers/developers is inadequate and software engineering principles are not fully applied [15]. Indeed, a first and fast prototyping phase rarely precedes systematic development steps; on the contrary, software implemented for a specific project cannot be reused in other projects only because of insufficient generalization of problems and user needs [14].

The objective of the work carried out in collaboration between the CoPhi-Lab and LaRI groups is to tailor a set of software components to the needs of humanists. The process which formalizes the users' requirements into a library of components can be summarized in the following step.

(1) **Gathering functional and non functional requirements.** The role of the humanists is crucial since they provide the necessary requirements that are generalized using *pattern techniques* cf. Fig. 1 and example in Listing 1.1. The resulting entities and models are then formalized in UML diagrams;

(2) **Refining the fundamental entities of the application model.** This phase refines the models and the entities in order to identify core structures;[16]

(3) **Defining the APIs to make each component interoperable.** This phase defines the general Application Programming Interfaces and how various agents (human or software) interact with services and components.

Listing 1.1. Simple pattern

```
As <Role X> I want to do <Action Y> [Using <Resource A>,
[through] <Tool B>, [on/with] <Infrastructure C>]
[so that <Happens W>] to obtain <Result Z>
```

---

[15] Abstract Data Types are values (data type) and operations (on them) without specifying how the data type is implemented (encapsulation) [23,39]. Designing reusable Abstract Data Types is strategic since they generalize the domain requirements in term of behavior and separation between implementation and interface.

[16] We strongly apply software design techniques such as analysis pattern, architectural pattern, design pattern …

1	**Manage Content**
1.1	As a content manager, I want to add a primary source text to the repository so that it is accessible by users for reading, curation, annotation and research.
1.2	As a content manager, I want to add a derivative work to a repository so that it is accessible by users for reading, curation, annotation and research.
1.3	...

2	**Research, Learn, Produce**
2.1	As a user I want to view a text and related named entity annotations to explore real word people, places and objects associated with the text.
2.2	...

Fig. 1. User requirements (Courtesy of Bridget Almas, Alpheios Project)

3.1 High Level Architecture

The resulting architecture consists of a set of components, at various levels, which provide services for the agents and intercommunicate using Application Programming Interfaces and services (cf. Figs. 2 and 3).

4 Cooperative Philology WordNet Platform

The Cooperative Philology WordNet Platform (CoPhiWordNet) is based on the need for a lexico-semantic resource (specifically a WordNet) for Ancient Greek, as noted in [5]. At the moment, CoPhiWordNet connects different WordNets in both modern and classical languages. Each WordNet in the platform is modeled on Princeton WordNet (PWN) which is used also as a *pivot* resource. In addition to PWN, CoPhiWordNet manages and connects the Ancient Greek WordNet, the Latin WordNet, the Italian WordNet [37], the Croatian WordNet [36] and the Arabic WordNet [6,20]. The Cooperative Philology WordNet Platform is accessed through a Web application[17] which allows users to browse and edit the WordNets: the platform is used as a means of assembling new linguistic resources (such as the WordNet for Ancient Greek) as well as of extending existing WordNets while preserving the integrity of the originals (as with Latin and Arabic).

CoPhiWordNet is the result of a collaboration between LaRI and CoPhi-Lab groups. Experts in Language Resources (LRs) from former group provided philologists in the latter with the necessary *know-how* on managing LRs suitable for their requirements while software engineers/developers, with experience in both LRTs and philology, defined the architecture and implemented the required solutions. We have followed the three steps of the process which formalizes user requirements into a library of components (cf. Sect. 3).

The CoPhiWordNet fulfills the requirements to have translations of classic terms into both modern languages and classic languages more accessible and

---

[17] GUI beta-version at http://www.languagelibrary.eu/new_ewnui.

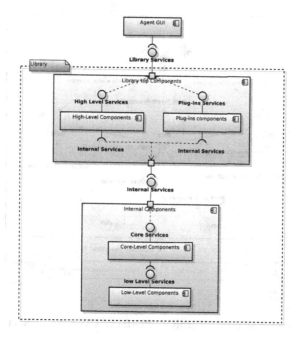

Fig. 2. Basic layers and modules of the CoPhiLib components

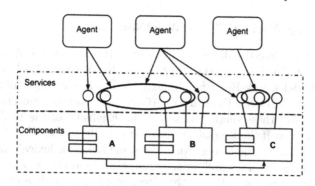

Fig. 3. Components and services

vice versa. Moreover, it provides APIs to be connected to other platforms, such as Perseids[18] as developed by Alpheios Projects, as well as providing semantic annotations. The core model and entities are mapped on the model of PWN while mapping entities follow the model of Interlingual Index (ILI) [42]; the use of Web Services makes the functions of the platform interoperable: each mapping service between $WordNet_i$ and $WordNet_j$ (WN_i2j_IndirectMapping_Ws in Fig. 4) is the composition of the ILI mapping between PWN and $WordNet_j$, (PWN_DirectMapping_Ws in Fig. 4).

---

[18] http://www.perseids.org/.

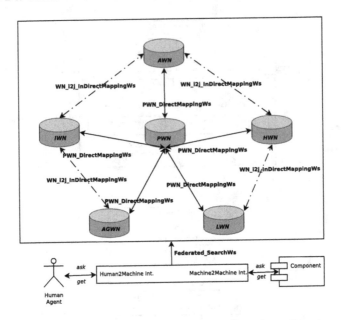

Fig. 4. Cooperative Philology WordNet Platform Overview: Direct and Indirect mappings

4.1 Enhancing Ancient Greek WordNet

In this section we describe different procedures to enhance the Ancient Greek WordNet. As outlined in [5], the creation of the Ancient Greek WordNet is based on digitized Greek-English bilingual dictionaries made available by the Perseus Project. The Greek-English pairs (Greek words and English translations) are extracted from these dictionaries and the English word is projected onto Princeton WordNet. If the English translation is in Princeton WordNet, then its synsets are assigned to the Greek word; the same holds for lexical and semantic relations with other lemmas and senses respectively. On the contrary, when the English translation is not in PWN, the Greek word of the pair is excluded from AGWN. This strategy thus strongly reduces the coverage of AGWN for the entire Greek lexicon to c.a 30 %. For example, sákos (σάκος) which is glossed by *shield* is successfully inserted in AGWN as a synonym of aspís ἀσπίς, while boágrion (βοάγριον) glossed by *a **shield** of wild bull's hide* is missing.

In order to improve the coverage, [8] describe the use of the Stanford parser to identify the *head* of the English translation and assign the corresponding Greek translation as an hypernym of the missing Greek word. In the previous example:

$$βοάγριον \ \textit{is\_a} \ ἀσπίς$$

A different strategy used to increase the precision of the resource is based on comparing Greek-Latin mapped pairs extracted from the CoPhiWord-Net with Greek-Latin pairs extracted from other, more controlled, resources.

Each Greek-Latin pair of the controlled resource is projected into CoPhiWord-Net and all pairs that are already in the platform are extracted along with their pivot (English) synset(s). The resulting triples $T = (g, l, s)$[19] are examined by domain experts responsible for validating the corresponding Greek and Latin synsets.

5 Cooperative Philology WordNet Platform and Linked Open Data

The Semantic Web offers a means of publishing datasets online and making them freely accessible as well as of facilitating the enrichment of such data with information from other resources; it thus helps to avoid the problem of so called 'data islands' or 'data silos' and makes the reuse of data much more straightforward. The benefits of Linked Open Data (LOD) for cultural resources, in particular for heritage resources in languages like Ancient Greek, Latin, and Classical Arabic are clear especially when one considers the possibilities of interlinking different datasets. The development of models to permit an appropriate representation of cultural heritage resources on the Semantic Web is an important and burgeoning area of research.

In this section we will focus on the RDF representation of the WordNets in CoPhiWordNet exploiting the possibilities that such representation offers to datasets for classical languages such as Greek, Latin and Arabic in order to facilitate their use in linguistic and philological research. Firstly however we will recap the Resource Description Framework (RDF) which is the model used to structure data on the Semantic Web. The RDF [29] model represents facts or statements by subject predicate object triples. Each member of such a triple is a so called resource with a unique identifier referred to as its Uniform Resource Identifier (URI). Each of these URI can be 'dereferenced' which means each URI will give us access to a description of the entity in question in lieu of the actual entity addressed.

As mentioned above the linked data paradigm enables the linking together of lots of different kinds of information using categories and relations that originate from diverse datasets. This is especially useful when it comes to lexical resources where we are dealing with sets of lexical entries in one or more languages. Using the RDF model we can attach various kinds of information to each lexical entry respecting the morpho-syntactic properties associated with the entry, for example its part of speech, its declensions, etc., using concepts and relations from various other online vocabularies. What's more we are able to represent the meaning of each entry by linking the entry itself to a concept in an ontology. This allows us to relate the concept associated with the word to a network of other concepts described in a formal ontology language such as OWL.

---

[19] Where g stands for Greek word, l for Latin and s is the id of the English synset which bridges g into l.

The *lemon* model (see Sect. 2) is a follow up to previous work in computational lexicography such as the Lexical Markup Framework [21, 22] and lexinfo,[20] and provides a model for describing lexical resources on the Semantic Web. One of the innovations of *lemon* is that it represents the meaning of words using so called sense objects which allow the linking of a computational lexicon with an ontology.[21]

According to this perspective, we aim to link the WordNets in CoPhiWordNet to other resources such as, for example PAROLE SIMPLE CLIPS [13] for Italian and the classical texts provided by the Perseus Digital Library for Ancient Greek. To achieve this goal, we are planning to complete the serialisation of the WordNets[22] in CoPhiWordNet in *lemon*-RDF [3, 32] and use the *lemon:reference* and *lemon:example* properties to connect those resources. The projected results should be as in Figs. 5 and 6.

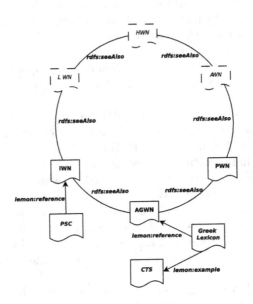

Fig. 5. Cooperative Philology WordNet Platform: RDF and interlinked resources

5.1   Adding Temporal Information to CoPhiWordNet

lemon allows the addition of temporal information via the use of the *usedSince* property. This can address one of the possible problems a digital humanist

---

[20] http://www.lexinfo.net/ontology/2.0/lexinfo.owl.

[21] Where the ontology provides the semantics for the lexical entries in the lexicon.

[22] So far, only Italian WordNet (IWN) is available in RDF - http://www.languagelibrary.eu/owl/italWordNet15/download/italWordNet15.tar.gz-, but, given the fact that each WordNet (WN) in CoPhiWordNet has the same structure as PWN their conversion is straightforward.

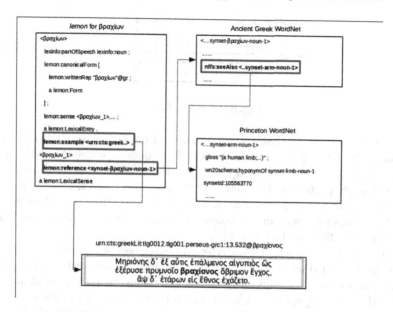

Fig. 6. Interaction between AGWN, PWN and CTS through *lemon*

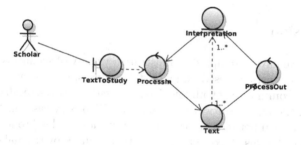

Fig. 7. Approaching a new interpretation of a text

encounters during his/her activities, i.e. the semantic shifting of a specific sense: the sense of a given word at different stages over time is crucial for text interpretation. For instance, the shift between positive and negative connotations in the term *otium* (cf. Figs. 7 and 8) is a compelling example.

The *usedSince* property may not be sufficient, however, for describing information relating to the temporal validity of the different senses of a word or for tracking how different word senses evolve one into another – something which is particularly important in representing historical languages like Latin. It is useful to have a more detailed representation of the evolution of word senses when it comes to constructing lexica for classical languages (or even explicitly diachronic lexica for modern languages like English or French) in which we want to represent the evolution of a language at different stages over time.

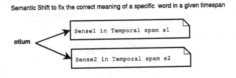

Fig. 8. Semantic Shift

It transpires however that adding a temporal dimension to RDF triples can be notoriously challenging given we are in effect confined within the RDF model to binary relations and breaking up n-ary relations into binary relations raises a number of other problems. The best solution seems to be to take a higher level, conceptual, approach namely, to work with perdurants, that is, entities with an associated temporal span, in the course of which individual properties can or can not hold at different intervals [43].

In previous work [17] we have devised an extension of *lemon* in which sense objects are modelled as perdurants. These different sense entities can then be combined in one meaning shift entity allowing us to explicitly represent and thus to query the meaning shifts that words can take on. With this explicit encoding of word senses as temporal entities it becomes easier to represent the dynamic semantic aspects of the lexicon.

6   Conclusion

In conclusion, we have attempted to illustrate a variety of scenarios in which the community of linguists, focused on linguistic analyses, lexico-semantic resources etc. meets the community of philologists, focused on texts, multiple interpretations etc. In the age of software components, Web Services and Linked Open Data, the interaction between these two communities can lead to a fruitful cross-fertilization, which aims at extending linguistic resources by textual evidence and enhancing scholarly editions by linguistic tools and lexico-semantic resources.

Acknowledgments. The present research has been partially supported by the Italian National Project Memorata Poetis (PRIN-2010/2011-2010NK2ACB). The work is part of a wider research panorama that is focused on models, resources, instruments and infrastructures for the Digital Humanities, namely CLARIN- and DARIAH-ERIC. The authors would also like to thank Bridget Almas, Harry Diakoff (Alpheios Project) and Gregory Crane (Perseus Project and Open Philology Project) who provided insight and expertise that greatly inspired important aspects of the research.

References

1. Del Grosso, A.M.: Designing a Library of Components for Textual Scholarship. Ph.D. thesis, University of Pisa (2015)
2. Arthur, P., Bode, K. (eds.): Advancing Digital Humanities: Research, Methods, Theories. Palgrave Macmillan, Basingstoke (2014)

3. Assem, M., Gangemi, A., Schreiber, G.: Conversion of WordNet to a standard RDF/OWL representation. In: Proceedings of the Fifth International Conference on Language Resources and Evaluation (LREC 2006), pp. 237–242, May 2006. http://www.cs.vu.nl/~mark/papers/Assem06a.pdf
4. Babeu, A.: Rome Wasn't Digitized in a Day: Building a Cyber Infrastructure for Digital Classics. Council on Library and Information Resources (2011)
5. Bizzoni, Y., Boschetti, F., Diakoff, H., Del Gratta, R., Monachini, M., Crane, G.: The Making of Ancient Greek WordNet. In: Calzolari, N., Choukri, K., Declerck, T., Loftsson, H., Maegaard, B., Mariani, J., Moreno, A., Odijk, J., Piperidis, S. (eds.) Proceedings of the Ninth International Conference on Language Resources and Evaluation, LREC 2014. European Language Resources Association (ELRA), Reykjavik, May 2014
6. Black, W., Elkateb, S., Vossen, P.: Introducing the Arabic WordNet Project. In: Proceedings of the Third International WordNet Conference (GWC-06) (2006)
7. Blackwell, C., Smith, N.: Four URLs, Limitless Apps: Separation of Concerns in the Homer Multitext Architecture. Donum natalicium digitaliter confectum Gregorio Nagy septuagenario a discipulis collegis familiaribus oblatum: A Virtual Birthday Gift Presented to Gregory Nagy on Turning Seventy by His Students, Colleagues, and Friends (2012)
8. Boschetti, F., Del Gratta, R., Lamé, M.: Computer Assisted Annotation of Themes and Motifs in Ancient Greek Epigrams: First Steps. In: CLIC, La prima Conferenza Italiana di Linguistica Computazionale, Pisa, Italy, December 2014
9. Boschetti, F., Del Grosso, A.M., Khan, A.F., Lamé, M., Nahli, O.: A top-down approach to the design of components for the philological domain. In: Digital Humanities 2014: Book of Abstracts, pp. 109–111 (2014)
10. Boschetti, F., Del Grosso, A.M.: TeiCoPhiLib: A Library of Components for the Domain of Collaborative Philology. J. Text Encoding Initiative (8) (2015). http://jtei.revues.org/1285
11. Burnard, L.: The evolution of the Text Encoding Initiative: from research project to research infrastructure. J. Text Encoding Initiative (5) (2013). http://jtei.revues.org/811
12. Crane, G.: Generating and parsing classical Greek. Literary Linguist. Comput. 6(4), 243–245 (1991)
13. Del Gratta, R., Frontini, F., Khan, F., Monachini, M.: Converting the PAROLE SIMPLE CLIPS lexicon into RDF with lemon. Semantic Web J. 6(4), 387–392 (2015)
14. Del Grosso, A.M., Boschetti, F.: Collaborative Multimedia Platform for Computational Philology, CoPhi Architecture. In: Davis, P. (ed.) Proceedings of the 5th International Conferences on Advances in Multimedia (MMEDIA), Venice, Italy, pp. 46–51. International Academy, Research, and Industry Association, IARIA, April 2013
15. Del Grosso, A.M., Nahli, O.: Towards a flexible open-source software library for multi-layered scholarly textual studies: an Arabic case study dealing with semi-automatic language processing. In: Proceedings of 3rd IEEE International Colloquium, Information Science and Technology (CIST), Tetouan, Marocco, pp. 285–290. IEEE, Washington, D.C., October 2014. http://dx.doi.org/10.1109/CIST.2014.7016633
16. Dombrowski, Q.: What Ever Happened to Project Bamboo? Literary Linguist. Comput. 29(3), 326–339 (2014). http://llc.oxfordjournals.org/content/29/3/326.abstract

17. Khan, F., Boschetti, F., Frontini, F.: Using lemon to Model Lexical Semantic Shift in Diachronic Lexical Resources. In: LDL-2014 3rd Workshop on Linked Data in Linguistics (2014)
18. Boschetti, F., Lamé, M., Del Gratta, R.: Few notes on the domain and subdomains of Collaborative and Cooperative Philology. In: Proceedings of First Digital Humanities and Antiquity Conference (DHANT-2015) (2016, to appear)
19. Federmann, C., Georgantopoulos, B., Del Gratta, R., Magnini, B., Mavroeidis, D., Piperidis, S., Speranza, M.: META-SHARE functional and technical specification (deliverable d7.1). Tech. report, METANET, dissemination Level: Open, January 2011
20. Fellbaum, C., Alkhalifa, M., Black, W.J., Elkateb, S., Pease, A., Rodríguez, H., Vossen, P.: Building a WordNet for Arabic. In: Proceedings of the 5th Conference on Language Resources and Evaluation, LREC 2006, May 2006
21. Francopoulo, G.: LMF - Lexical Markup Framework, 1st edn. ISTE Ltd., Wiley, New York (2013)
22. Francopulo, G., Laurent, R., Monica, M., Calzolari, N.: Lexical Markup Framework (LMF ISO-24613). In: Proceedings of the 5th International Conference on Language Resources and Evaluation (LREC 2006), Genova, Italy (2006)
23. Gabbrielli, M., Martini, S.: Programming Languages: Principles and Paradigms. Undergraduate Topics in Computer Science. Springer, London (2010)
24. Gibbs, F., Owens, T.: Building Better Digital Humanities Tools: Toward broader audiences and user-centered designs. Digital Humanit. Q. **6**(2) (2012). http://www.digitalhumanities.org/dhq/vol/6/2/000136/000136.html
25. Hinrichs, E., Krauwer, S.: The CLARIN Research Infrastructure: Resources and Tools for eHumanities Scholars. In: Chair, N.C.C., Choukri, K., Declerck, T., Loftsson, H., Maegaard, B., Mariani, J., Moreno, A., Odijk, J., Piperidis, S. (eds.) Proceedings of the Ninth International Conference on Language Resources and Evaluation (LREC 2014). European Language Resources Association (ELRA), Reykjavik, May 2014
26. Isaksen, L., Simon, R., Barker, E.T., de Soto Cañamares, P.: Pelagios and the emerging graph of ancient world data. In: Proceedings of the 2014 ACM Conference on Web Science, pp. 197–201. ACM (2014)
27. Kemman, M., Kleppe, M.: Too Many Varied User Requirements for Digital Humanities Projects. In: The 3rd CLARIN ERIC Annual Conference, 24–25 October 2014, Soesterberg, The Netherlands (2014)
28. Kozar, O.: Towards Better Group Work: Seeing the Difference Between Cooperation and Collaboration. Engl. Teach. Forum **48**(2), 16–23 (2010)
29. Lassila, O., Swick, R.R.: Resource Description Framework (RDF). Model and Syntax Specification. Tech. report, W3C (1999). http://www.w3.org/TR/1999/REC-rdf-syntax-19990222
30. Mambrini, F., Passarotti, M.: Non-projectivity in the Ancient Greek Dependency Treebank. In: DepLing 2013, p. 177 (2013)
31. McCarty, W.: Signs of times present and future. Human Discussion Group, vol. 22, no. 218 (2008)
32. McCrae, J., Fellbaum, C., Cimiano, P.: Publishing and Linking WordNet using lemon and RDF. In: Proceedings of the 3rd Workshop on Linked Data in Linguistics (2014)
33. McGillivray, B.: Automatic selectional preference acquisition for Latin verbs. In: Proceedings of the ACL 2010 Student Research Workshop, ACL student 2010, pp. 73–78. ACL (2010). http://dl.acm.org/citation.cfm?id=1858913.1858926

34. Minozzi, S.: The Latin WordNet Project. In: Anreiter, P., Kienpointner, M. (eds.) Latin Linguistics Today. Akten des 15. Internationalem Kolloquiums zur Lateinischen Linguistik. Innsbrucker Beiträge zur Sprachwissenschaft, vol. 137, pp. 707–716 (2009). http://www.dfll.univr.it/documenti/Iniziativa/dall/dall234343.pdf
35. Passarotti, M.: LEMLAT. Uno strumento per la lemmatizzazione morfologica automatica del latino. J. Latin Linguist. **9**(3), 107–128 (2007)
36. Raffaelli, I., Tadić, M., Bekavac, B., Agić, Ž.: Building Croatian WordNet. In: GWC 2008 4th International Global Wordnet Conference, pp. 349–360 (2008)
37. Roventini, A., Alonge, A., Bertagna, F., Calzolari, N., Girardi, C., Magnini, B., Marinelli, R., Zampolli, A.: Italwordnet: building a large semantic database for the automatic treatment of Italian. Computational Linguistics in Pisa, Special Issue, XVIII-XIX, Pisa, Roma, IEPI, vol. 2, pp. 745–791 (2003)
38. Schmitz, P., Pearce, L., Dombrowski, Q.: DH-CASE II: Collaborative Annotations in Shared Environments: Metadata, Tools and Techniques in the Digital Humanities. In: Proceedings of the 2014 ACM Symposium on Document Engineering (DocEng), Fort Collins, Colorado, USA, pp. 211–212. ACM, New York, September 2014. http://doi.acm.org/10.1145/2644866.2644898
39. Shaffer, C.A.: A Practical Introduction to Data Structures and Algorithm Analysis, 3rd edn. Prentice Hall, Upper Saddle River (2010)
40. Teehan, A., Keating, J.G.: Appropriate Use Case modeling for humanities documents. Literary Linguist. Comput. **25**(4), 381–391 (2010). http://llc.oxfordjournals.org/content/25/4/381.abstract
41. Terras, M., Nyhan, J., Vanhoutte, E. (eds.): Defining Digital Humanities: A Reader. Ashgate, Farnham (2013)
42. Vossen, P. (ed.): EuroWordNet: A Multilingual Database with Lexical Semantic Networks. Kluwer Academic Publishers, Norwell (1998)
43. Welty, C., Fikes, R., Makarios, S.: A reusable ontology for fluents in owl. In: FOIS, vol. 150, pp. 226–236 (2006)

Effectiveness of Keyword and Semantic Relation Extraction for Knowledge Map Generation

Virach Sornlertlamvanich[1(✉)] and Canasai Kruengkrai[2]

[1] Sirindhorn International Institute of Technology,
Thammasat University, Bangkok, Thailand
virach@siit.tu.ac.th
[2] Graduate School of Information Sciences, Tohoku University,
Sendai, Japan
canasai@ecei.tohoku.ac.jp

Abstract. We explore the named entity (NE) recognition and semantic relation extraction technique on the Thai cultural database. Within the limited domain and well-structured database, our proposed method can perform in an acceptable high accuracy to generate the tuples of semantic relation for expressing the essence of the record in terms of infobox and knowledge map. In this paper, we propose a semantic relation extraction approach based on simple relation templates that determine relation types and their arguments. We attempt to reduce semantic drift of the arguments by using named entity models as semantic constraints. Experimental results indicate that our approach is very promising. We successfully apply our approach to a cultural database and discover more than 18,000 relation instances with expected high accuracy.

Keywords: Named entity extraction · Semantic relation extraction · Cultural database · Infobox · Knowledge map

1 Introduction

Targeting on the user generated content (UGC) e.g. Thai Cultural Information Center website,[1] we are interested in relating the document units semantically to generate a network that can express in a knowledge map manner. In our approach, we focus on keyword and semantic relation extraction. Some language dependent problems have to be solved especially in handling the Thai language, which has no word delimiter or punctuation mark. We apply general tools for word segmentation and POS tagging, then extract the keyword according to the model trained from named entity (NE) tagged corpus.

The size of this cultural database has gradually increased to around 100,000 records (from November 2010 to December 2014). Each record contains a number of fields describing a specific cultural object. The content includes four main components: (1) cover image and thumbnails, (2) title, (3) description and (4) domain. We need to

---

[1] http://www.m-culture.in.th/.

© Springer International Publishing Switzerland 2016
Y. Murakami and D. Lin (Eds.): WLSI 2015, LNAI 9442, pp. 188–199, 2016.
DOI: 10.1007/978-3-319-31468-6_14

extract facts (hereafter referred to as relation instances) from the description. One can view relation instances as formal meaning representations of corresponding texts. These relation instances are useful for question answering and other applications i.e. summary as an infobox, or a network of information in knowledge map.

Recent research in semantic relation extraction has shown the possibility to automatically find such relation instances. Some approaches rely on high-quality syntactic parsers. For example, DIRT [10] and USP [12] discover relation instances based on the outputs from dependency parsers. Such parsers and annotated training corpora are difficult to obtain in non-English languages. Pattern-based approaches [1, 2, 11] seem to be more practical for languages with limited NLP resources. For example, TEX-TRUNNER [2] can efficiently extract relation instances from a large-scale Web corpus with minimal supervision. It only requires a lightweight noun phrase chunker to identify relation arguments. More advanced approaches like SNE [7], RESOLVER [17] and SHERLOCK [13] exploit the outputs of TEXTRUNNER for learning.

Our cultural database allows us to make two assumptions:

(A1) Each record belongs to only one main cultural domain.
(A2) Each record has only one subject of relations.

The assumption (A1) seems to hold for most of records. We adopt the assumption (A2) from [6] that try to extract infobox-like relations from Wikipedia. Also, the assumption (A2) seems to hold for our data since the description provides the details about one cultural object whose name is expressed in the record title.

Based on the above two assumptions, we propose our strategy to semi-automatically extract relation instances from the cultural database. We focus on unary relation extraction similar to [4, 6]. We assume that the subject of the relation is the record title. Each relation remains only one argument to be extracted.

The Thai cultural database has been collected in the structure as described in Sect. 2. We describe our relation template in Sect. 3 and how to effectively find relation texts in a large database in Sect. 4. We use named entities to reduce semantic drift of the target arguments in Sect. 5. We examine the effect of the distances between the relation surfaces and the target arguments in Sect. 6.1 and provide preliminary results of our experiments in Sect. 6.2. The results indicate that our strategy of semantic relation extraction is very promising for real-world applications by applying to generate infobox and knowledge map of the Thai cultural database as described in Sect. 7.

2   Thai Cultural Database

The portal is hosted by Thai Ministry of Culture providing for cultural rural office to collect culture information online. The cultural information is structured to follow a template guideline mainly adopted from Dublin Core Metadata Element Set, Version 1.1.[2]

---

[2] http://dublincore.org/documents/2012/06/14/dces/.

There are 15 elements that have been introduced to annotate the record as elaborated in Table 1. The record is allowed to contain text, image, and video. In the period of November 2010 to December 2014, the number of uploaded records has already exceeded 100,000 records.

Table 1. The elements for annotating the content of the cultural information

Label	Definition
dc.title	Name of the culture resource
dc.subject	Set of tags or keywords representing the category of the resource
dc.description	Detail about the resource
dc.type	Type of attaching media i.e. image, video, sound, SWF
dc.relation	Reference identification to other resource
dc.coverage	Location of the resource
dc.creator	Person primarily responsible for making the resource
dc.publisher	Person responsible for making the resource available
dc.contributor	Person responsible for making contributions to the resource.
dc.rights	Information about rights held in and over the resource
dc.date	Point of time describing the last updating, creating, submitting, approving, contributing the detail of the resource
dc.identifier	Unambiguous reference to the resource within a given context
dc.language	Language of the resource
dc.source	Name of the attached media file
dc.format	File format, physical medium, or dimensions of the resource

As an example, Fig. 1 shows an excerpt of the front-end web page of the record number 35860 about the Phra Samut Chedi; (1) is the photo images of the record, (2) is the title of the record, (3) is the description of the record, (4) is the subject of the record.

The annotated information of title, description, and subject are the essential key fields that we use to identify the NE for keyword and semantic relation extraction. Subject is used to filter for the records of attraction (location), person, and artifact. These are the group of NE in which we are interested in this paper. Title is the target NE according to our assumption to identify the semantic relation to any occurrence of related NE in the description.

3   Relation Template

Table 2 shows the relation template. There are five main cultural domains in the database, and each main cultural domain has several sub-domains.

In our work [9], we focus on three cultural domains, including attraction, person and artifact, as shown in the first column. Based on these cultural domains, we expect that the subject of relations in each record (i.e., the record title) should be a place, a human or a man-made object, respectively. As a consequence, we can design a set of relations that correspond to the subject. For example, if the subject is a place, we may

Fig. 1. An excerpt of the front-end web page of the record number 35860 about the Phra Samut Chedi

Table 2. Relation template (LOC denotes location; PER denotes person; ORG denotes organization; DATE denotes date)

Domain	Relation	Surface	Argument
Cultural attraction	ISLOCATEDAT	ตั้งอยู่ที่	LOC
	ISBUILTIN	สร้าง(ปืน)*ใน สร้าง(ปืน)*เมือ ตั้ง(ปืน)*เมือ	DATE
	ISBUILTBY	สร้าง(ปืน)*โดย ตั้ง(ปืน)*โดย	PER, ORG
	HASOLDNAME	เดิมชื่อ ชื่อเดิม	LOC, ORG
Cultural person	MARRIEDWITH	สมรสกับ	PER
	HASFATHERNAME	บิดาชื่อ	PER
	HASMOTHERNAME	มารดาชื่อ	PER
	HASOLDNAME	เดิมชื่อ ชื่อเดิม	PER
	HASBIRTHDATE	เกิด(เมือ)*	DATE
	BECOMEMONKIN	อุปสมบทเมือ	DATE
Cultural artifact	ISMADEBY	ผลิต(ปืน)*โดย ทำ(ปืน)*โดย ผลงานโดย	PER, ORG
	ISSOLDAT	จำหน่ายที่	LOC, ORG

need to know where it is, when it was built and who built it. We can formally write these expressions by ISLOCATEDAT, ISBUILTIN and ISBUILTBY. The second column shows our relations that are associated with the subject domains. The third column shows relation surfaces used for searching relation texts in which arguments may co-occur. The word in parentheses with an asterisk indicates that it may or may not appear in the surface.

The answers to where, when and who questions are typically short and expressed in the form of noun phrases. Using noun phrases as relation arguments can lead to high recall but low precision. For example, the noun phrase occurring after the relation ISBUILTIN could be a place (is built in the area of…) or an expression of time (is built in the year of…). In our case, we expect the answer to be the expression of time, and hence returning the place is irrelevant. This issue can be thought of as semantic drift. Here, we attempt to reduce semantic drift of the target arguments by using named entities as semantic constraints. The forth column shows named entity types associated with the subject domains and their relations. Each relation can be expressed in more than one surface in the text. However, the surface list in Table 2 is not thoroughly expressed. Many other more can be extracted from the corpus.

4   Surface-Relation Mapping

Mapping text segments containing a given relation surface (e.g., "สร้างโดย" (is built by)) in a large database is not a trivial task. Here, we use Apache Solr[3] for indexing and searching the database. Apache Solr works well with English and also has extensions for handling non-English languages. To process Thai text, one just enables ThaiWordFilterFactory module in schema.xml. This module invokes the Java BreakIterator and specifies the locale to Thai (TH). The Java BreakIterator uses a simple dictionary-based method, which does not tolerate word boundary ambiguities and unknown words. For example, the words "สร้าง" (build) and "ก่อสร้าง" (construct) occur in the Java's system dictionary. Both convey the same meaning (to build). We can see that the first word is a part of the second word. However, these two words are indexed differently. This means if our query is "สร้าง" (build), we cannot retrieve the records containing "ก่อสร้าง" (construct). In other words, the dictionary-based search returns results with high precision but low recall.

In our work, we process Thai text in lower units called character clusters. A character cluster functions as an inseparable unit, which is larger than (or equal to) a character and smaller than (or equal to) a word. Once the character cluster is produced, it cannot be further divided into smaller units. For example, we can divide the word "ก่อสร้าง" (construct) into 5 character clusters like "ก่-อ-ส-ร้า-ง". As a result, if our query is "สร้าง" (build), we can retrieve the records containing "ก่อสร้าง" (construct). We refer to [16] for more details about character cluster based indexing. In our work, we implement our own ThaiWordTokinizeFactory module and plug it into Apache Solr by replacing the default WhitespaceTokenizerFactory. Our character cluster generator class is based on the spelling rules described in [8].

In Thai, sentence boundary markers (e.g., a full stop) are not explicitly written. The white spaces placing among text segments can function as word, phrase, clause or sentence boundaries (see the "รายละเอียด" (description) section in Fig. 1 for example).

---

[3] http://lucene.apache.org/solr/.

To obtain a relation text, which is not too short (one text segment) or too long (a whole paragraph), we proceed as follows. After finding the position of the target relation surface, we look up at most ±4 text segments to generate relation texts. This length should be enough for morphological analyzer and named entity recognizer.

5 Named Entity Recognition

We control semantic drift of the target arguments using named entities. We build our named entity (NE) recognizer from an annotated corpus developed by [15]. The original contents are from several news websites. The corpus consists of 7 NE types. We focus on 4 NE types according to our relation templates in Table 2. Once we obtained the NE corpus, we checked it and found several issues as follows:

1. Each NE tag contains nested NE tags. For example, the person name tag contains the forename and surname tags.
2. The corpus does not provide gold word boundaries and POS tags.
3. Each NE type is annotated separately.

For the first issue, we ignored the nested NE tags and trained our model with top NE tags (PER, ORG, LOC, DATE). For the second issue, we used a state-of-the-art Thai morphological analyzer [8] to obtain word boundaries and POS tags. In this work, we trained the morphological analyzer using ORCHID corpus [14] and TCL's lexicon [3]. We then converted the corpus format into the IOB tagging style for NE tags. Thus, the final form of our corpus contains three columns (word, POS tag, NE tag), where the first two columns are automatically generated and of course contain a number of errors. For the third issue, we trained the model separately for each NE type. We obtained 33231, 20398, 8585, 2783 samples for PER, ORG, LOC, DATE, respectively.

To ensure that our NE models work properly, we split samples into 90 %/10 % training/test sets and conducted some experiments. We trained our NE models using k-best MIRA (Margin Infused Relaxed Algorithm) [5]. We set $k = 5$ and the number of training iterations to 10. We denote the word by w, the k-character prefix and suffix of the word by $P_k(w)$ and $S_k(w)$, the POS tag by p and the NE tag by y. Table 3 summarizes all feature combinations used in our experiments. Our baseline features (I) include word unigrams/bigrams and NE tag bigrams. Since we obtained the word boundaries and POS tags automatically, we introduced them gradually to our features (II, III, IV) to observe their effects.

Figure 2 shows F1 results for the NE models. We used the `conlleval` script[4] for evaluation. We observe that PER is easy to identify, while ORG is difficult. Prefix/suffix features dramatically improve performance on ORG. Using all features (IV) gives best performance on PER (93.24 %), ORG (68.75 %) and LOC (83.78 %), while slightly drops performance on DATE (85.06 %). Thus, our final NE models used in relation extraction are based on all features (IV). Although these results are from the

---

[4] http://www.cnts.ua.ac.be/conll2000/chunking/conlleval.txt.

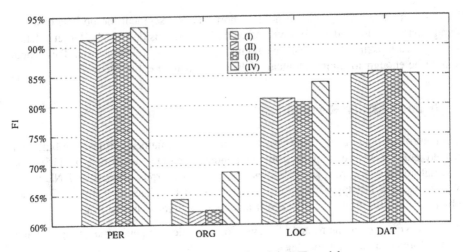

Fig. 2. F1 evaluation results of the NE models

news domain, we could expect similar performance when applying the NE models to our cultural domains.

We summarize our strategy as follows. After selecting the subject domain, we send its relation surfaces (shown in the 3rd column of Table 2) to Apache Solr. We then trim the resulting record descriptions to obtain the relation texts (described in Sect. 4). Next, we perform word segmentation and POS tagging simultaneously using our morphological analyzer and feed the results into our NE models (described in Sect. 5). We invoke the appropriate NE model based on our relation templates (described in Sect. 3). Finally, our system produces outputs in the form of RELATION(a, b), where a is a record title, and b is an argument specified by its NE type in the templates.

Table 3. NE features

(I): word 1, 2 grams + label bigrams $\langle w_j \rangle, j \in [-2, 2] \times y_0$ $\langle w_j, w_{j+1} \rangle, j \in [-2, 1] \times y_0$ $\langle y_{-1}, y_0 \rangle$	(III): (II) + POS 3 grams $\langle p_j, p_{j+1}, p_{j+2} \rangle, j \in [-2, 0] \times y_0$
(II): (I) + POS 1,2 grams $\langle p_j \rangle, j \in [-2, 2] \times y_0$ $\langle p_j, p_{j+1} \rangle, j \in [-2, 1] \times y_0$	(IV): (III) + k-char prefixes/suffixes $\langle P_k(w_0) \rangle, k \in [2, 3] \times y_0$ $\langle S_k(w_0) \rangle, k \in [2, 3] \times y_0$ $\langle P_k(w_0), S_k(w_0) \rangle, k \in [2, 3] \times y_0$

6   Experiments

6.1   Effect of the Distances Between Relation Surfaces and Arguments

In this section, we examine the number of extracted instances for each relation (without considering its accuracy). Our assumption is that the target argument tends to be relevant if it is adjacent (or close) to the relation surface. The relevance weakens with the distance. In our first example, the target argument "ตำบลปากน้ำ" (Tambon Paknam, a subdistrict name) is adjacent (distance = 0) to the relation surface "ตั้งอยู่ที่" (is located at). This target argument is relevant. Suppose there are intervening words (white space or punctuation mark) between them. The relevance tends to decrease. However, if we only select adjacent named entities to be the target arguments, the coverage may be limited. In our experiments, we varied the distances from 0 to 5 intervening words for observation.

Table 4 shows the numbers of relation instances when the distances are varied. For all relations, we observe that the numbers of relation instances do not significantly change after one word distance. For example, we cannot extract more relation instances for MARRIEDWITH + PER, even we increased the distance. This indicates that using named entities helps to bound the number of possible arguments.

Table 4. Numbers of relation instances when the distances are varied

Relation	Argument	Distance					
		0	1	2	3	4	5
Cultural attraction							
ISLOCATEDAT	LOC	356	574	591	624	678	757
ISBUILDIN	DATE	3825	11487	11538	11573	11633	11667
ISBUILDBY	PER, ORG	131	202	218	234	249	257
HASOLDNAME	LOC, ORG	0	9	21	26	27	29
Cultural person							
MARRIEDWITH	PER	132	177	177	177	177	177
HASFATHERNAME	PER	120	372	372	373	373	373
HASMOTHERNAME	PER	97	383	383	383	383	383
HASOLDNAME	PER	51	259	273	277	277	283
HASBIRTHDATE	DATE	4122	4745	4801	4947	4966	5075
BECOMEMONKIN	DATE	346	435	435	436	436	436
Cultural artifact							
ISMADEBY	PER, ORG	62	107	109	125	129	130
ISSOLDAT	LOC, ORG	31	31	56	59	62	64

6.2 Preliminary Results

To inspect the quality of relation instances extracted by our strategy, we randomly selected at most 50 instances of each relation for evaluation. Our evaluation procedure is as follows. Based on the assumptions (A1) and (A2), we expect that the subject (record title) of an instance should be relevant to its domain. We ignored instances whose subject is irrelevant. For example, the subject of the record no. 8026 is a person, but the volunteer assigned it to the cultural artifact domain. Note that this case rarely occurs, but exists. Next, a relation instance is considered to be correctly extracted if its argument exactly matches the fact. For example, if our system only extracts the first name while the fact is the whole name, then we consider this instance to be incorrect. Finally, we set the maximum distance between the relation surface and its argument to 5. Table 5 shows the performance of our relation extraction. The overall results are surprisingly good, except those of HASOLDNAME and ISMADEBY. Table 6 shows some samples of relation instances produced by our system.

Table 5. Performance of the relation extraction

Relation	Argument	#Sample	#Correct	#Incorrect	Accuracy
Cultural attraction					
ISLOCATEDAT	LOC	50	49	1	98 %
ISBUILDIN	DATE	50	48	2	96 %
ISBUILDBY	PER, ORG	50	48	2	96 %
HASOLDNAME	LOC, ORG	27	23	4	85 %
Cultural person					
MARRIEDWITH	PER	50	49	1	98 %
HASFATHERNAME	PER	50	48	2	96 %
HASMOTHERNAME	PER	50	49	1	98 %
HASOLDNAME	PER	50	47	3	94 %
HASBIRTHDATE	DATE	50	48	2	96 %
BECOMEMONKIN	DATE	50	50	0	100 %
Cultural artifact					
ISMADEBY	PER, ORG	50	44	6	88 %
ISSOLDAT	LOC, ORG	50	49	1	98 %

7   Knowledge Map Generation

Relations between NE (or keyword) are successfully extracted as shown in the result in Table 6. The accuracy is acceptably high, ranging from 85 % to 100 % corresponding to the type of the relation. The tuples of relation are stored attaching to the record they belong to. Though the tuple of semantic relation is extracted from a part of the description, it determines the semantic modification to the title of the record. From the set of tuples of each record, the infobox of the record is generated to express the essence of the title we are looking for. NE's are used to modify the title which is also included in the set of NE. By mapping the NE found in the database, we can extensively trace the semantic modification of any target NE. Finally, the knowledge map, which is a network of the NE can be express to understand the relation among all NE's in the database.

Figure 3 shows the tuples of semantic relation extracted from the record of Phra Samut Chedi i.e.

ISBUILDIN(พระเจดีย์กลางน้ำ, พ.ศ. 2403)
Lit. ISBUILDIN(Phra Samut Chedi, BE 2403), and
ISLOCATEDAT(พระเจดีย์กลางน้ำ, ตำบลปากน้ำ).
Lit. ISLOCATEDIN(Phra Samut Chedi, Tambon Paknam).

Table 6. Relation instances produced by the system

Record no.	Relation instance
Cultural attraction	
38481	ISLOCATEDAT(วัดโพธิ์ศรี, บ้านโพธิ์ศรี ต.อินทร์บุรี)
114585	ISBUILDIN(วัดเขาวงกฎ, ประมาณปี พ.ศ.2471-2573)
114333	ISBUILDBY(วัดปิตุลาธิราชรังสฤษฎิ์, กรมหลวงรักษ์รณเรศร์)
61446	HASOLDNAME(วัดหนองกันเกรา, วัดหนองตะเกรา)
Cultural person	
14125	MARRIEDWITH(นายเนาวรัตน์ พงษ์ไพบูลย์, นางประคองกูล อิศรางกูร ณ อยุธยา)
32530	HASFATHERNAME(พระครูประยุตนวการ, นายเหยม เดขมาก)
45389	HASMOTHERNAME(หลวงฟอลิ้ง สุทสสโน, นางพริ้ง แก้วแดง)
144574	HASOLDNAME(พระครูมงคลวรวัฒน์, สวัสดีบพุศิริ)
145771	HASBIRTHDATE(อาจารย์ธนิสร ศรีกลิ่นดี, วันจันทร์ที่ 23 มกราคม 2494)
123678	BECOMEMONKIN(พระครูพิจิตรสิทธิคุณ, วันที่ ๑๖ เมษายน พ.ศ. ๒๔๒๘)
Cultural artifact	
160974	ISMADEBY(หนังสือประวัติคลองดำเนินสะดวก, พระครูสิริวรรณวิวัฒน์)
94286	ISSOLDAT(ข้าวเกรียบปากหม้อ, ตลาดเทศบาลพรานกระต่าย)

Fig. 3. Tuples of semantic relation extracted from the record of Phra Samut Chedi

In the infobox as shown in Fig. 4(1), it notifies when and where the Phra Samut Chedi was constructed. The summary information about the record in the form of infobox can help the audience to grasp the information about the record in quick. By knowing that the pagoda (Chedi) was founded in Tambon Paknam, we can trace further for what else are related to the NE of Tambon Paknam. As a result, we can find that many other attractions are located in this Tambon Paknam. These records can then be attached to the location name of Tambon Paknam. The example of the knowledge map expression is shown in Fig. 4(2). The audience can traverse for other related information about the focus topic and understand the relation among the records. Further level of relation can be expended as far as they are connected with the extracted tuples of semantic relation.

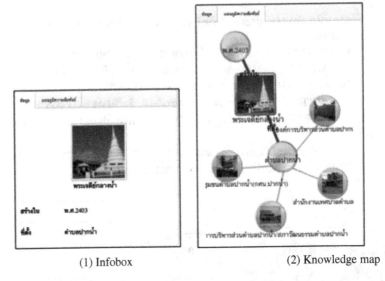

(1) Infobox   (2) Knowledge map

Fig. 4. Infobox and knowledge map extracted from the cultural database for the record of Phra Samut Chedi

8   Conclusion

We successfully applied our approach to a cultural database and could discover more than 18,000 relation instances with expected high accuracy. The outputs of our NE and relation extraction can be useful for other applications such as question answering or suggesting related topics based on semantic relations. For an example, attaching the tuples of semantic relation to the corresponding record, we can express the essence of the record in terms of infobox. In addition, by mapping among the NE's, a network of NE can be generated to form a knowledge map for better understanding the content of the cultural database.

In future work, many more other semantic relations are interested, especially in the cultural artifact domain. As an example, the relations like ISMADEOF, which requires the NE type like materials, can help in understanding the raw materials from what the artifacts are made. However, this NE type is not available in the current NE corpus. We will explore other techniques to constrain the noun phrases to prevent the semantic drift problem.

Acknowledgement. The experiments in this paper are conducted on the Thai Cultural Database of the Ministry of Culture, developed under the central information project since November 2010.

References

1. Agichtein, E., Gravano, L.: Snowball: extracting relations from large plain-text collections. In: Proceedings of ICDL, pp. 85–94 (2000)
2. Banko, M., Cafarella, M.J., Soderl, S., Broadhead, M., Etzioni, O.: Open information extraction from the web. In: Proceedings of IJCAI, pp. 2670–2676 (2007)
3. Charoenporn, T., Kruengkrai, C., Sornlertlamvanich, V., Isahara, H.: Acquiring semantic information in the TCL's computational lexicon. In: Proceedings of the Fourth Workshop on Asia Language Resources (2004)
4. Chen, H., Benson, E., Naseem, T., Barzilay, R.: In-domain relation discovery with meta-constraints via posterior regularization. In: Proceedings of ACL-HLT, pp. 530–540 (2011)
5. Crammer, K., McDonald, R., Pereira, F.: Scalable large-margin online learning for structured classification. In: Proceedings of NIPS Workshop on Learning with Structured Outputs (2005)
6. Hoffmann, R., Zhang, C., Weld, D.S.: Learning 5000 relational extractors. In: Proceedings of ACL (2010)
7. Kok, S., Domingos, P.: Extracting semantic networks from text via relational clustering. In: Daelemans, W., Goethals, B., Morik, K. (eds.) ECML PKDD 2008, Part I. LNCS (LNAI), vol. 5211, pp. 624–639. Springer, Heidelberg (2008)
8. Kruengkrai, C., Uchimoto, K., Kazama, J., Torisawa, K., Isahara, H., Jaruskulchai, C.: A word and character-cluster hybrid model for Thai word segmentation. In: Proceedings of InterBEST: Thai Word Segmentation Workshop (2009)
9. Kruengkrai, C., Sornlertlamvanich, V., Buranasing, W., Charoenporn, T.: Semantic relation extraction from a cultural database. In: Proceedings of The 3rd Workshop on South and Southeast Asian NLP (2012)
10. Lin, D., Pantel, P.: Dirt-discovery of inference rules from text. In: Proceedings of KDD, pp. 323–328 (2001)
11. Pantel, P., Pennacchiotti, M.: Espresso: leveraging generic patterns for automatically harvesting semantic relations. In: Proceedings of ACL, pp. 113–120 (2006)
12. Poon, H., Domingos, P.: Unsupervised semantic parsing. In: Proceedings of EMNLP, pp. 1–10 (2009)
13. Schoenmackers, S., Etzioni, O., Weld, D.S., Davis, J.: Learning first-order horn clauses from web text. In: Proceedings of EMNLP, pp. 1088–1098 (2010)
14. Sornlertlamvanich, V., Charoenporn, T., Isahara, H.: ORCHID: Thai part-of-speech tagged corpus. Technical report TR-NECTEC-1997-001, NECTEC (1997)
15. Theeramunkong, T., Boriboon, M., Haruechaiyasak, C., Kittiphattanabawon, N., Kosawat, K., Onsuwan, C., Siriwat, I., Suwanapong, T., Tongtep, N.: THAI-NEST: a framework for Thai named entity tagging specification and tools. In: Proceedings of CILC (2010)
16. Theeramunkong, T., Sornlertlamvanich, V., Tanhermhong, T., Chinnan, W.: Character cluster based Thai information retrieval. In Proceedings of IRAL, pp. 75–80 (2000)
17. Yates, A., Etzioni, O.: Unsupervised methods for determining object and relation synonyms on the web. J. Artif. Intell. Res. **34**, 255–296 (2009)

Author Index

Printed in the United States
By Bookmasters